THE

FACTS AND PRINCIPLES

OF

GEOLOGY

GEOGNOSY

OR THE

FACTS AND PRINCIPLES OF GEOLOGY

AGAINST

THEORIES

BY

DAVID N. LORD

NEW YORK
FRANKLIN KNIGHT
138 NASSAU STREET
1855

W. H. Tinson, Printer & Stereotyper.

PREFACE.

How is it that, at a period when unusual efforts have been made for the religious instruction of the young and the general diffusion of sacred knowledge, a distrust of the inspiration of the Holy Scriptures and doubt of their authenticity has sprung up and gained a wide diffusion among the classes who have enjoyed, in a large degree, the means of an enlightened and religious education? Of the fact there is no room for doubt. It is so conspicuous as to attract the notice of observers in every direction, and excite surprise and alarm. It cannot be regarded as resulting from the exertions that are made by the avowedly infidel to propagate their sentiments; as their influence is chiefly expended on those of a different circle. It springs undoubtedly from doctrines that are taught them by persons of their own sphere, and that enter as elements into the system of popular education, and doctrines that, instead of being openly hostile to revelation, are masked under the form of facts or truths of natural science, metaphysics, or some other branch of knowledge that is not directly connected with religion. It were easy to verify this by a multitude of proofs, but it cannot be necessary. It is known to all familiar with the subject that speculations respecting the structure of the universe, the nature of the mind, the causes of perception, the laws of life, the principles of language, and other kindred subjects, are often made the medium of promulgating sceptical views; and that doctrines are advanced by physiologists, chemists, professors of the several branches of natural philosophy, and writers on the higher metaphysics, that contravene the teachings of revelation, and naturally lead those who adopt them to doubt its divine origin. This fact renders it peculiarly important that the false principle by which they thus become the instruments of undermining the authority of the Scriptures should be pointed out, and the means indicated by which they may be counteracted. It is to such a purpose that the present work is to be devoted.

CONTENTS.

CHAPTER VII.

CHAPTER VIII.

CHAPTER IX.

CHAPTER X.

CHAPTER XI.

CHAPTER XII.

CHAPTER XIII.

CHAPTER XIV.

CHAPTER XV.

CHAPTER XVI.

THE STRUCTURE OF THE EARTH.

CHAPTER I.

The Geological Theory of the Age of the Earth—The Criteria by which it is to be Tested.

Among the various speculations that are adverse to the teachings of the Bible, and naturally lead those who accept them, to doubt and reject its inspiration, the theory of modern geology in respect to the age of the world, holds, we believe, a conspicuous place; and from the title and air with which it is invested of an inductive science, from the great number of interesting and extraordinary facts that are alleged as demonstrating it, and from the acquiescence and sanction it receives from men of learning and worth, is one of the most imposing and seductive.* Geolo-

* We are aware that this statement will be received by some, not simply with incredulity, but with offence, as though it carried with it an implication that geologists are intentionally the authors of the

gists have not confined themselves to the discovery and description of the great facts of the science;—that the crust generally of the continents and islands

scepticism which their theory is the means of generating; while a still greater number—who, indeed, are of little consideration either on the score of religion or learning—will denounce it as the mere ebullition of ignorance and bigotry, which the least tincture of science would have been sufficient to suppress. There is no class of the learned perhaps so intolerant of criticism in this relation as the cultivators of the natural sciences, and none who have the misfortune to have so large a share of ostentatious vindicators and eulogists among infidels themselves, and that grade of paragraphists and critics—whose advocacy is almost equally undesirable—who only forage and skirmish in the suburbs of knowledge, and attempt to make themselves of consequence by affecting to be the patrons of learning, dogmatizing on subjects with which they have little acquaintance, and assailing and aspersing those whom they think they may safely abuse. The question has been largely debated by geologists themselves ever since the dawn of the science, and is still in dispute. Scarce a volume appears on the subject without a chapter on this theme. Have they acquired an exclusive right to treat it? Have all others forfeited their title to receive what God has revealed respecting the origin of the world, and to vindicate that revelation from the impeachment which lies couched in the geological theory? If not, why is it not as legitimate a subject of inquiry and criticism as any other? The extreme sensitiveness which a certain class of geologists exhibit on the subject is the result, we apprehend, of weakness, rather than of strength; it has its origin in the consciousness that they are not able satisfactorily to reconcile their theory with the teachings of the Scriptures; not in a lofty feeling of injured innocence—not in a cloudless conviction that their system is not justly obnoxious to the charge.

We scarcely need say that we shall not confound the distinction between geologists themselves and the doctrines which they teach. The question we are to debate respects the import of their theory, not their personal reception or rejection of Christianity. That many of them are sincere believers in the inspiration of the Scriptures and of genuine piety, notwithstanding their geological theory, we do not

has received its present form since the creation of plants and animals; that it consists of a series of different rocky and earthy beds, in many places very numerous and of great depth, which have either been deposited from the ocean or thrown up from beneath; that many of them are interspersed with the relics of other rocks, and of plants, shells, the bones of fish, and the skeletons of land quadrupeds, a large share of which are of species and genera that no longer exist; and that subsequently to their formation, most of them have been raised into new positions, contorted, dislocated, and broken into fragments; but they have, on the ground of these facts, framed theories respecting the causes of which they are the result, and the sources from which their materials were derived, that have led them to conclusions that conflict with the inspired account given in Genesis of the creation. Proceeding on the assumption that they are the product of forces like those that are now giving birth to somewhat similar effects, as on vol-

doubt; that on some of them that theory, nevertheless, has a very unhappy influence, we regard as equally indisputable. But of that we shall, for the present, leave others to judge, and address ourselves exclusively to the bearings of the doctrines and implications of their theory on the inspired history of the creation and deluge, without deeming it necessary to offer any apology for stating and maintaining what the sacred word teaches on the subject, or pointing out the elements of their hypothesis, which are, in our judgment, at war alike with that record and with their own principles. To a candid discussion of the subject, no fair-minded man should object.

canic mountains, at the mouths of rivers, and on the shores of seas, they have inferred that their deposition must have occupied a period immensely larger than that which is assigned to the earth by the Mosaic record. If they are the result, they reason, of the chemical and mechanical forces that are now in activity, and operating with only their present intensity, instead of being the work of but six thousand years, they must have required an almost inconceivable duration; they must have been the growth of an incalculable round of ages.* And thence, unfor-

* Thus Dr. Buckland says:

"The truth is, that all observers, however various may be their speculations respecting the secondary causes by which geological phenomena have been brought about, are now agreed in admitting the lapse of very long periods to have been an essential condition to the production of these phenomena."

"My fire now burns with fuel, and my lamp is shining with the light of gas, derived from coal that has been buried for *countless ages* in the deep and dark recesses of the earth."

"We shall view them with less contempt when we learn from the records of geological history that there was a time when reptiles not only constituted the chief tenants and most powerful possessors of the earth, but extended their dominion also over the waters of the seas; and that the annals of their history may be traced back through *thousands of years, antecedent to that latest point in the progressive stages of animal creation, when the first pair of the human race were called into existence.*"—*Bridg. Treat.* pp. 13, 66, 167.

Professor Sedgwick, of Cambridge, England, holds the same theory:

"We see, from the form and structure of the solid masses on the surface of the earth, that many parts of it have been elaborated during successive periods of time; and if we cannot point out the first traces of organic life, we can find at least an indication of its beginning. During the evolution of *countless succeeding ages*, mechani-

tunately, mistaking that conclusion from a mere hypothesis for a scientific induction from those facts, and elevating it to the rank of a demonstrated truth, they have exhibited geology as contradicting the Scriptural history of the creation, and prepared the way for the inference that that history is not true, and cannot therefore have proceeded from God.

cal and chemical laws seem to have undergone no change ; but tribes of sentient beings were created and lived their time upon earth. *At succeeding epochs* new tribes of beings were called into existence, not merely as the progeny of those that had appeared before them, but as new and living proofs of creative interference ; and, though formed on the same plan, and bearing the same marks of wise contrivance, oftentimes as unlike those creatures which preceded them as if they had been matured in a different portion of the universe, and cast upon the earth by the collision of another planet. At length, within a *few thousand years* of the days in which we live (*a period short indeed if measured by the physical monuments of the past*) man and his fellow beings are placed upon the earth."—*Discourse on the Studies of the University of Cambridge*, 1833.

"By the geometer were measured the regions of space and the relative distance of the heavenly bodies ; by the geologist *myriads of ages* were reckoned, not by arithmetical computation, but by a train of physical events—a succession of phenomena in the animate and inanimate worlds—signs which convey to our minds *more definite ideas than figures* can do of *the immensity of time*."—*Lyell's Principles of Geology*, p. 63.

"We cannot but believe that every impartial mind, which fairly examines this subject, will be forced to the conclusion that the facts of geology do teach, as conclusively as any science not founded on mathematics can teach, that the globe must have existed during a period *indefinitely long* anterior to the creation of man. We are not aware that any practical and thorough geologist doubts this, whatever are his views in respect to revelation."—*Hitchcock's Geology and Revelation*, p. 22.

For that conclusion is the logical consequence of their theory. It is incredible, they themselves admit, that the truths of science should be at war with the teachings of a divine revelation. It is impossible that God should make a communication to us through one medium, which he contradicts and confutes in another. But we know, they assert, that the great volume of nature, the vast monuments of the material world, proceeded from his hand; and on those indestructible tablets he has inscribed a record, which announces in the most unequivocal and emphatic terms that the earth and its organized and living races, with the exception of man, instead of having been summoned into being, as Moses relates, only some six thousand years ago, had at that epoch existed through myriads and millions of ages. And contemplated thus, the inference is inevitable that the contradictory testimony of Moses is false, and cannot be from God. That Hebrew writer, it is said, may have been ignorant of the date of the creation; God cannot. Moses may have deliberately framed a fiction; it is impossible that God should not have spoken the truth.

The question then, whether the conclusion geologists thus draw in respect to the age of the world, is legitimate, or not, is of the greatest moment. If founded on just grounds, it disproves the inspiration not only of the record in Genesis of the creation, but of the whole of the writings of Moses, and thence, as we shall show, of the whole of the Old and New Testament, and divests Christianity itself of its title to be received as a divine institution. The whole Revelation is changed at once from a heaven-descended reality, into a fable; from the most glorious of God's works, into a device of man. This geological doctrine deserves therefore to be carefully and effectively tested, that if mistaken, and unscientific, the false principle on which it proceeds may be pointed out, and the Scriptures vindicated from the objections of which it is the source: and that if, on the other hand, it be found to be just, the friends of Christianity may be apprised of the blow with which it strikes away the object of their faith. And its merits are to be determined manifestly, not by specious appearances merely, plausible conjectures, showy hypotheses, or vague and shadowy speculations: it is to be tried by the laws of nature, the great facts of the strata, and the forces that are now and have been at work in modifying the earth's surface. If supported by these, in a clear and demonstrative manner, it must stand, so far as its truth is to be decided within the sphere of nature; if not supported by them, if irreconcilable both with the facts of the strata and the laws of nature, it must fall, and the objection against Christianity fall with it, of which its doctrine of the great age of the world is the source. That question we propose to try.

The theory on which geologists found their inference of the great age of the earth is, that the materials of which the strata consist, were derived from mountains and continents of granite and other rocks; that those rocks were gradually disintegrated by the action of the air, water, and heat; that they were borne down from those mountains and continents by rains, currents, and rivers to the ocean, and distributed over its bed in successive layers; and that they were at length elevated from the bottom of the ocean to their present position: that the agents by which these vast effects were wrought, were those by which the somewhat similar changes that are now taking place, are produced; and that the number and thickness of the strata, the vast multitudes of vegetable and animal remains that lie buried in them, and the slowness with which similar processes of erosion and deposition now advance, prove that an immense series of ages must have been required for their formation. This inference of the age of the world, is thus founded on a theory of the sources from which the materials of the strata were derived, the agents by which they were transferred to the bottom of the ocean, and the forces by which they were raised to their present position;—not irrespective of that on the strata themselves.

On the other hand, we reject their hypothesis respecting the derivation of the materials of the strata, and the mode in which they were distributed over the bed of the ocean, as a mere assumption, inconsistent with the laws of nature, and the facts of the strata, and subversive of itself: and thereby confute the inference they found on it of the great age of the world, as unproved and unscientific.

The question then we are to debate is, not whether the strata that have been formed since the earth was created, are such in nature and number as geologists represent; nor whether such vegetable and animal relics lie entombed in them. These facts are indisputable, and are admitted as freely in our reasonings as in theirs. But the question between us is, whether their hypothesis respecting the formation of the strata is legitimate; and thence whether the conclusion which they found on that hypothesis respecting the age of the world, is just and authoritative.

In order that the hypotheses and reasonings on which geologists build their inference of the age of the world, may be legitimate and fill the office which they assign them, they must possess, it will be admitted on all hands, certain characteristics, and be free from certain faults.

1. They must be consistent with—not contravene—the laws of nature. Geologists must not assume, for example, as a preparative for their hypothesis

respecting the formation of the strata, that the world originally existed in a state that is incompatible with its present nature. Such as that it was created a gas or an assemblage of gases; as that implies that there was an immensely greater amount of caloric in it originally than now belongs to it; which is wholly unauthorized and unscientific. Geologists have no more right to assume that it was imbued originally with thousands and millions of times its present sum of heat, than they have to assume that it had thousands and millions of times its present bulk of water, air, quartz, lime, or any other ingredient that enters into its composition. It is against the great principle also, on which they proceed in their attempts to account for the changes which the surface of the earth has undergone: namely, that the effects that have been wrought in it, were the work of identically the agents—air, water, and heat,—that are now producing changes on the earth's surface, and acting on their present scale both of extent and of intensity. It is to contradict the laws of matter likewise, to assume that the world was created in the form of gas. Matter with the exception of a few species—such as the elements of air and water—is raised to a gaseous form only by intense heat. But heat is naturally latent. It is developed or made perceptible only by chemical action. To suppose the world to have been created in a gaseous form, is therefore to suppose it to have been created in a condition in which it could not—according to the present laws of matter—have existed, except as a secondary state; or as a consequence of the action of its elements on each other after they were created. That supposition therefore contradicts the laws of heat and the formation of gaseous bodies. It is as unphilosophical and absurd to suppose the matter of the globe to have been created in the form of a gas, as it is to suppose that it was created in the form of vegetables and animals; organic structures which matter never assumes until after it has existed in another form. An inference of the great age of the world, founded on an assumption, on the one hand, of the creation of its matter in a state in which by its laws it could not exist, until after it had existed in another form; and on the other, of its originally containing a far larger share of one of its elements than now belongs to it, can have no claim to be regarded as legitimate and authoritative.

2. They must not assume as a basis of their inference of the age of the world, that it once existed in a form of which they have no proof; such as that it was in a state of fusion; and that a granite crust was formed over its molten ocean, by the cooling of its surface. Such a supposition is forbidden, indeed, by the consideration to which we have already referred; that it implies that the earth originally had a far greater proportion of combustible matter than now belongs to

it; as at present there is not—so far as can be judged, —a hundredth, and probably not a millionth part of the combustible matter in the globe, that would be requisite, if ignited, to reduce its whole mass to a state of fusion. On the assumption, however, that there is no lack of combustible matter in the earth for the fusion of all its substances; there yet, is no proof nor probability that it ever was in a state of universal fusion. It is as impossible to prove that it ever was in such a state, as it is to prove that it once existed in a gaseous form. To build an inference of the age of the world on such an assumption, is therefore to build it on an hypothesis, of what cannot be shown to have been a fact; and that is to build it on nothing, and render it wholly unscientific and worthless.

3. They must not found their inference of the age of the world, on the assumption of a condition of the globe, which if it is supposed to have existed, instead of contributing to the formation of the strata, would have made their construction impossible: such as the supposition that the materials of the strata, were drawn from mountains of granite, that were ten or fifteen miles above the level of the ocean. The strata of the earth are held by geologists, to be on an average, about ten miles in depth. To maintain therefore, that their materials were derived from continents and mountains of granite, and were

borne from them by torrents and rivers to the ocean, is to imply that those granite continents and mountains,—even if they covered as large an area as the strata now occupy—were at least ten miles above the level of the ocean; and if the mountains from which it is represented the matter of the strata was chiefly drawn, were of but half, or two-thirds the extent of the strata that are supposed to have been formed from them, then they must have been elevated at least fourteen or fifteen miles above the level of the ocean. But mountains elevated to such an enormous height and extending over vast areas, could never have been disintegrated by the action of the air, water, and heat. There would have been no air, except of the most attenuated kind, and no water at all probably at that elevation. On the supposition that vapors could have ascended to such a height, and fallen in the form of snow, they would for ever have remained congealed. No heat could have been developed there, sufficient to dissolve them. No rivers therefore could have flown from them, and consequently no detritus could have been borne from them to the sea, to be distributed over its bottom, and form layers, like our present strata. The supposition of such mountains, as the source of the materials of the strata, defeats itself, and renders the inference from it of the great age of the earth, unscientific and absurd.

4. They must not assume that the effects for which they attempt to account, are the work of agents, that are wholly inadequate to produce them: such as that the torrents and great rivers which they represent as having borne the materials of the strata from mountains and continents, entered the ocean with such a rush, as to diffuse the gravel, mud, and vegetable matter, with which they were loaded, through all its waters, and cause their deposition in layers co-extensive with its bed. None of the present rivers of the globe enter the ocean with such an impulse. So far from it, the currents of all the principal rivers are greatly checked as they approach the sea, divided into numerous channels, and brought to a dead pause, at the distance usually of fifty to one hundred miles from the shore; and consequently the detritus with which they are charged, falls to the bottom within a narrow space. The great mass of the ocean is no more affected by them, than the continents are, that lie opposite to the points where the rivers enter it. To assign to the rivers therefore, or the tides and currents of the sea, the distribution of the materials of the strata, throughout their whole domain, is to ascribe to them an effect, that wholly transcends their power.

5. They must not found their inference of the age of the world on an hypothesis, respecting the *mode* in which the strata were formed, instead of the strata

themselves. To found their inference of the age of the world on the hypothesis, for example, that the strata were formed by the agency of heat, air, and water, acting only on the scale, and with the intensity, with which they are now disintegrating rocks, and bearing their detritus to the sea—is to beg at the outset, the very point which they affect to prove. For if the strata were formed by no other agents, than those which are now acting on the land, and the sea, and their deposition proceeded at no more rapid rate, than similar strata are now forming at the bottom of the ocean, then of course, a vast series of ages must have passed before their construction could have been completed; not to say that it could never have taken place. But such a method of establishing the antiquity of the globe, has no title to be regarded as demonstrative or logical. Geologists must first prove by irrefragable evidence, that the strata were formed by the slow process, which the hypothesis represents, before they can make that mode of their formation, the ground of an inference of the vast age of the world. To assume that hundreds or thousands of years were necessary for the structure of any one of the layers, of which the strata consist; and that therefore, as many hundreds or thousands of years were consumed in the construction of the whole, as there are layers in the whole of the strata—is to take for granted—not to prove the vast antiquity of the earth.

6. They must not assume any condition of the world, the existence of any agents, or the occurrence of any events, the reality of which they cannot demonstrate; and all their assumptions and reasonings must be consistent with all the facts, and all the laws of nature, which the question affects.

To these, axioms geologists themselves will undoubtedly assent; and it results from them, that if the strata demonstrate that the world has subsisted through a vast series of ages, it must be by what they themselves are, in composition, bulk, and number—not by any theory of an antecedent state of the earth, or the processes by which they were formed. If they do not prove the great age of the world, by what they themselves are, irrespective of any speculations, in regard to the agents by which they were formed, they cannot prove it at all; precisely as, if the nature and number of the elements of which the great pyramid of Egypt consists, and the fact that it was erected by human hands—do not prove that millions of ages were occupied in its erection; no theory, respecting the agents by whom it was built, and the method of their procedure, can demonstrate, that such a period was occupied in its construction.

QUESTIONS

RESPECTING THE POINTS DISCUSSED IN THIS CHAPTER.

What is the doctrine of modern geology respecting the age of the world? What great truth does that doctrine contradict? What is the mischievous influence which it exerts? Is what it asserts, a geological fact that is discovered by the eye, as the natures and numbers of the strata are; or is it a mere inference from an hypothesis respecting the mode in which the strata were formed? Is the question, whether it is true or not, one of great moment? What is the conclusion to which, if true, it must lead, in respect to the record in Genesis of the creation, and the inspiration of the Scriptures? By what criterion is the question, whether it is true or not, to be tried? State the theory of geologists respecting the formation of the present crust of the globe—in reference, 1st, To the sources from which the materials of the strata were derived; 2d, To the agents by which they were conveyed to the places of their deposition; 3d, To the scale of intensity on which those agents acted. Is their inference of the age of the earth founded on that theory; or is it drawn from the facts of geology which the theory respects? State the language in which geologists express their estimate of the age of the world.

What part of their system is it that we reject? What are the grounds on which we reject it? State then the question we are to debate. Does it respect the reality of the great facts of geology? Or does it simply concern the truth of the hypothesis by which geologists attempt to account for those facts, and ascribe a vast age to the world?

There are certain axioms from which geologists must not depart; there are certain errors into which they must not fall, in order that their conclusion respecting the age of the world may be legitimate. What is the first error from which they must keep free? Specify one of their assumptions that is chargeable with that error. In what

2

respect does the supposition that the earth was created in a gaseous form, contradict nature? Has the geologist any more right to assume that there was once ten thousand times as much combustible matter, or ten thousand times as much latent heat in the globe, as there now is; any more than he has to suppose there was once ten thousand times as much quartz, feldspar, or lime? Is it against a great principle on which they themselves proceed in their speculations, as well as inconsistent with the condition of nature? What is that principle? Is it inconsistent also with the laws of matter, to assume that the material parts of the earth were created in the form of gas? What law of heat does that theory contradict?

What is the next error which they must avoid? State an assumption that is chargeable with that error. What is the first objection to that assumption? What is the second?

What is the third mistake from which they must keep free? Give an instance of a supposition in which an error of that kind lurks. Why would it have been impossible that the materials of the strata should ever have been drawn from lands of such an elevation, as that supposition ascribes to the continents and mountains of the earth?

What is the fourth error which they must avoid in their speculations? Specify one of their assumptions which is chargeable with that error. Prove that the torrents and rivers that convey sand, mud, and vegetable matter to the ocean, are inadequate to distribute them over its bed.

Point out a fifth ground which they must not make the basis of their inference of the great age of the earth. What is the objection to their deducing the antiquity of the earth from such an hypothesis? Prove that they assume in their premise what they infer in their conclusion. What must they demonstrate to be a fact—before their inference can be legitimate?

What is the last thing which they must not gratuitously assume, if they would make their inference of the age of the world conclusive?

Will geologists themselves assent to these axioms? What then results from them in respect to the nature of the proof by which the great age of the world is to be established, if established at all? If there is nothing in the strata themselves, that proves that a vast period was occupied in their formation, is it not clear that no hypothesis respecting the rate at which their formation was accomplished, can demonstrate it? May it not be as conclusively proved by their mode of reasoning, that innumerable ages were employed in the erection of the pyramids of Egypt, as that such a series of ages were requisite to the construction of the strata of the earth?

CHAPTER II.

The Geological Theory contradicts the Sacred History of the Creation.

THAT the theory of the creation which geologists entertain and hold is graven on the strata, contravenes the sacred history, is fully admitted and asserted, not merely by those of them who are avowedly sceptical, but by many who receive the Scriptures as a revelation. Thus a writer in a foreign journal, in vindicating their theory, says:

"Geology is accused of inculcating views with respect to the formation of the planet we inhabit, irreconcilable with those statements which may be gathered from the book of Genesis.

"We have always thought the wisest and most consistent course for divines to pursue with regard to this delicate question, would be that of maintaining, to the full extent, the inspiration of the sacred volume on all facts involving the history, prospects, and *moral condition of man;* but allowing a greater latitude in regard to those portions which relate to *natural phenomena*, with which these facts are in no wise concerned. It seems reasonable to expect that a book, intended for our moral guidance, should be exempt from error wherever we are to look into it for the regulation of our conduct; but that the deity, who does not interfere unnecessarily, should have withheld any extraordinary assistance from such portions as relate to *natural phenomena,* in which man has no vital concern. Indeed, any revelation on such points as those would have been not only superfluous, but subversive of some of the great ends for which the book of nature has been unfolded, which appears to have been intended to awaken our appetite for inquiry, to afford a fit and healthy exercise for our reasoning faculties, and to impart glimpses of the great designs of the Creator in the system of the universe. Granting this to be the case, there seems an *a priori* improbability that the writings of Moses should contain any precise information on such subjects as these; for the condition of the globe before the creation of man is clearly as irrelevant to the objects for which revelation was specially intended, as the question whether the moon has inhabitants or is endowed with an atmosphere."—*Literary Gazette,* 1834, p. 770.

The irreconcilableness of the history of the creation in Genesis with the views of geologists, is thus exhibited as so clear and indisputable that no safe course is left to divines but to admit that those portions of "the sacred volume which relate to *natural phenomena*" are not inspired, nor free from error, and that there is an intrinsic improbability, from the nature of the subject, that "the writings of Moses should contain any precise information" respecting such events. As "natural phenomena" include not only the effects produced by the omniponent fiat in the six days of the creation, but all that were observable by the senses, and the theophanies, therefore, miraculous works and historical events recorded in the Scriptures; this sweeping doctrine, which surrenders all that the most eager infidel could ask, would not have been advanced had not its author felt the most unhesitating conviction that the narrative of the creation in Genesis cannot be conciliated with his views of the facts of geology.*

* That such is the result to which that supposition leads, is indicated by another British journalist, in animadverting on it.

"If the Bible speaks at all, it speaks truly; and it is utterly subversive of its authority to make one degree of inspiration for its moral declarations, and a lower, which is none at all, for its physical statements. Many geologists think that they can so explain the first chapter of Genesis as, without violence, to reconcile it with the known facts of geology; in this there is no shadow of scepticism. Others go further, and confess that they have no hypothesis by which they can do so; but even this, *if this be all*, is only a confession of ignorance; but to advance one step beyond this, *is to open the floodgates of infidelity;* as even some professed Christians have allowed themselves to do, by treating the Mosaic cosmogony as a tradition or allegory, and not as a correct record of actual facts. Thus we find the Rev. Baden Powell, the Savilian Professor of Geometry at Oxford, in a sermon entitled Revelation and Science, saying:

"'If we look at the actual case of the writings of Moses, it is surely in every way the most probable supposition that tradition had preserved some legendary memorial of primeval events, and that the origin of the world had been recorded in a poetical cosmogony. As introductory to the revelation, Moses then put a religious application

Professor Sedgwick, a clergyman of the establishment and a distinguished geologist, indicates in an equally emphatic manner his conviction that it is wholly impracticable to harmonize the sacred record with the doctrines of the science. He says:—

"The only way of escape from all difficulties pressing upon the question of cosmogony, is to consider the old strata of the earth as monuments of a date long anterior to the existence of man and to the times contemplated in the moral records of his creation. The Bible is then left to rest upon its own appropriate evidence, and its interpretation is committed to the learning and good sense of the critic and commentator; while geology is allowed to stand on its own basis, and the philosopher to follow the investigations of physical truth wherever they may lead him, without any dread of evil consequences."—*Discourse on the Studies of the University of Cambridge*, p. 108.

No terms could show more decisively that the history the Bible gives of the creation, is felt to be wholly irreconcilable with his geological theory. If coincident with each other, if not in the most palpable collision, why, in order to escape pressing difficulties, assume, in direct contravention of the

upon such memorials, for the stronger sanction of the enactments of that law to the Israelites, and adopted them for the illustration of religious truths, and as the vehicles of moral instruction to the chosen people.'"—*Ch. Obser.*, June, 1834, pp. 369, 370.

It is thus, according to Professor Powell, in every relation, a mere fiction.

fact, that the Bible utters nothing on the subject of the earth's creation?*

Though the conviction of these writers of the impossibility of reconciling those two views of the creation, is, in our judgment, legitimate, and had better be acknowledged than disguised, a great number of geologists recoil from it, and the startling and self-contradictious methods proposed by them for evading the abandonment, with which it is felt to be fraught, of the inspiration of the Scriptures, and maintain, some on one supposition and some on another, that the sacred narrative and the geological theory are consistent with each other.

* It is not easy, however, to see what way this expedient presents "of escape from all difficulties pressing upon the question." How is a consideration of "the old strata of the earth as monuments of a date long anterior to the existence of man, and the times contemplated in the moral records of his creation," to prevent them from being regarded as contradicting that record? To admit and proclaim that they are totally incompatible with each other, is a singular method of escaping the difficulties of their irreconcilableness, or of suppressing debate respecting it! The fact that geologists may adopt that hypothesis respecting their relations to each other, cannot exempt the critic and commentator from the necessity of interpreting the Bible by its proper laws, and defending it from the imputation of error, which that hypothesis casts on it. How, moreover, is "the Bible to rest upon its own appropriate evidence," if that evidence is admitted to be confuted by "the old strata of the earth?" An extraordinary expedient really of avoiding an impeachment of the truth and inspiration of the Bible! Professor S. is here guilty, we apprehend, of what he denounces as a "sinful indiscretion" in those who attempt to evade the difficulty by extending the periods of time implied in the six days of the creation.

The principal hypotheses which have been advanced for the purpose of reconciling them are stated in the following manner by the Rev. W. D. Conybeare, England, a clergyman of the establishment, and an eminent geologist:—

"We may, perhaps, without real violence to the inspired writer, regard the period of the creation recorded by Moses, and expressed under the term of days, not to have designated ordinary days of twenty-four hours, but periods of definite but considerable length. . . . . Those who embrace this opinion will, of course, assign the formation of the secondary strata, in great part at least, to those *days of creation*, and we have the authority of several divines for such an interpretation.

But "it does not seem inconsistent with the authority of the sacred historian to suppose that, after recording in the first sentence of Genesis the fundamental fact of the original formation of all things by the will of an intelligent Creator, he may pass, sub silentio, some intermediate state, whose ruins formed the chaotic mass he proceeds to describe, and out of which, according to his further narrative, the present order of our portion of the universe was educed. Upon this supposition, the former world, whose remains we explore, may have belonged to this intermediate æra."*—*Outlines of the Geology of Eng. and Wales.* introd. pp. lix., lx.

* He adopts the last of these hypotheses, as is seen from the

These expedients, however, have only served to show in a more decisive manner the impracticability of their conciliation. Thus the assumption that the word day, in the narrative of the successive acts of the creation, instead of signifying the time of a revolution of the earth on its axis, denotes a vast indefinite period of cycles, or centuries, is in direct contradiction to the passage itself, which defines each of the six days as consisting of an evening and morning; *i. e.* the period of a complete revolution of the earth on its axis. "And God divided the light from the darkness; and God called the light Day, and the darkness he called Night; and the evening and the morning"—which were the darkness and light of twenty-four hours—"were the first day."—Chap. i. 4, 5. This is confirmed also by the announcement at the institution of the law at Sinai, that "in six days the Lord made heaven and earth, and the sea, and all that in them is."—Exodus

following passage in an article from him in the *Christian Observer*, May, 1834:—

"Not the mere theoretical views of geologists alone, but the conclusions which appear by the most cogent logical necessity to result from the phenomena of the structure of the earth's surface, and the variety and order of the very numerous series of organic remains imbedded in the strata, do undoubtedly appear to require periods of very considerable duration, and to indicate that very many ages had elapsed before 'the diapason closing full in man,' a new exertion of the creative energy, made in its own image a being of higher intellectual and moral capacities as the head of its other terrestrial works," P. 308.

xx. 11. As we have thus the explicit testimony of the Most High himself that the days of the creation were ordinary days, to assign to the word so totally different and unnatural a meaning, is to contravene his own definition and use of it. It is, in fact, nothing less than to impeach the veracity of his declaration in one passage, in order to save his word from a charge of falsehood in another. So self-confuting a device, instead of answering its purpose, could only serve to impress those who carefully scrutinized it with a profounder feeling of the contrariety of the two representations, and of their hopeless perplexity who could rely on such an expedient for their conciliation. Accordingly, though advanced with much confidence, and for a time accepted by many, it was soon seen to be untenable, and is now, we believe, generally rejected by geologists.*

The other expedient†—the assumption that the

* Thus Professor Sedgwick discards it, and pronounces those guilty "of a sinful indiscretion" "who have endeavored to bring the natural history of the earth into a literal accordance with the book of Genesis, first by greatly extending the periods of time implied by the six days of creation; and secondly, by endeavoring to show that under this new interpretation of its words, the narrative of Moses may be supposed to comprehend and describe in order the successive epochs of geology."—*Discourse.*

† This view is held by Dr. Buckland:—

"The Mosaic narrative commences with a declaration that 'in the beginning God created the heaven and the earth.' These few words

creation of the heavens and the earth in the beginning, announced in the first verse, was not included in the first of the six days' work, but took place at

of Genesis may be fairly appealed to by the geologist as containing a brief statement of the creation of the material elements, at a time distinctly preceding the operations of the first day; it is nowhere affirmed that God created the heaven and the earth in the *first day*, but in the *beginning*; this beginning may have been an epoch at an unmeasured distance, followed by periods of undefined duration, during which all the physical operations disclosed by geology were going on."—*Bridgewater Treat.*, p. 20.

It is maintained also by Professor Sedgwick and many others.

"The Bible instructs us that man and other living things have been placed but a few years upon the earth, and the physical monuments of the world bear witness to the same truth. If the astronomer tells us of myriads of worlds not spoken of in the sacred records, the geologist in like manner proves (not by arguments from analogy, but by the incontrovertible evidence of physical phenomena) that there were former conditions of our planet, separated from each other by vast intervals of time, during which man and the other creatures of his own date had not been called into being. Periods such as these belong not therefore to the moral history of our race, and come neither within the letter nor the spirit of revelation. Between the first creation of the earth and the day in which it pleased God to place man upon it, *who shall define the interval?* On this question Scripture is silent. But that silence destroys not the meaning of those physical monuments of his power that God has put before our eyes; giving us at the same time faculties whereby we may interpret them and comprehend their meaning. If the Bible be a rule of life and faith, a record of our moral destinies, it is not, I repeat, nor does it pretend to be, a revelation of natural science."—*Discourse on the Studies of the University of Cambridge.*

A writer in the *Christian Observer* also advances it in the following form, quoted from a friend:—

"I regard Genesis i. 1 as an universal proposition, intended to contradict all the heathen systems, which supposed the eternity of

the distance of innumerable ages, and that, in the interval between that and the creation narrated by Moses, there was a series of creations and destructions of vegetable and animal races—is equally at variance with the representation in v. 4, 5, that the darkness, which was divided from the day—which must have embraced that of the whole space between the first creative fiat and the production of light—was called night, and formed part of the first day. It is also in direct contradiction to the declaration of the Almighty at Sinai, that "in six days he made heaven and earth, the sea, and all that in them is;" in which the creation of the heavens and earth is as specifically assigned to the six days, as the plants, fish, fowls, and beasts are, with which the earth and sea were peopled. It is, like the former, accordingly nothing else than an attempt to bring this passage into harmony with the theory of geology, by impeaching the veracity of the other; or to clear the word of God from the charge of falsehood, by transferring that charge to himself!

Apart from this consideration, also, the supposition

matter, or polytheism, or any notion inconsistent with the infinite perfections of the one great Creator; and ver. 2 I regard as proceeding to take up our planet *in a state of ruin from a former condition*, and describing a succession of phenomena, effected in part by the *laws of nature* (which are no more than our expressions of God's observed method of working), and in part by the immediate exercise of divine power directing and creating."—*Christian Observer*, *May*, 1834.

of such an omission is unnatural and improbable. If such a vast interval, and occupied by such a stupendous series of creative acts, intervened between the fiat which called the heavens and earth into existence, and the six days of the Mosaic creation, why should the Most High, in professedly giving a history of his work, pass them in total silence, and frame the narrative so as necessarily to mislead his creatures in respect to the date and history of the earth? If, as geology asserts, the strata form an indubitable record of those creations, the recital of them in the history in Genesis, so far from unimportant, was obviously necessary, both to his vindication, and to the just instruction of his creatures. To exclude it, was to place them under an unavoidable necessity either of misconceiving or distrusting him, and prepare the way for their being betrayed into the most fatal errors. For as the sole creation in our system which he claims is that of the six days, including the fiat by which the heavens and the earth were called into existence, if there were other previous creations equally important, what could suggest itself so naturally as the reason that they were not claimed by him, as that they were not in fact his? But it is wholly unlike his procedure, and incompatible with his perfections, thus to place them under a seeming logical necessity of doubting that he is the author of his own works. The supposition of such an omission in the narrative he has given of the creation, is thus in every relation wholly improbable.

These considerations, then,—which are hereafter to be confirmed by others equally decisive and emphatic,—sufficiently show that the expedients by which it has been supposed that the narrative in Genesis is brought into harmony with the doctrines of geology, so far from answering that end, only serve to demonstrate that their reconciliation is impossible.

The theory of the existence of the earth and its races through innumerable ages, is thus in direct antagonism with that part of the Mosaic record which defines the period of the creation, and if held to be true, renders the conclusion natural and unavoidable, that that record is not. And such, it is well known, is the result to which it carries great numbers of those to whom it is taught. Wherever advanced by a popular lecturer, and exhibited as a truth that is demonstrated by the strata of the earth, there it will be found it has left the impression very generally on the hearers that the Mosaic account of the creation is convicted of error; and thence cannot be regarded as having been written by inspiration. It has, indeed, been so boldly and speciously taught for many years in books, in laboratories, in lyceums, in popular lectures and sermons, that it has become a very common impression with the young that the first chapter of Genesis is mistaken and without authority.*

But that inference, if adopted, cannot be restricted

* "The circulation of systems of natural history contrary to the Mosaic revelation has been greatly extended by representing them," as the theory held by Dr. Buckland, Professor Sedgwick, and others does, "as wholly unconnected with Christianity, the certainty of which, it is said, is independent of that of the Jewish religion, or at least of the first chapters of Genesis: an assertion which even a number of Christian ministers have been made to believe. It is thus that a great number of individuals have allowed themselves to be carried away by pretended natural science, without being aware of its tendency; that it has become a kind of fashion; that its general results, exhibited as demonstrated propositions, have been circulated through all classes of society; and that, at length, the greater part of those who pretend to any information, are fearful of incurring the charge of ignorance, if they do not side with those who consider the first of our sacred books as a fiction. . . . The consequence is that men of letters who are not naturalists, putting implicit faith in what is so positively asserted to be the evidence of nature, have reproduced some arguments against revelation, which otherwise would not have had any influence."—*De Luc's Letters to Blumenbach*, pp. 46, 47.

A writer in the Christian Observer, for May, 1834, says of the difficulties of the question: "We are come to where four cross-roads meet; for, first, we must deny the geological facts and inferences; or, secondly, we must give up the popular interpretation of the first chapter of Genesis, and reconcile the facts to the sacred text by a new one; or, thirdly, we must deny that the Bible touches at all upon the question; or, fourthly, *we must give up the inspiration of the Bible as to its physical statements.*"

"If some plan of reconciliation be not devised, *we are at the mercy of the infidel*, who, in spite of all our protests and reasonings, will not fail to prejudice the cause of revelation, by appeals to persons of education and influence, setting before them the physical facts and conclusions, and telling them that their religious instructors refuse to listen to them, and instead of showing them that the inspired narrative is not opposed to actual phenomena, would at once stop investigation as heretical and blasphemous."—Pp. 313, 314.

to that chapter. To pronounce the history there given a fiction, because of its representation that the heavens, the earth, and the sea and all that in them is, were created in six days, is to make it logically necessary to deny the inspiration of every other part of the book, and of the law that is associated with it; as that representation was expressly reaffirmed by the Most High himself at Sinai, incorporated in the law of the sabbath, and presented as the reason of the consecration of that day to rest; and was renewed again to Moses, on delivering to him the tables on which it was written. "Six days shalt thou labor and do all thy work; but the seventh day is the sabbath of the Lord thy God: in it thou shalt not do any work, thou, nor thy son, nor thy daughter, thy man-servant, nor thy maid-servant, nor thy cattle, nor the stranger that is within thy gates: For in six days the Lord made heaven and earth, the sea and all that in them is, and rested the seventh day, and hallowed it." Exodus xx. 11. "Wherefore the children of Israel shall keep the sabbath to observe the sabbath throughout their generations, a perpetual covenant, a sign between me and the children of Israel for ever; for in six days the Lord made heaven and earth, and on the seventh day he rested and was refreshed." Exodus xxxi. 16, 17. It is incredible that God should have thus with his own voice repeated that declaration on his revealing himself in glory to the Israelitish people at Sinai, and institution of the law, and graven it with his own finger on the tables of stone, if it was not true; if it were such a sheer and enormous error as modern geology represents. It is impossible from his rectitude. There would then have been no conceivable motive for founding the institution of the sabbath on such a reason. As he had a perfect right to establish it, independently of the consideration whether he created the world and its vegetable and animal races in six days, or any other period, why should he offer his having accomplished it in six days, and rested the seventh, as the reason of his consecrating the seventh as a day of rest, unless he had actually wrought it in those six days? It is infinitely impossible that he should have renewed and ratified that declaration in so solemn a manner, and made it an element of his legislation that was for ever to be kept before the eyes of mankind, if, as geology teaches, it is confuted by his natural works, that are equally open to their inspection; if the strata of the earth which they were soon to explore and read, contain a record which shows that the date of the creation was innumerable ages earlier. It would have been to overthrow his authority, instead of establishing it. If, then, as geology contends, the record on the table of the law is convicted of falsehood by another record which he has graven in ineffaceable characters on the strata of the earth, it is impossible that the law can have proceeded from him, and the whole system of legislation associated with it must, like the first chapter of Genesis, be rejected as a fiction. To suppose it can be otherwise, is to suppose that he has, in the most momentous act of his administration, proclaimed a falsehood which was soon to be detected by his creatures, and place them under an inevitable necessity of distrusting his truth, his uprightness, and his wisdom.

Nor does that conclusion terminate at this point. If that announcement from Sinai, and ratification of the history of the creation given in Genesis, is held to be a fiction, it must of necessity lead to the rejection of the whole Pentateuch as a fabrication. If, without any conceivable motive, and against every consideration that would govern a wise and holy being, a misrepresentation so stupendous, and so sure to be detected and exposed, is incorporated in the decalogue itself, both as it is represented to have been pronounced by the Almighty Lawgiver, and written by him on the tables of stone, what certainty can be felt that any of the other recitals or declarations are not equally false? If no trust is to be placed in the awful attestations which God is represented to have given to that part of the law, no other attestations which he is said to have given the other enactments and institutions can be entitled to reliance. Neither visible theophanies, audible voices, miracles, nor prophecies, which are declared to have attended the communication of commands, and to have shown that they were from him, can yield them any corroboration. Indeed, it would be absolutely incredible that the whole was not in an equal measure a fabrication.

But the rejection of the Pentateuch as false in its claims to a divine origin and authority, would necessarily draw after it the rejection also of all the other books of the Old Testament; for they all recognize the truth of the Pentateuch, and proceed on its histories, enactments, and institutions, as verities. They exhibit the Israelitish nation as sustaining that relation to God which the Pentateuch represents; and the priesthood, the sacrifices, the covenants, the promises, and the whole system of laws, as instituted by God, as that record relates. If they are not his work, it is impossible that the other should be. But their rejection draws after it also as necessarily the rejection of the New Testament; for the latter ratifies, in the fullest manner, all the great historical statements, enactments, and religious institutions of the former, and it is on them that the work of redemption which it reveals is founded. If the Mosaic history of the creation and fall, the destruction of the ancient world, the adoption of the Israelites as a peculiar people, their deliverance from Egypt, the proclamation of the law at Sinai, the institution of the priesthood sacrifices and rites of worship, and the interpositions, commands, and revelations that are recorded by the prophets that followed, are not from God, it is impossible that the New Testament can be, which everywhere recognizes them as realities, and is dependent on them for its truth and propriety.

The whole Bible, as a revelation, thus stands or falls with the first chapter of Genesis. This intimate connexion with other parts of the word of God, is, in a great degree, peculiar to that record of the creation. The histories, narratives, and even the enactments of many other chapters might be supposed to be supposititious, without necessarily destroying the credibility of the inspiration of the remainder. But the subversion of this, from its incorporation in the law of Sinai, necessarily carries with it the subversion of all that follows.

These considerations sufficiently show, that the contradiction which the modern theory of geology presents to the record of the creation by Moses, naturally leads those who assent to it, to regard that record as erroneous, and prepares the way for a distrust and rejection of the whole Bible. The scepticism which it is known to excite and foster, is not gratuitous and causeless, but the logical result of such an impeachment of that part of the word of God, which is the foundation of all the rest. The question, therefore, between the Bible and that theory, is one of the utmost interest. It is the question whether Christianity is credible and true, or whether it is contradicted and convicted of falsehood by the material works of the Creator. If it cannot be vindicated from the impeachment offered by the geological theory, it cannot be vindicated at all; but scepticism is unavoidable, and nothing is left for those who would be consistent, but to adopt and propagate it. The subject is entitled, therefore, to the most serious consideration of all believers in revelation, and especially of the ministers of the gospel, whose office it is to teach and enforce the doctrines, laws, promises, and predictions of the Scriptures as communications from God. They cannot, rationally, satisfy themselves with mere presumptions, vague hopes, or undefined impressions, that the Bible is God's word, although it may be contradicted by his works. They cannot consistently act as his ministers, unless they can defend it from this imputation, and show that it is entitled to be received as a divine revelation. They cannot fulfill their duty to those of their people who have been betrayed into scepticism, or are in danger of becoming its victims, unless able to point out the fallacies and errors of the system which impeaches it, and show that the works of God, instead of confuting or contravening it, are both in perfect harmony with it, and offer it the most clear and ample corroboration.

QUESTIONS.

Is it admitted by many geologists of intelligence and reputation, that the theory of the great age of the world, is irreconcilable with the history of the creation in Genesis? Is that admitted, even by some who still regard the Scriptures as the word of God? How does the Literary Gazette account for the admission of what it believes to be a false history of the creation, into the Pentateuch, while it still holds the Bible to be in the main, an inspired book? What is Professor Sedgwick's method of accounting for what he regards as the errors of Genesis, i. ii, while he receives the Scriptures in the main, as the word of God? Are there other geologists who maintain, that though the theory they hold of the great age of the world, is apparently at variance with the Mosaic history of the creation, it is not in fact irreconcilable with it? What is the first hypothesis by which they attempt to prove them to be consistent with each other? What is the other expedient by which they endeavor to bring them into harmony? How will you prove that the word day in Genesis i. is not used to denote an indefinitely long period? How will you show from the narrative, Genesis, i. 1—5, that a vast period cannot, according to their second hypothesis, have intervened between the creation announced Genesis, i. 1, and that which is detailed, vs. 3, 4, and 5? If such a space had intervened between the creation of the heaven and earth recorded, v. 1, and the creation of light recorded, v. 3—5, is it credible that it would not have been mentioned by the sacred writer? Do these attempts then, fail to reconcile the sacred text with the geological theory, and leave the conclusion unavoidable, that if the theory is correct, the narrative of the sacred writer is not? But if geology proves that narrative to be false, does it not make it impossible to believe that the remainder of the book is inspired? Show how the truth of the narrative, of the six days creation, is recognized and ratified in the institution of the sabbath? But if the inspiration of Genesis is given up, must not that of the whole Pentateuch be likewise rejected? Show how the disbelief of the one must necessarily lead to the disbelief of the other? But if the Pentateuch is proved to be uninspired, must not the claim of every other part of the sacred volume to a divine origin be rejected? Does the geological theory then naturally lead those who assent to it, to doubt the inspiration of the Bible? Is the question whether the theory is true, equivalent to the question, whether the Bible is not a fiction? Is not the inquiry then one of the greatest moment?

CHAPTER III.

False Notions of Geology—It is not a Science—It has no Laws—Geologists have not an Exclusive Right to treat of the subject.

UNDER the conviction that the geological theory which thus conflicts with the word of God, is wholly mistaken, and may be easily refuted, and that its refutation and abandonment are demanded both by the interests of religion and the credit of geology, we shall proceed to point out the fallacy on which it rests; indicate proofs both from the record of Moses and from the earth, hitherto overlooked by geologists, which demonstrate it to be erroneous; and finally suggest the view of the subject, which seems to us to be required alike by the word of God and the facts of the science.

To prepare the way for the discussion, it is important to correct several misapprehensions and prejudices that extensively prevail, and are obstacles to a candid consideration of the question.

In the first place, the language which geological lecturers and writers are accustomed to use, has produced the impression that geology is a demonstrative science, having laws peculiar to itself, that are verified by the facts discovered in the strata of the earth; and thence, that the conclusions which they deduce from the strata, and embody in their systems, are the legitimate results of those laws, and as incontrovertible as the truths that are derived from the axioms or principles of other sciences. No misapprehension could be greater. Geology has no laws that are peculiar to itself. It professedly treats of the nature of the substances that constitute those parts of the crust of the globe that are accessible to our observation, and of the causes or forces to which they owe their present combinations and positions; and those forces are expressly defined as either chemical or mechanical; or those of attraction, by which particles that have an affinity are united in crystals and other solid forms; and those of fire and water, by which they are fused or disintegrated, and transported from one place to another.

This is seen from the following quotations:—

"The history of the earth forms a large and complex subject of inquiry, divisible at its outset into two distinct branches, the first comprehending the history of the unorganized mineral matter, and of the various changes through which it has advanced from the creation of its component elements to its actual condition; the second embracing the past history of the animal and vegetable kingdoms, and the successive modifications which these two great departments of nature have undergone, *during the chemical and mechanical operations* that have affected the surface of our planet.

"In tracing the history of these natural phenomena, we enter at once into the consideration of *geological dynamics*, including *the nature and mode of operation of all kinds of physical agents*, that have at any time and in any manner affected the surface and interior of the earth. In the foremost rank of these agents we find *fire* and *water*—those two universal and mighty disorganizing forces which have most materially influenced the condition of the globe.

"The state of the ingredients of crystalline rocks has, in a great degree, been influenced by *chemical and electro-magnetic forces*, whilst that of stratified sedimentary deposits has resulted chiefly from *the mechanical action of moving water*, and has occasionally been modified by large admixtures of animal and vegetable remains."—*Buckland's Bridgewater T.*, pp. 34–37.

"It is the province of geology to investigate the ancient natural history of the earth. To this purpose geologists must observe the effects of *terrestrial agencies*, both organic and inorganic, which are *now in progress*, in order to understand those which have been performed in earlier periods; they must inquire what changes *now take place* upon the land and in the sea; and whether these be due to *mechanical, chemical, or vital agency;* and compare these effects with the monuments of *more ancient revolutions*, and thus endeavor to trace the physical conditions of the globe from the *earliest period to the present date,* so as to present a correct history of the successive steps by which it has been brought to its actual state, and made fit for the purposes which it now fulfills.

"In the modern system of nature we recognize two great agencies employed in producing changes on the face of the globe. WATER, which wastes away grain by grain the elevated portions of the land, and deposits its spoils in lower situations, thus ever tending to equalize the levels of the surface. FIRE, which raises matter in masses from the interior of the earth, and thus tends to increase the inequalities of its surface. Both of these agents are chemical; water dissolves, heat fuses ; both act mechanically. The mechanical effects of water depend on the general force of gravitation, and ever tend downwards ; but the mechanical force of heat is independent of gravitation, and ever struggles to overcome it."—*Phillips's Guide,* pp. 3, 25.

"Geology was defined to be the science which investigates the former changes that have taken place in the organic, as well as in the inorganic kingdoms of nature. As vicissitudes in the inorganic world are most apparent, and as on them all the fluctuations in the animate creation must in a great measure depend, they may claim our first consideration. The great *agents* of change in the inorganic world may be divided into two principal classes, the aqueous and the igneous. To the aqueous belong rain, rivers, torrents, springs, currents, and tides ; to the igneous, volcanoes and earthquakes. Both these classes are instruments of decay as well as of reproduction; but they may also be regarded as antagonist forces. For the aqueous agents are incessantly labouring to reduce the inequalities of the earth's surface to a level; while the igneous are equally active in restoring the unevenness of the external crust, partly by heaping up new matter in certain localities, and partly by depressing one portion and forcing out another of the earth's envelope."—*Lyell's Principles*, p. 191.

Sir Charles Lyell holds not only that all the facts which it is the province of the science to explain, are to be referred to these causes, but that they are to be regarded as having been produced by an agency of essentially the same energy as that by which these causes are now giving birth to similar effects; as the result "of one uniform system of change in the animate and inanimate world," that has been in progress "from the remotest periods," and is to continue through all future time.—P. 188.

The following is from Mr. Macculloch:—

"The materials of this inquiry are objects and actions; the result constitutes inferences; and these are retrospective, as well as present and future. The retrospect is the material for a theory of the earth.

OBJECTS.

"The objects are the materials of the earth; the materials are rocks and fragments. Rocks and the larger fragments are composed of earths or of minerals, and of animal and vegetable matters compacted. They are compacted by *mechanical approximation*, or *by chemical action*, or by both united.

ACTIONS.

"Actions are the results of *animal and vegetable life and destruction*, of *water* and the force of *gravity*, or of *fire*. By organic production and destruction its objects become portions of the fragments, or form strata, or parts of these. By water and gravity the solid rocks are broken into fragments, and deposited on the land or beneath the water. By water animal remains are mineralized, and vegetable ones bituminized. Fire acts in volcanoes which are visible or invisible. It elevates the superincumbent materials of the earth, whether solid or otherwise.

RETROSPECT.

"The inferences from objects and actions connect the present with the past. The fragments and solution of former rocks and earths in former water, produced the present stratified rocks. The effects of former fire produced the unstratified rocks with the consequences attributed to them. Former races of living animals and vegetables in different waters and on different lands, produced the objects of this nature now found in rocks and fragments. The successive connexions of distinct parallelisms among the stratified rocks infer as many distinct conditions of the globe. The time requisite for the production of stratified rocks, and for the reproduction of animals and vegetables, implies long intervals between each condition.

"With respect to the future, it is inferred that the present actions are tending to produce a new condition analogous to that which is just past."—*J. Macculloch's Geol.* vol. i. pp. 11–15.

"A practical observer . . . needs no labored argument to satisfy him that if the stratified rocks were deposited *in the manner the work is now going on, immense periods* of time were requisite. Even if he admit, what we are not disposed with some geologists to deny, that *the causes now in operation* did formerly *act with greater energy than at present;* yet he will still see the necessity of allowing periods of time vastly extended to form the fossiliferous rocks, unless he admit without proof that the laws of nature have been changed." *Hitchcock's Geology and Revelation*, p. 20.

Some geologists hold the necessity of regarding the rate at which those causes are now generating their several effects, as the measure of the rapidity with which they produced them at all former periods as so imperative, that to deny it were to strike from our hands all means of reasoning respecting them.

"All agree that the deposition of thick beds of limestone or clay replete with the exuviæ of successive generations of marine or terrestrial animals, interrupted too by several periods of convulsion, during which the existing races were in many cases destroyed, and new ones afterwards substituted, could not have been accomplished, consistently with the *present laws of nature,* within a very short space of time. And if it be said that the processes which produced them may be imagined to have proceeded *at a more rapid rate, and in a different manner at that period,* than they do at present, we reply, that such a supposition *would strike at the root of every species of evidence;* for if the author of nature should have imparted to the constituents of the globe those characters and relations which at the present time would result from the operation of known causes continued during a period of at least a certain duration, and yet have chosen to employ other agencies, of whose character and laws we know nothing, or have accomplished the whole by the immediate fiat of his omnipotence, there then is an end to all reasoning on the subject."—*Literary Gazette,* 1834, p. 771.*

They thus unite first in maintaining that geology treats simply of the materials of which the crust of the earth consists, and of the forces from which they received their present form; and next, in regarding the effects which they attempt to explain, as not only produced by the chemical and mechanical forces

* He thus assumes that the causes to which the strata are to be referred, cannot have acted on any larger area, nor with any higher energy, than they now do; and that to suppose "the processes" to have taken place at a more rapid rate than at present, is to suppose that they were produced either by agencies of whose character we know nothing, or by the fiat of omnipotence; a mistake as obvious and absurd as it were to maintain that there can be no diversity in the strength and activity of chemical and mechanical forces.

that are now giving birth to somewhat similar changes on the earth's surface, but by agencies of essentially the same energy as those which they are now exerting.

Geology, it is thus seen from these statements of its objects, is not a demonstrative science. It is not a system of principles or laws by which a share of the great processes of nature are explained, and can, like the movements of the bodies of the solar system, be made the subject of exact calculation, and traced back through the past, or forward to the future. Instead, it is a mere statement or description of the stratified and other rocks which compose the crust of the globe, with a reference of them to the agents by which they are supposed to have been produced. It has no axioms or principles that are peculiar to itself, as the laws of optics are to light, and of gravity and motion to the phenomena of the solar system. In chemistry, experiments are made by which it is ascertained what substances have such an affinity for each other as to enter into combination; what the circumstances are in which their attractive powers act, what the proportions are in which they unite, and what the forms are which they assume. In like manner experiments have been made with bodies dropped from a height, and projected into the atmosphere, by which it has been ascertained what the motions are of bodies in space acted on by gravity, and by gravity and a projectile force; and the laws of those motions taken as indicating the laws of all material bodies moving in space, have been generalized and employed in the solution of the movements of the bodies of the solar system. But no analogous experiments are made in geology, by which it is ascertained from what quarter materials must be drawn to form such strata as those of which the transition, carboniferous, and tertiary systems consist, or what the periods are which are required for their formation. No laws, consequently, can be deduced from the strata themselves by which it can be demonstrated, that vast periods have been employed in their deposition. They present no data from which that conclusion can be scientifically deduced. If drawn at all as a logical conclusion from a premise, it must be from an assumption or hypothesis, not from an ascertained fact or demonstrated law of such formations.

Geology, indeed, has no axioms, or generalized facts whatever, except those, first, which respect the materials of which the different strata of the earth consist; secondly, the relations which they sustain to each other, or the order in which they are superimposed; and, thirdly, the agents or media through which they were formed and placed in their present positions; and *they* furnish no means of a scientific demonstration of a different and higher class of truths, such as the existence of the world through an immeasurable round of ages. The facts, for example, that the strata are often very numerous and of great thickness, that they consist of certain substances, and are arranged in a specific or uniform order, is no basis for the logical deduction of such a conclusion, just as the fact that the great pyramid of Egypt consists of a certain series of stones of certain specific characters, and arranged in a certain order, is no logical ground for the inference that a vast series of ages was occupied in its erection—inasmuch as the time required for its formation did not depend on the magnitude of the effect, but on the measure of the forces by which it was accomplished.

It is not, therefore, a demonstrative science, in the usual sense of the term. Its facts do not furnish the media of deducing a set of general laws peculiar to itself, by which all the phenomena of which it treats can be explained. And consequently, it cannot, by possibility, furnish a scientific confutation of the Mosaic account of the creation. The fancy of such a demonstration is a mere fallacy, veiled under the forms of a philosophical induction ; and stated arithmetically, is simply equivalent to the following problem in the rule of three :—As the depth of the primary strata or any one of them is to the period which was employed in its formation, so is the depth of the whole series to the periods which their deposition occupied—in which, as the second term, on which the problem turns, must be arbitrarily assumed, or guessed on only probable grounds, the result, instead of being scientifically demonstrated, is necessarily a mere deduction from a conjecture, and without value.

Geology, accordingly, in place of a systematic body of truths deduced from a few primary axioms or laws, that are demonstrated by experiment, and furnish a scientific solution of all the phenomena presented by the strata of the earth, consists only of facts or truths that are ascertained by *observation.* It is no more a demonstrative science than any other branch of knowledge that is acquired solely by that method, such as the topography of countries. The investigation of the fallen capitals of Assyria, by Botta, Layard, and others, and their statements respecting their date and destruction, present a very exact parallel to it. Instead of an affair of axioms or laws, it is simply a question of substances and their relations and conditions, that is determined by inspection. It is entitled, therefore, to the name of a science in no higher sense than that it presents a minute and accurate description of the elements of which the crust of the earth is composed, the order in which the strata are arranged, their depth and extent, and the vegetable and animal relics that are imbedded in them, and in some instances gives a probable hypothesis of the sources whence their materials were drawn, the means by which they were originally arranged horizontally, and the forces by which they have since been modified in structure, and thrown into their present conditions. To accomplish anything beyond this, to demonstrate that the date of the creation was infinite ages ago, is wholly without its sphere. It might almost as well be assigned the task of determining any other date in chronology, or resolving any other question with which it has no logical connexion.

Another impression that needs to be corrected, to which the language and representations of writers on the subject have given birth, is, that no person can be competent to offer objections to the theories that are formed respecting it, except professed geologists themselves. An attempt by men of other pursuits to controvert their deductions, and especially by expositors and theologians, is treated as an ill-judged and absurd intrusion into a sphere for which they can have no qualifications—as nothing else indeed than an attempt to solve the problems of one branch of knowledge by the principles of another with which it has no affinity. It is, accordingly, often met by mere appeals to prejudice, repelled with sneers as unworthy of consideration, or denounced in terms of discourtesy and passion quite inconsistent with the calmness and impartiality of philosophers who regard themselves as able to verify their doctrines by scientific processes, that have the force of unanswerable demonstration. That the works that are usually quoted as specimens of the ill-judged attempts of "the divine and man of letters" to treat of the subject, such as those of Penn, Nolon, and Cole, betray a very unfortunate inacqaintance with many of the topics which they discuss, and indulge in unjustifiable imputations on those whom they assail, we shall not deny. That they undertook a task for which they were inadequately qualified, is no ground, however, for the conclusion that no others who are not professors of the science can be warranted in discussing it. Great as their errors are, they are not greater than those into which some of the geologists of their period fell; nor do the asperities in which they indulged, transcend those that have disfigured the controversies which geologists have waged with each other. The objection is absurd indeed, in the absolute form in which it is often presented, inasmuch as the question whether an argument against the geological theory is entitled to consideration or not, must depend on its character, not on the class from which it proceeds.

In the first place, this opposition to the criticism of their theory by any except of their own profession, is chargeable with much the same inconsideration and injustice which they impute to the divines who venture to arraign their doctrines at the bar of the Bible, and show that they contradict the history God has there given of the work of the creation. For it certainly lies within the proper province of the sacred interpreter and theologian to ascertain what the import is of the record in Genesis, and of other parts of the sacred volume which treat of the creation, and to determine whether the dogmas of geology contravene it or not. They do not step out of their sphere in that part of their labors. It is their proper and peculiar province. They are equally in their sphere also when, on finding that the teachings of the sacred word are contradicted by the speculations of geologists, they point out the error, and defend the Bible from the inferences which might otherwise be drawn against its inspiration. It is a task to which their profession directly calls them, and which they cannot refuse to fulfill, without a gross dereliction of their office. When, therefore, these objectors charge them in doing this with transcending their proper profession, they are themselves guilty of the unfairness which they unjustly impute to them. It is the mere geologist, plainly, who quits his proper sphere, when he attempts to decide that the record of the creation in Genesis is not inconsistent with his theory of the age of the world—not the philologist and theologian who venture to decide that it is. How is it that geologists have any higher right to determine what the meaning of the first chapter of Genesis is, than divines have to pronounce on the true theory of geology? How, indeed, is it that they have an exclusive title to treat of the subject, while divines are guilty of transcending their province, when they venture to interpret and maintain what God has revealed respecting the creation? This important question seems not to have occurred to these objectors; but while in effect denying to divines the right not only to treat of geology, but even to interpret and teach the word of God, which is the peculiar business of their office, they themselves not only claim it as their special function to treat authoritatively of geology, but usurp the right also of determining the philological meaning of the inspired history of the creation, which lies out of their peculiar sphere.

This objection, then, to the interference of divines and philologists with the subject, so far as the interpretation of the first chapter of Genesis, and a protest against the theories of geology which contradict the testimony God has there given, are concerned, should be withdrawn. It is not only unauthorized and unjust, but it is more obnoxious to the charge of illiberality and intolerance, than the most intemperate denunciations in which "the divine and man of letters" have indulged, whom they spurn with so much contemptuousness and resentment.

In the next place, the objection indicates an unfortunate misapprehension of the premise from which geologists deduce the vast age they ascribe to the world. They proceed in it as though there were a class of direct and specific evidences of the existence of the earth through vast periods, graven, as it were, on the strata themselves, that can be learned only by inspection, in the same manner as the number, position, depth, and contents of the strata themselves are. But that is altogether mistaken. The age of the strata is not to be ascertained by the hammer or pickaxe, by chemical analysis, by touch, or by inspection. The chronology which they represent as inscribed on the rocks, instead of being wrought by the finger of the Almighty, is the work in a great measure of metaphor and fancy. The strata themselves are not, in fact, the premise from which they deduce the age they ascribe to the earth. They furnish no direct data for such a conclusion, as may be seen from the form the argument from them assumes, as in the following premise and conclusion.

The strata which have been deposited since the creation of the earth are numerous, and in many places of great depth, and are interspersed with vegetable and animal fossils, which indicate that much time was occupied in their formation. Therefore the creation itself must have taken place innumerable ages ago.

But this inference is plainly irrelevant to the

premise. There is nothing in the facts stated in the proposition that can generate such a conclusion. Inasmuch as the period occupied in the deposition of the strata is not determinable from their number, depth, and contents, but depends on the species and energy of the agents by which they were formed; to treat the inference from such an irrelative premise as a truth established by scientific deduction, is an extraordinary inaccuracy. Instead of being graven in legible characters on the strata themselves, or directly deduced from the facts of geology, their alleged chronology of the world is in reality drawn from *a mere hypothesis* respecting the forces or processes by which the strata were constituted, as is seen from their argument when expressed in a syllogistic form.

Each of the several strata deposited since the creation of vegetables and animals, having been formed by essentially the same forces as are now in activity, and thence by a very slow process, must have occupied a long period.

But in many localities the series of separate beds amounts to several hundreds and even thousands.

Therefore the period which the deposition of the whole series has occupied, must be immense beyond computation—a round of innumerable years—myriads and millions of ages.*

* Thus Mr. Macculloch: "We have every reason to know, *from*

This, or an equivalent proposition is the only one from which that conclusion can be logically deduced. It is not possible to frame a major excluding the element of time, that shall be a logical ground for the induction of such an age of the earth. But here the inference is drawn plainly, not from the number, dimensions, and contents of the strata, but from an hypothesis respecting the nature of the forces and processes by which they were formed. Take away that hypothesis, and the inference becomes, like the other, a non sequitur. But that hypothesis is not found graven on the rocks, nor is it legitimately deduced from them; as there is nothing, as we shall hereafter show, in the strata themselves that compels or authorizes the assumption that they were formed by a slow process, but instead, their structure indicates that they were deposited very rapidly, and under the agency of forces immensely more energetic than those of the fire, water, and chemistry that are now in activity.

what is now taking place on our own earth, that the accumulation of materials at the bottom of the ocean is a work *infinitely slow:* we are sure that such an accumulation as should produce the primary strata as we now see them, must have occupied a space, *from the contemplation of which the mind shrinks.* Whatever that may be, *the geological depth of the consecutive series of any one stage of the surface is* THE MEASURE OF THE TIME *through which it was deposited:* it is *the measure of the duration of that world* which immediately preceded the one of which it forms the latest stratified portion."—*Geol.* vol. i. p. 473.

As the inference of the age of the world which geologists dignify with the name of a scientific induction, is thus drawn from *a premise that lies out of the facts of geology*, and is a fallacy, it is plain, that philologists, and "the divine, and man of letters," if logicians, are as competent to detect its deceptive character and criticise and confute it, as though they were practical geologists. It is entirely within their sphere as reasoners. A minute inspection of the strata of the earth is not requisite to it. Though an intimate acquaintance from observation with all the great facts of the science must naturally give a more vivid apprehension and realization of them, yet it is not necessary in order to avoid the error into which geologists themselves have fallen, of confounding them with an hypothesis respecting the processes of their formation. It is not the great facts themselves of geology, let it be considered, that are in question. It is not a direct and logical deduction from those facts even. It is only a deduction from an assumption respecting *the causes* to which they owe their origin, which men "of letters" and theologians capable of distinguishing a fallacy from a legitimate induction, are as adequate to confute as those of any other profession. That this consideration, which, of itself, overturns their theory respecting the age of the world, should have been overlooked by geologists, and an objection thus confidently urged which indicates such a misapprehension of the point at issue, is truly singular, and shows that however eminent they may be in their peculiar sphere, it is not the part of prudence to acquiesce in their deductions and hypotheses, without an examination of the grounds on which they rest.

But in the third place, the objection, if legitimate, is applicable in a large degree to geologists themselves, and invalidates their speculations as effectually as it can the views and reasonings respecting them, of those who are not of their profession. For what share of the facts on which geologists professedly found their theories, have they severally themselves observed? Not one probably in fifty, perhaps not in five hundred. It is physically impossible that such a writer, for example, as Sir Charles Lyell, should have personally inspected all the localities of which he treats, all the processes he describes, and all the facts which he alleges in support of his theories. Of the localities, those of South America, the islands of the Pacific and Indian Oceans, the seas, rivers, lakes, mountains, and plains of Eastern Asia, to say nothing of many others, he has never seen. Of the processes, many have extended through centuries, and could not have been inspected through their whole period by a single individual; and many of the facts had their dates ages ago, and are not now within the sphere of observation. And so of other writers. Instead of relying exclusively on their own personal investigation, they avail themselves of the observations and discoveries of others, and build their speculations with as much confidence on the facts of which they thus gain a knowledge, as on those which they derive directly from their own examination. And this is as legitimate, as safe, and as indispensable as it is in mineralogy, chemistry, geography, history, or any other branch of knowledge. It were to impeach geologists themselves of inaccuracy, and invalidate their reasonings, to suppose that the descriptions they give of the facts they have severally observed, are not intelligible and entitled to reliance. What claims can their systems have to be regarded as scientific deductions, if the facts on which they professedly found them are of a doubtful nature, or questionable reality? They are not, however, generally obnoxious in any measure to doubt. The number of practical geologists during the last thirty years has been very large; many of the most important localities have been explored by the most competent observers, and their descriptions are distinguished in a high degree, by minuteness, intelligibleness, and accuracy, and fully justify the use that is made of them by such authors as Lyell, La Beche, Murchison, Buckland, Conybeare, Sedgwick, Phillips, Macculloch; and together with theirs, and the works of other eminent writers, furnish the most ample means to such as are not professed geologists, of an accurate knowledge of all the great facts of the science, and just judgment of the validity of the inductions that are founded on them. Were it otherwise; were a practical acquaintance with all the facts that are made the basis of theoretical geology necessary, there is not a solitary treatise on the subject, that would not be in a large measure obnoxious to the objection, and as unworthy of consideration as the counter speculations are of the mere "divine and man of letters." This objection is thus in every relation ill-considered and unfortunate.*

* This is verified by the mode which is usually pursued by geological professors, in teaching the science to their classes. It is by verbal descriptions, specimens, and pictorial representations, such as are given in books, that they present the great facts of the system to their pupils, not by conducting them to the scenes where those facts can be ascertained by inspection. Thus Professor Phillips, of King's College, London, and one of the distinguished geologists of England, says:—

"Geology founded upon *observations* of the effects of terrestrial agencies upon a grand scale, *admits of being taught*, first, by actual demonstration of the phenomena as they are laid open by nature in mountains and valleys, cliffs and ravines; secondly, *by the aid of specimens of natural products and representations and descriptions* of the manner of their occurrence. As we cannot transport a pupil to the summit of the Alps, the glens of the Grampians, or the caverns of the Peak; as we cannot at pleasure show him the bold cliffs of Hastings, Whitby, or Charmouth, the wasting shores of Norfolk, or the extension of new land along the margin of the Adriatic, he must be taught *to reason upon these characteristic phenomena by the aid of pictorial or verbal representation.* With this view we

QUESTIONS.

What is the first false notion that has been extensively spread respecting the nature of geology? Has geology any laws by which it can be demonstrated that the strata of the earth were formed in a particular way, and that a vast series of ages was occupied in their structure? What is it of which geology professedly treats, according to Dr. Buckland? What is the definition which Professor Phillips gives of its object? What is Sir C. Lyell's? What is Mr. Maccul-

found museums of specimens, publish sections and maps and models, and endeavor by lectures on these examples and imitations of geological occurrences, to lead the student *to the contemplation of the magnificent objects themselves.* Could we dispense with these artificial aids, were it possible to compress into a short geological tour an actual inspection of the most important facts, much of the technical language which is now found so convenient might be dispensed with; many explanations might be spared; the monuments yet remaining of the changes which the earth has undergone, would tell their own history, and never require the little aid of words. But the writer and the lecturer must have recourse to other methods, and by a studied arrangement of representations and reasoning, strive to impress the same truths, *with equal force of conviction*, which are directly gathered from the more vivid, though less regular lessons in the glorious theatre of nature."—*Guide to Geology*, pp. 1, 2.

And this, we may add, is the method also in which the professors of the science prepare themselves to give instruction respecting it. The usual course is to attend the lectures of some distinguished geologist, and study books and specimens. The information derived from the direct inspection of the strata, is slight, generally, compared with that which is drawn from these sources. And this method is not only as justifiable, but as indispensable to success in this branch of knowledge as any other. It were as absurd in a geologist, as it were in a chemist or astronomer, to neglect the discoveries others have made, and attempt to build up a system exclusively on his own observations. The objection often put forth with a very imposing air, thus shrinks, when properly considered, into very moderate dimensions.

loch's? Has it then, according to the definitions of these writers, any laws peculiar to itself, by which it can be proved that the strata were formed by the slow processes, and that the earth is of the great age, which their theory asserts? If geology, then, has no laws, and deals only with mere facts, what are the great facts of which it takes cognizance? Do those facts furnish any means of demonstrating the immense age of the world? Is it a mistake then to regard it as a demonstrative science? Exemplify the fallacy of attempting to prove the vast age of the world by it. What sort of a science then is it, if it is not a demonstrative one? Name some other subject, the knowledge of which is of the same kind as that of geology.

What is the second false impression respecting it that needs to be corrected? Are geologists accustomed to sneer at criticisms on their theory by persons of other professions, and denounce them as unworthy of notice? What is the first objection to that course? Is not the interpretation of the sacred text, Genesis i. and ii., within the proper sphere of the theologian? Has not the theologian quite as good a right to maintain the truth of the inspired narrative against the speculations of the geologist, as the geologist has to endeavor to sustain his theory against the testimony of the sacred text?

What is the second objection to the claims of geologists that none but persons of their profession are competent to criticise their theory? What is the error in the reasoning by which geologists attempt to prove the great antiquity of the world, which shows that they themselves are not masters of their own logic? State the first premise from which they infer the great age of the world. Point out its fallacy. What then is it, in fact, on which their inference of the age of the world from this premise rests? Is it on the facts of *the strata themselves*, or a mere *hypothesis* respecting the forces by which they were formed? State their argument in a syllogistic form. What is it now, in that syllogism, from which the inference of the age of the world is drawn—from the strata themselves, or from an hypothesis respecting the processes by which they were constructed? Is that hypothesis, however, found graven on the strata? Is not the inference of the age of the world drawn from a premise then *that lies out of the facts of geology?* Is it not, therefore, a fallacy, instead of a legitimate scientific conclusion?

What is the third objection to their claim of an exclusive competence to criticise their own theory?

CHAPTER IV.

The Principles of Geologists—Their Theory tried by their own Criteria, irreconcilable with the History of the Creation in Genesis.

We will now proceed to try the question between the Scriptures and the theory of the geologists, by showing first what the facts are that are indicated by the Mosaic account of the six days' creation; and next by pointing out the contradictions both to that record and to the principles of geology itself, presented by the postulates and implications of that theory.

By the principles of geology are meant the principles on which the authors of that theory found their systems; or, in other words, the axioms on which they proceed in their explanations of the facts of the science; first, that the processes which have taken place since the creation of the world, such as the formation of strata, and their subsequent modifications, are to be referred entirely to such forces as are now in activity, and producing similar changes on the earth's surface, namely: gravity, chemical affinity, and the mechanical forces of water and fire.

Secondly, That those forces are to be regarded as having acted on essentially the same scale, both as to extent and intensity, as that on which they have given birth to similar effects since the date of authentic history, and are now producing them.

It is on this postulate, unsupported by evidence, and inconsistent, as we shall hereafter show, with many of the great facts of the science, that they found nearly the whole of their reasonings.

As it follows from this definition, that nothing falls within the sphere of the science, except effects that are the products of those forces, acting as far as the formation of strata is concerned, with much their present energy, it results,

Thirdly, that no geological events can be assumed by them to have taken place, except such as may have been produced by those forces. As they are held to be the only causes of geological effects, and the scale on which they are now acting is taken as the exponent of their capacity to produce their several classes of effects—as well as the measure of the rapidity with which the processes that are referred to them have been accomplished—no geological changes can be assumed and made a basis of induction, except such as may have resulted from those causes.

And finally, it results also, that no geological events can be assumed to have been wrought by those causes, and made the basis of induction, except such as can be proved from the present condition of the strata, to have actually taken place.*

* It results also from these positions, not only that all effects, if there are such, that cannot be referred to those agents, are excluded from the sphere of the science, but that all those of the species produced by them are also, that happen to transcend the effects of the same class which they are now generating. If the effects that are at present resulting from those causes, are the measure of their power to produce such effects, then none of the effects of the same species that required causes of higher energy, can have been the product of their agency. They must lie out of the sphere of the science, therefore, as absolutely as though they were the product of a supernatural power. This, which is the necessary result of their postulate, is indeed a solecism, and overturns the whole theoretical fabric which they have employed themselves in rearing. It contradicts the first great principle of inductive science, which requires that all effects of the same species, no matter what their dimensions are, should be referred to the same cause or causes of the same class. As it is plainly necessary that all effects that are from their nature referable to the force of gravity, such as the deposition of earthy and mineral substances that have been held in solution or suspension by water, which cannot be assigned to any other known power, should be ascribed to that force; so it is equally that all effects of the classes that are produced by chemical agencies, such as crystallization and the union of crystallized and other solidified matter in masses, should, without any consideration of the scale on which they exist, be referred to those agents; and in like manner that all of the several species which fire and water mechanically produce, should be regarded as the result of their agency. The great axiom on which they build their speculative system is thus in contradiction to a first great law of philosophy. Unscientific and solecistical as it is, however, they are compelled to adhere to it in order to give a color of validity to the conclusion they deduce from it of the vast age of the world; as the moment they admit a sliding scale of those forces, and assume that they rose or sank in energy, and acted on a larger or smaller area, proportional to the magnitude of the effects that are referable to them, that moment they quit the postulate on which they found their deduc-

Such being the great postulates or axioms which they acknowledge as the criteria of the truth or error of their inductions, let us now look at the facts which are presented by the Mosaic history of the creation, and see how they consist with the views of these writers.

"In the beginning God created the heaven and the earth," v. 1. By the heaven is meant, not all other worlds besides the earth, i. e. the universe; as it is implied in the temptation of the first pair by Satan that there were worlds and creatures before this creative fiat; and it is expressly indicated (Job xxxviii. 4–7), in which all the sons of God—implying that there were several orders of them—are represented as having shouted for joy when the

tion of the immense age of the world. If it is admitted that, at the period when the strata were formed, those forces acted on a scale as much greater in extent and energy than they now do, as those effects are greater than the corresponding classes that are now in progress, the whole ground is abandoned of the assumption, that they were the work of a slow process, and required a vast series of ages for their completion.

They do not, in fact, however, adhere to that postulate, which would exclude the deposition of strata and most other important processes from the sphere of geology, and circumscribe it to a few of late date that are of comparatively little moment; but, instead, attempt to account for all formations of the classes to which those forces give birth, whatever their magnitude may be, and however vast the energies were that called them into existence. Some of them, indeed, candidly admit the impossibility of accounting by such slight forces for many of the most important of the phenomena they are required to explain, and others swerve from the conditions they prescribe to themselves, whenever an exigency requires it.

foundations of the earth were laid. Nor does it denote simply the orbs of our solar system; as it is stated in a subsequent verse that the stars—by which are meant those that are visible to the unaided eye—were placed in the firmament at the same time as the sun and moon. Heaven denotes, therefore, doubtless, the vast cloud of worlds to which our system and the glittering arch that spans our evening sky belong, that till within a few years comprised all that were known to the inhabitants of our world.

"And the earth was waste and desolate," or unfurnished with organic bodies, "and darkness was upon the face of the deep; and the Spirit of God moved upon the face of the waters," v. 2. That which is here the subject of predication is the *earth*, the same identical earth that now exists, and in essentially its present shape and solidity; not as some maintain, the mere materials of which it consists in the form of gases, or in solution in a vast ocean. This is seen from a variety of considerations. As gravity is a property or law of all matter, the earth must have been subject to it from the moment of the creative fiat, and not only to that share of it which was inherent in itself, and drew its particles to its own centre, but that also which is exerted on its mass by the sun, moon, and other orbs of our system. It is seen, also, from its rotation on its axis. That it was created with that motion is shown by the fact that a whole night and day had passed, that is a complete revolution on its axis, at the close of the first day. It must, therefore, have been under the full force of the gravitating power, or its rapid whirl would have thrown off not only the ocean from its bosom into the surrounding space, but a large share, if not the whole, of its earthy and rocky mass, and left them, if the other bodies of the system were exerting their attractive force, to be drawn away to them.

That it was then as solid as it now is, and of essentially the same dimensions and shape, is shown also by the fact that the ocean enveloped and formed a deep around it. It appears from the narrative of the third day that there was no dry land until the waters were gathered into the seas. The waters of the original deep were those that were then collected into seas, and constitute the present waters of the globe. The earth cannot, therefore, have been larger than it now is, or they would not have been adequate to cover its whole surface, and to such a depth as to form an abyss. Had it been three or four times its present diameter, they would have formed only a thin stratum around it. It must also have been in a spheroidal form, or of greater diameter at the equator than at the poles, or they would not have retained their position on every part of its surface; as a perfect sphere enveloped by an ocean of only such a depth, and revolving on its axis, would immediately throw its water towards the equator in such a manner as to uncover the poles. It was thus created essentially what it now is, in shape, dimensions, and solidity, and its waters were what waters now are, and were those of our present seas.

These truths lie on the face of the narrative, and cannot be set aside by any legitimate process. It has been supposed, indeed, by some, that the language of the narrative is metaphorical, and denotes a different event from the creation of the material earth. But that has arisen from a misconception or ignorance of the nature of the metaphor. That figure, in the first place, always lies exclusively in the predicate of a proposition. The subject or nominative to which it is applied, or of which the affirmation is made, is always used in its literal sense, as in the expressions: God is a shield; all flesh is grass; the winds sigh; the fields smile. But the nominative of the affirmation in the first verse is God, and in the second the earth. Whatever the meanings of the affirmations are, therefore, of which they are the nominatives, *they*, and nothing else, are the subjects of those affirmations; or in other words, God was literally the agent of that which is ascribed to him; and the earth was really the subject of that which is asserted of it. And next, the figure consists in the ascription to the agent or subject to which it is applied, of a nature, act, or condition, that is not proper to it, but that is peculiar to a being or thing of a different species; and the object of its use is, to indicate in an emphatic manner, that the agent or object to which it is applied, presents a strong resemblance to that which the terms used by the figure literally signify; as when a hero is called a lion, to indicate his courage; and a statesman a pillar of the republic, to express the support he yields to its institutions. But there is no such transference here of the words create, waste, desolate, deep, waters, which are the terms of the predicates, from their natural sphere, to one that is proper only to another class of words. It is proper to God, and his peculiar and exclusive prerogative, to create, and to create worlds like heaven and the earth. It is equally consonant to the nature of the earth to be created, and created a waste, that is without vegetables or animals, enveloped at every point by an ocean, and shrouded in darkness. There is no other body of which those affirmations could be more truly and appropriately made. The fancy, therefore, that they are used metaphorically, can only be entertained by persons who are altogether unaware of these laws of the figure. The only term in the passage that is employed metaphorically is *face*, which properly denotes the human countenance, but is here used instead of surface, as is shown by the noun that follows, and does not vary the general sense of the passage.

The narrative is demonstrably, therefore, literal, and teaches that the earth, as called into existence by the creative fiat, was essentially what it now is in shape, dimensions, solidity, and motion on its axis. What a crowd of absurd speculations which divines as well as geologists have indulged, are dispersed by this inspired announcement!

"And God said, Let there be light: and there was light. And God saw the light, that it was good; and God divided the light from the darkness. And God called the light Day, and the darkness he called Night: and the evening and the morning were the first day," v. 3–5.

This act was not the creation of the sun and other light-giving bodies, as they are not the subject of the fiat, "let there be light," and their creation had already been announced in the first verse; but the light itself of the sun, and probably of all the other similar orbs which to us are fixed stars, and constitute the vast circuit of worlds clustered most numerously in the line of the milky-way, to which our solar group belongs; and included not only the creation of the light-giving atmosphere of the sun, and all the other bodies of that class, but of the medium also, or element throughout the realms occupied by the system—if, as philosophers suppose, such an element exists—by acting on which it is that the light becomes perceptible. That it was the light of the sun that was then created, is seen from the fact that it is called day, in contradistinction from night. No illumination of the earth by other celestial bodies, or by other causes, ever bears that name. If an element, such as some hold is the instrument of illumination, had been diffused through space, it would not have been perceptible, unless acted on by the sun, or some similar agent. That it was the light of the sun is shown, moreover, from the fact that its commencement formed a morning, and that the period of its shining, together with the night, constituted the first day. Morning is never caused by any other light than that of the sun. In order to a morning, evening, and day, the earth must, as already stated, have revolved on its axis; and the space which elapsed from the first creative fiat to the close of the first day, must have been twenty-four hours, or the period of one complete revolution. The expression—evening and morning were the first day—is equivalent to the expression: the period of darkness and sunshine were the first day. It would have been to use the term in a double sense, to have said, night and day were the first day.

These *facts* plainly preclude the supposition of a

prior existence of the earth and its vegetable and animal races. The geological theory which ascribes to the globe a previous existence, is as directly and irreconcilably in contradiction to them, as it is to the inspired representation that the whole work of creation was accomplished in six days. The testimony of the text is that the earth was created on the first day. The theory asserts that its creation took place innumerable ages earlier, and that in the interspace it had been the theatre of vegetable and animal life, and passed through a series of destructive revolutions. The text declares that the heavenly orbs and light were created on the first day. The theory asserts that they had then existed through a duration whose length we cannot estimate.

This contradiction cannot be evaded by the supposition which some have made, that the language is metaphorical. Nothing but a total ignorance of the law of the metaphor could have betrayed any one into so absurd a notion. In order to prove that the words light, evening, morning, and day, are used metaphorically, it must be shown that they are applied to something wholly unlike that which they literally denote. Light, accordingly, on that supposition, does not mean light that is perceptible by the eye, but something analogous, and knowledge, therefore, or the means of intellectual illumination; as that is the only instrument that produces an effect that simply resembles that of light on the eye. On the same principle, evening and morning must mean, not the dark and light portions of twenty-four hours of the earth's revolution, but analogous parts of a period in the existence of some other agent or object, such as the late and early parts of a person's life, or old age and youth.* The meaning of the expression, And the evening and the morning were the first day, must accordingly be:—And the old age and youth of the earth were the first day. The corresponding statement in the following verses must, in like manner, mean:—And the old age and youth of the earth were the second day, the third day, and so to the sixth! And finally, to complete the climax of absurdity, the word *day* must, to be consistent, be taken to mean the whole period of the earth's existence; for what period can it be supposed to have after its youth and old age? The expression, accordingly translated so as to give the terms a metaphorical meaning, becomes: and the old age and youth of the earth were its first whole existence; and the old age and youth of the earth were its second whole

* This construction is indeed formally advanced by De Luc and others. "As morning and evening are expressions used to denote likewise *the beginning and end* either of *a life*, or of *a certain period*, there can be no doubt that it is necessary, without reference to anything but the immediate sense contemplated by the inspired writer, to take the days in question for indefinite periods."—*Letters to Prof. Blumenbach*, p. 91.

existence; and so of the remaining four days! Such is the absurd perversion of the passage to which this contrivance to reconcile it with the demands of the geological theory leads. It indicates a very crude state of the art of interpretation that writers of reputation should have sanctioned so extraordinary a construction.

But the supposition that the passage is metaphorical is set aside by the further consideration, that terms, when metaphorically used, are always applied to agents or objects of which that which they literally mean, cannot be properly predicated; as when God is called a sun; knowledge is called light; youth, the morning of life; old age, its evening; and death, its night. But in applying the terms light, evening, morning, and day, to the earth, no such transferrence of them is made from a different set of objects of which they alone can be literally predicated. They are as applicable in their literal sense to the earth, as they are to anything else. The fancy that they are here used by that figure is thus, in every relation, mistaken and absurd. The contradiction, therefore, of the theory to the passage is direct and absolute.

This however, is but one of the objections to which their construction of it is obnoxious. It is as contradictory to the principles of geology as it is to the sacred text. As light is necessary to plants and animals, and dry land also to many of the species that are found imbedded in the earth, geologists, in assuming that the earth was the theatre of vegetable and animal life through vast ages anterior to the creation here narrated, assume that light and dry land also existed through those immeasurable periods. Consequently, as at the epoch of this narrative there was no light in being, until created on the first day, and no dry land till the waters were drawn into seas on the third, they assume or imply that the light they suppose to have existed previously, had been annihilated, and the dry land submerged under the ocean. But those suppositions are not merely unauthorized, but forbidden by their principles. The axioms on which they professedly found their system prohibit, in the first place, their assuming as a ground of induction, the occurrence of any event since the creation of the earth, that is not directly indicated by the strata themselves in their present condition. But they do not pretend to find any traces in the strata of which they treat, that an annihilation of light and submergence of the continents and islands of an inhabited earth had taken place anterior to the Mosaic epoch. They find indubitable proofs in the depths of the earth, that light and dry land were contemporaneous with those races; but none that at a later epoch they were struck from existence. The supposition, indeed, of the existence of such proofs, in the condition of the rocks, earths, and fossils, is preposterous. What conceivable effect could the annihilation of light have produced on the strata at a distance below the surface, to which not a ray ever penetrated after the superposition of the rocks and earths that intervene between them and the atmosphere?

In the next place, they are prohibited by their principles from assuming that any geological events have taken place, except such as have resulted from the chemical and mechanical forces to which they refer the formation of the strata. But they cannot account for the annihilation of light by those forces. Whether it is held to be an emanation from the sun, or an effect produced by that orb on an ether diffused through space, its annihilation would involve the annihilation either of the light-giving atmosphere of the sun, and all the similar orbs of our star system, or else of that ether, or both. But such a stupendous effect could not be wrought by chemistry, fire, or water, raised to any energy of which they can be thought to be capable, much less in acting only on the scale on which they are now producing effects. Light itself is a chemical agent, and can no more be annihilated by others than it can annihilate them. Water acts only on bodies with which it comes in contact, and fire only on such as are either in contact with it, or within the reach of the heat which it imparts. The sphere of chemical forces is equally limited. They are exerted only between particles of matter that are in absolute contact, or separated from each other by a very slight space. No greater contradiction, therefore, can be offered to their nature, than the supposition that the imagined annihilation of light was the work of their agency. It is to suppose that they extended their influence not only through the space that immediately surrounds the earth, but through the immeasurable realms which our star system occupies, and robbed the sun, and all other light-giving orbs, of their luminiferous atmospheres! A beautiful postulate, truly, of a theory which announces the conclusions it advances in contradiction to the Mosaic record, as the result of a "scientific induction."

The supposition of the obliteration of continents and islands by those agents, acting with their present energy, or a thousand times higher force, is equally absurd. It would involve the erosion or depression of every mountain and hill, and reduction of the surface universally to a geological level, by agents, as inadequate to the production of such an effect, as they are to annihilate the light of the countless suns and constellations that glitter in our heavens. Do these writers find any traces in the condition of the earth of such a catastrophe anterior to the Mosaic creation? Did philosophers, arrogating, as many of them do, an exclusive right and competence to treat of the subject,* ever before present such an extravagance to the faith of men?

Such are the extraordinary contradictions to their principles which they offer in these assumptions; such the stupendous postulates, wholly unproved, wholly incapable of proof, and irreconcilable with the genius of geology itself, which, by their own concessions, are requisite to a conciliation of their theory with the Mosaic record, and which, instead of reconciling them, only place them in a more complicated antagonism.

QUESTIONS.

What is the question now to be tried? What do geologists mean by the principles of their science? What is the first of those principles? What is the second? What is or ought to be a third axiom of their system? What is or ought to be a fourth? Are they forbidden by their principles from assuming or inferring any facts that are not consistent with these axioms? What is the first statement of Genesis i. which is to be compared with their theory? What is there meant by the heaven? Give the reason for assigning that

* It is scarcely necessary to say that this fault does not appear in the higher class of writers. Notwithstanding what we deem their errors, the volumes of Bakewell, Buckland, Lyell, Sedgwick, De la Beche, Murchison, Daubeny, Conybeare, Mantell, Phillips, and many others, instead of an affectation of knowledge, and intolerance of all opinions that differ from theirs, are, like the works of the great chemists, zoologists, and astronomers, distinguished for good sense, modesty, and candor. If Macculloch is sometimes splenetic and reproachful, he generally has the justice to vent his sarcasms on those of his own profession. The pretence to learning and contempt of criticism, are generally in the inverse ratio of talents and attainments.

sense to the word. What is the next declaration of the sacred narrative? What is meant by the earth? What is the first consideration which proves that the same earth is meant that now exists, and essentially in its present shape and solidity? What is the second? What is the third? Can these proofs be set aside by the pretext that the language is metaphorical? State the first law of the metaphor. Show by it that God, the name of him who is declared to have created the heaven and earth, is used literally. State the second law of the metaphor. Show that the words create, earth, waste, waters, and others, are used also in their literal sense. What is the only term in the passage that is used by a metaphor? Does the use of that term to denote the surface of the waters indicate that the other terms of the passage are not used in their literal sense? What is the next declaration of the sacred text, v. 3, 4? What is it that is there said to have been called into existence? Is the light of the sun and stars clearly distinguishable from the sun itself and the stars? Is the fact that light was created after the sun itself and the stars from which it emanates, were called into existence, credible and consistent with the nature of those bodies? What is the first reason which proves that it was the *light* of the sun that was then created, not the sun itself? What other considerations prove it? Do these facts preclude the supposition of a prior existence of the earth, and its vegetable and animal races? Are the text and the geological theory here in direct contradiction to each other? Designate the points of their opposition. Can this antagonism be set aside by the pretext that the language of the sacred writer is metaphorical? Show why the word light cannot be used metaphorically. Show why evening and morning cannot. Show why day cannot. What further consideration proves that those words are not used by a metaphor? Is the construction put by geologists on the passage inconsistent also with the principle on which they professedly proceed, as well as with the sacred text? What do they assume or imply had been annihilated? How does this contradict their principles? How does their third axiom prove that their assumption of such an annihilation of light is unauthorized? How does it show that their assumption of the obliteration of continents and islands, and reduction of the globe to a geological level, so that the whole was immersed in the ocean, is absurd?

CHAPTER V.

Difficulties of Geologists in respect to an Extinction of Light, and the Creation of the Atmosphere.

How now do geologists extricate themselves from the difficulty in which they are thus involved by the supposition of an extinction of light, and an obliteration of continents and islands? We might justly expect that it would engage their profoundest attention, and a satisfactory solution be felt to be indispensable before those supposed catastrophes would be assumed to be facts, and incorporated as fundamental elements in the inductive processes by which they rear the vast fabric of their system. No such justification, however, of the great postulates on which they proceed, have they thought necessary. Not a syllable of proof has been alleged; not a pretence has been uttered, that any evidence exists that those events in fact occurred. Not the faintest attempt has been made to reconcile them with the principles of geology. By most they are assumed without any intimation of the causes by which they can have been produced; and the few who have offered any suggestions in respect to the mode of the suppression of light, have only contradicted the laws of matter, and shown the inextricable embarrassment in which their postulate involves them. The existence of light, contemporaneously with the plants and animals, which they refer to ages anterior to the creation recorded in Genesis, is fully admitted and asserted by them. Dr. Buckland says:—

"The first evening may be considered as the termination of the indefinite time which followed the primeval creation announced in the first verse, and is the commencement of the first of the six succeeding days, in which the earth was to be fitted up and prepared in a manner fit for the reception of mankind. We have in the second verse a distinct mention of earth and waters as already existing, *involved in darkness.* Their condition also is described as a state of confusion and emptiness—*tohu bohu,* words which are usually interpreted by the vague and indefinite Greek term 'chaos,' and which may be *geologically considered as designating* THE WRECK AND RUINS OF A FORMER WORLD. At this intermediate point of time, the preceding undefined geological periods had terminated, a new series of events commenced, and the work of the first morning of this new creation was *the calling forth of light from a temporary darkness, which had overspread the ruins of the ancient earth.*

"We have evidence of the presence of light during long and distant periods of time, in which the many extinct fossil forms of animal life succeeded one another upon the early surface of the globe ; this evidence consists in the petrified remains of eyes of animals found in geological formations of various ages. In a future chapter I shall show that the eyes of Trilobites, which are preserved in strata of the transition formation, were constructed in a manner so closely resembling those of existing crustacea, and that the eyes of Ichthyosauri in the lias contained an apparatus so like one in the eyes of many birds, as to leave no doubt that these fossil eyes were optical instruments, calculated to receive in the same manner impressions of the same light which conveys the perception of sight to living animals. This conclusion is further confirmed by the fact that the heads of all fossil fishes and fossil reptiles, in every geological formation, are furnished with cavities for the reception of eyes, and with perforations for the passage of optic nerves, *although the cases are rare* in which *any part of the eye itself has been preserved.* The influence of light is also so necessary to the growth of existing vegetables, that we cannot but infer that it was equally essential to the development of the numerous fossil species of the vegetable kingdom, which are coextensive and coeval with the remains of fossil animals."—*Bridgewater Treatise*, i. pp. 26, 31.

He thus assumes as geological facts the wreck of the former world, and the extinction or disappearance of light after the burial of the plants and animals that are found fossilized, and makes them the basis of his whole system, without attempting to offer either the slightest evidence of their occurrence, or explanation of the causes by which they were produced. This is truly extraordinary. Can it be that it did not occur to him to inquire whether such an assumption is authorized either by the laws of interpretation, or the axioms of geology? Is it possible that he can have been wholly unconscious that the towering structure he was rearing had but a mere groundless hypothesis for its foundation, and must at the first shock of criticism give way and fall to ruins? A reconciliation of the geological theory with the Mosaic record, accomplished by an assumption that not only is not proved, and does not admit of proof, but that both directly contradicts that record and the principles of geology itself! Was there ever a more singular mistake! He can no more assume the wreck of the earth and the extinction of light betwixt the creative fiats of the first and the third verses, than he can assume that originally those events were recorded in the text, and were subsequently erased by some extraordinary catastrophe. It is truly surprising that so obvious a consideration should have escaped his notice, and the notice of the writers who preceded and followed him in this ascription to the earth of a long existence prior to the epoch of the Mosaic creation. The vast chasm which he thought to bridge over so easily, thus instead of supporting, ingulfs his whole theory. No deductions can hold that are detached from their premise by such an impassable abyss. By his failure to verify this assumption on which he proceeds, his argument from the fossil plants and animals becomes an argument against him, and overthrows his system. As light indisputably existed during the life of those plants and animals—and there is not only no geological proof that it was subsequently annihilated, but the principles of the science forbid the supposition—those vegetables and animals must be taken as evidences that the light that was contemporaneous with them, was that which was created on the first of the six days, and thence that their period of existence was subsequent to that date.

Several authors attempt to justify the supposition that betwixt the epochs of the first and the third verses a vast period of vegetable and animal life intervened that was followed by a wreck of the earth and annihilation of light, by instances of the omission in other narratives of occurrences that are known to have taken place in an interval between the events that are narrated; and they allege Exodus ii. 1, 2, as an example.

"So far from its being contrary to the usage of Scripture, in its succinct and even in its detailed narratives, to pass over much intervening matter without notice in an apparently consecutive history, it is one of its most remarkable features. We might bring numerous proofs, especially from the early books. Take for example the following, which we select because it happens to occur near the opening of the very next book of Holy Writ, and is from the pen of the same inspired writer ; so that as far as we may safely speak of individual style in a volume all the facts of which were indited by one omniscient mind, it points out the characteristic style of Moses, the inspired historian both of the creation and of Exodus. We read thus, Exodus ii. 1, 2 :—'And there went a man of the house of Levi, and took to wife a daughter of Levi. And the woman conceived and bare a son (Moses), and when she saw that he was a goodly child, she hid him three months.' Now suppose this were all that is related respecting Moses and his family, but that Professor Sedgwick, following the steps of Belzoni or the researches of Champollion, had discovered, by digging up certain antique Egyptian monuments, that Moses must have had an elder brother, and also a sister nearly ten years older than himself, and had set out from Cambridge some fine June morning to relate his discovery to Mr. Cole in London. With what a burst of indignation would he have been met! 'What! interpose two children where the sacred text indubitably consecutive passes over all mention of such an event, and clearly speaks of Moses as the first born, and apparently as having been born within a short time after the marriage of his parents! Who in his senses would dare to put such a construction on the passage?' Why no person, certainly, if it stood alone and bore upon nothing else. But if the supposed monuments were as clear in their indications as Professor Sedgwick considers are those of geology, the reply would be that though this is not the obvious *primâ facie* construction, yet there is nothing in it absolutely opposed to the text; and that if we do not admit it, the veracity of the narrative may seem to come into question; but since *that* is indubitable, and the monumental discoveries are irresistible, this appears to be a fair and consistent mode of reconciling the alleged but not real discrepancy."—*Christian Observer*, 1834, p. 387.

It seems to us to indicate a condition of extreme difficulty to resort to such an expedient to justify the imagined omission in Genesis. In the first place there is not an omission, as this writer indeed admits, in the narrative of Exodus of the fact that Moses had a sister older than himself. The verses he quotes are immediately followed by the statement that when Moses was placed in the ark of rushes, among the flags at the river's bank, his sister was stationed near by to see what befell him, and that on his being taken by Pharaoh's daughter, she ran and called her mother to become his nurse.

Next: But apart from this error, the supposed omission presents no parallel with that which it is employed to exemplify. We have specific evidence from Moses himself, Ex. ii. 4, 7, 8, iv. 1–14, Num. xxxvi. 59, that he had an elder brother and sister, Aaron and Miriam. But we have no such testimony from him, or any other writer in the Scriptures, that a vast series of ages intervened betwixt the epoch of the creation of the heavens and earth recorded in the first verse, and the creation of light narrated in the third; that the plants and animals that are entombed in the strata of the earth had their life in that remote period; and that at its close the earth was reduced to a "wreck," and light annihilated. To make the cases parallel, proofs of those events must be produced from the Scriptures, as direct and positive as they are which they present that Aaron and Miriam were children of the same family, and of an earlier birth than Moses. To assume, because an event mentioned in one passage is omitted in another that relates to the same family, that therefore events of the most momentous nature that are not mentioned at all, and of the occurrence of which no evidence exists, may be held to have actually taken place, though omitted from the narrative of the creation, and then make that assumption the basis of a train of such stupendous deductions, is truly an extraordinary procedure in men who claim, in a measure, a monopoly of knowledge on the subject, and announce—*Hitchcock's Geology and Revelation*, p. 30—that "geology is no longer a bundle of crude speculations and airy hypotheses, but a collection of most striking *facts, with inferences legitimately drawn according to the strictest rules of the Baconian philosophy.*"

Thirdly. But there is a still more formidable objection to this imagined illustration. The event omitted in the narrative (Exodus ii. 1–8), presents no contradiction either to the fact, that Aaron was an older son of the parents of Moses, or to the statements made of that fact in other passages; nor does it involve any inconsistency with his or their nature, or any of the events of their history. But the supposition of such an interval betwixt the creation of the heavens and earth narrated in the first verse, and the creation of light recorded in the third, is in direct contradiction to the declaration, that the darkness which preceded that creation of light, and the season of light that followed till evening, were the first day, or first period of a complete revolution of the earth on its axis; and to the declaration by God himself in the institution of the law, that in "six days he made heaven and earth, the sea and all that in them is," Exodus xx. 11; while the supposition of a wreck of the world and extinction of light after the existence of vegetables and animals, is in flagrant antagonism not only with the sacred narrative, but with the principles of geology, and in every respect infinitely incredible. These instances, therefore, instead of a parallel, are of such extreme dissimilarity, that no one except by the most unfortunate inconsideration, could possibly confound them. What a splendid exemplification of the exclusive competence which some of these writers claim to discuss the subject!

The suggestions they present of the modes in which the extinction of light may have taken place, are equally inconsistent with the sacred narrative, and with the principles of geology. Thus Dr. Buckland advances the *supposition* that it was occasioned by an accumulation of dense vapors.

"If we suppose all the heavenly bodies and the earth to have been created at the indefinitely distant time designated by the word beginning, *and that the darkness described on the evening of the first day was a temporary darkness, produced by an accumulation of dense vapors* 'upon the face of the deep,' an incipient dispersion of these vapors may have readmitted light to the earth upon the first day whilst the exciting cause of light was still obscured."—*Bridgewater Treatise*, pp. 29, 30.

But this supposition is in contravention of the narrative which exhibits the light as called into existence by a creative act. Though the word translated *created* is not used in the third verse, but a word equivalent to our verb *let be*, the sense is shown to be the same by the whole narrative, and by the express exhibition (Gen. ii. 4, 5) of the whole work of the six days, as a creation. "These are the generations of the heavens and the earth in their creation, in the day the Lord God made the earth and the heavens and every plant of the field before it was in the earth, and every herb of the field before it grew." Here the creation is represented as extending to the formation of the herbs of the field, though the verb created is not used in the fiat by which they were called into existence, but an expression equivalent to that employed in the creation of light. "Let the earth bring forth grass, the herb yielding seed; the fruit tree yielding fruit after his kind," chap. i. 11. Accordingly, in the description of the formation of man, both the verbs answering *to create* and *to make* are used as equivalent in meaning to signify his creation. It is inconsistent, also, with the representation that God then divided the light from the darkness, and called the one day and the other night, which implies that light had not before existed. It were an infinite misrepresentation to exhibit that separation as constituting them, if they had been distinguished from each other, and followed in a regular alternation every twenty-four hours through a round of countless ages.

To assume that light was not then created, but merely readmitted to the earth by a dispersion of dense vapors, that occasioned a temporary darkness, is to assume that the day had, in fact, returned at its regular period during that temporary darkness; as no vapors are ever known to envelop the earth so completely as to exclude the light. The diminution of light occasioned by the densest mists or clouds is very far short of an absolute extinction of it. Besides, if the sun shone in his full splendor on the exterior of the imagined body of vapors, there must not only have been perfect day there, but his rays must have penetrated the body of the clouds to a great depth, and rendered them luminous. What a perversion of the passage to hold that the darkness that wrapped the deep extended only a few feet or rods from the surface, while at a short distance above the vapors were basking in a dazzling effulgence! What a degradation of the sublime act of the Almighty, by which he called into existence the light not only of our sun, but probably of all the countless stars and constellations that sparkle in our firmament, to represent it as nothing more than a dispersion of dense vapors that had temporarily intercepted his beams from the face of the waters! It is a sad exemplification of the perverting influence of this false theory, that men of the fine powers and just taste Dr. Buckland usually displays, are betrayed by it into such misconceptions.

It is to divest the work of the six days of the character of a creation, to exhibit the production of light as nothing more than a re-admission of it to the earth by a dispersion of clouds. If that assumption may be made in respect to light, it may be equally in respect to the atmosphere, the seas, the dry land, plants, animals, and even man. No reason can be given to justify it in respect to the one that will not be an equal justification of it in respect to the others.

A scheme must be embarrassed with fatal difficulties that needs the aid of such an expedient for its support.

But not less unfortunately for his supposition—there was then no atmosphere in existence to support vapors above the waters, and render such an accumulation of clouds possible as to intercept the rays of the sun! It was not until the following day that God made the firmament, and "divided the waters which were under the firmament from the waters which were above the firmament," in the form of vapors and clouds. As, then, on the first day, there were no waters except those that were under the firmament, that is, the waters of the abyss, there cannot have been any vapors in the space above them to occasion the darkness in which the deep was enveloped. The supposition is as contradictory, therefore, to the laws of vapor as it is to the sacred narrative. And, finally, it is in contravention of the principles of geology, which forbid the supposition of any physical event as a condition or basis of its theories, that cannot be proved by geological evidence to have taken place, and to have resulted from the chemical or mechanical agencies to which geologists refer the facts of the science. But what geological proofs can Dr. Buckland produce that, on the first day of the creation, a mass of vapors enveloped the abyss so dense as to wrap it in absolute darkness, though the sun was shining above in unclouded effulgence? Or what evidence can he allege that, in the total absence of an atmosphere, the forces of chemistry, fire, and water, acting with only their present energy, could fill the void above the ocean to a vast height with a cloud of vapor so dense, as wholly to intercept the rays of the sun. Can a greater self-contradiction, a more extraordinary absurdity be imagined? Such is the inextricable embarrassment in which he involves himself by this attempt to bring the sacred word into harmony with his theory.

Dr. Hitchcock intimates that the darkness was occasioned by the absorption by matter of the light that previously existed.

"From the facts which modern science has developed as to the existence of light and heat in all bodies, we can hardly imagine that these were not created in the beginning *along with matter.* But these facts show us that they might have existed *without being visible,* or that, after *having been visible during ages, they might have been* ABSORBED *into matter,* and that it required the power of Almighty God to develop them to such an extent as was necessary to the new state of the earth; that is to say, it was rather a recreation than an original production of light that is described in the third verse."—*Geology and Revelation,* p. 91.

This group of errors is a fit associate of Dr. Buckland's. In the first place, not a syllable is uttered by

Moses to indicate that such an absorption of light actually took place, and caused the darkness which Dr. H. attempts to explain by it. It is deemed by him enough to determine the question at issue, to assert that it *might* have occurred. A very satisfactory verification truly of the assurance he gives on an earlier page, that geology, instead of "a bundle of crude speculations and airy hypotheses," is "a collection of striking *facts*, with inferences legitimately drawn according to the strictest rules of the Baconian Philosophy." With what disdain would an attempt by a "theologian" to controvert one of his facts or inferences by such an expedient be received! But in a geologist, "according to the strictest rules of the Baconian philosophy," it seems to be thought enough to invalidate the plainest testimony of the Bible, and invest it with a meaning that is at war alike with the laws of language and of nature.

But in the next place, as invisible light and imperceptible heat would not have exerted the influences that are necessary to plants and animals, we are not able to see how their existence "without *being visible*"—we were not before aware that *heat* is *visible*—can furnish any explanation of the life of vegetables and animals during the ages in which it is supposed they may have been in that latent state.

Thirdly. We are equally unable to understand what is meant by the declaration, that "after having been visible during ages, they might have been absorbed into matter." If the light of those ages was visible, it must have been the light of the sun, as it is sunlight alone, either direct or reflected, that is visible to animals, and ministers to the life of plants. Who ever heard that animals see light that is latent? Who ever held that it is latent light, not the light of the sun, that is requisite to the growth of vegetables? The light which "modern science" has shown, exists "in all bodies," is invisible and latent, not radiated into the atmosphere, so as to be the medium of a sight of other objects. But if the light which was visible during those imagined ages was the light of the sun illuminating an atmosphere with its effulgence, as his supposition must imply, what are we to understand by the extraordinary representation that it "might have been *absorbed into matter?*" Does he imagine that matter became inbued with a susceptibility of absorbing light, so vast as to detach the luminiferous atmosphere from the sun, and attract it into itself? If not, if the sun continued to shed forth its light with undiminished radiance, as its rays must have passed through the atmosphere—if it is held that one then existed—in order to reach the matter that was to absorb it, how is it that it would not have continued to illuminate that atmosphere, and been as visible therefore as it is now? Does Dr. H. deem himself entitled, in disregard of the laws of light, to assume that it might have lost its susceptibility of reflection from the surfaces on which it fell, or that "matter" might, in defiance of its established laws, have lost its power of reflecting it? What a splendid hypothesis for the reconciliation of his theory of an anterior existence of the world with the testimony of the Creator which it contradicts! But Dr. H. cannot, on the principles of geology, assume the existence of any physical fact that is not referable either to the chemical or mechanical forces that are now in activity, and acting with their present degree of energy. Is he aware, then, of any instances in which those forces have actually absorbed the light of the sun, so as to involve the world in absolute darkness? Are they now daily producing that stupendous effect? If not, his assertion that light, "after having been visible during ages, might have been absorbed into matter," is as inconsistent with the axioms of geology as it is contradictory to the laws of optics. Was ever before such a "bundle" of astounding errors couched in so narrow a compass, and dignified with the title of facts and inferences drawn according to the strictest rules of the Baconian philosophy?

But we are not yet at the end of the series. It is raised to a towering climax in the representation that the light which was created after that absorption, and denominated by the Most High day, was the identical light which had become latent in matter, and was developed by him out of the bodies by which it had been absorbed. "These facts show" that light and heat "might have been absorbed into matter, and that it required the power of Almighty God to develop them to such an extent as was necessary to the new state of the earth." It were in vain to attempt to lash such a blunder with the thong of ridicule. It transcends the power of satire. Optics, chemistry, physics, geology, are alike disregarded. Who ever before heard of a *day*, commencing with an evening and ending with a morning, being produced by a development of latent light from the matter of the earth's surface? As latent light is only developed from the matter in which it is absorbed by a chemical process by which that matter is resolved into its elements, or united in new combinations, that process must have extended over the whole surface of the globe. Will Dr. H. be good enough to inform us how either the waters of the ocean, or the rocks and earths that then formed, as he assumes, the crust of the mountains, hills, plains, and valleys, throughout the earth, were put into that chemical activity? Whence were the exciting forces drawn? If they existed at every point before, why is it that they remained inactive till that great crisis? It will not meet the difficulty simply to say, that they were developed by an act of Almighty power, or that "it was rather a re-creation than an original production of light." That is precisely the process of which we wish an explanation on the principles of chemistry. What is a development of latent light from matter in which it has been absorbed, that is rather a re-creation than an original production of it—while, in fact, by the terms, it can be neither—and on such a scale as to produce day at every point, like that of a brilliant sunshine? Is he aware of the existence in the immediate vicinity of each of the substances in the crust of the earth of elements that are capable of acting on them in such a manner? Was the globe dropped into a vast alembic, filled with powerful chemical agents that at once dissolved all the solids and fluids with which it came in contact, released their latent light, and radiated it into surrounding space? That would have made a "wreck" of the world undoubtedly, and rendered a new construction and a repopulation of it necessary. It is only by some process of that kind that such a result could have been produced. What an ingenious and philosophic conception to account for that illumination of the earth which God called Day! What a profound insight it indicates into the mysteries of nature! At what an infinite distance it is removed from "the crude speculations and airy hypotheses" in which theologians have indulged! And what glory it reflects upon the power of the Almighty! For what a delicate affair it must have been to form and adjust those forces in such a manner that they naturally, through three successive revolutions of the earth on its axis, intermitted their activity at every line of longitude at the proper moment for the commencement of evening, and resumed it again at the proper moment for the dawn of morning!

Such are the singular fancies by which these and other writers attempt to reconcile their theory of the world with the history which God has given us of its creation;—such the strange absurdities, the infinite contradictions to the principles of their own science and the universal laws of matter, assent to which is, by their own showing, a necessary condition of faith in their system! Was such a farce ever before passed off under the dignified and imposing names of "inductive science" and "Baconian philosophy?" Did men of talent and learning ever before confound in so extraordinary a manner the principles of their own profession? How is it to be accounted for, except that, misled by an excessive enthusiasm, they have misconceived the proper sphere of geology and the import of its facts, and assuming it to be a veritable science of ascertained and infallible laws peculiar to itself, have mistaken their unauthorized inferences for demonstrated truths; and thence, losing in a measure their sense of the sanctity of the divine declarations, and persuaded that their natural cannot be their real meaning, have presumed that they may be legitimately construed on any hypothesis that seems to make it possible to suppose them not at war with the dogmas of geology.

So much for the relation of their theory to the inspired narrative of the first day's creation. Instead of bringing them into harmony, they have only shown that they are in the most palpable and irremediable antagonism.

We proceed to the history of the second day.

"And God said, Let there be a firmament in the midst of the waters, and let it divide the waters from the waters. And God made the firmament, and divided the waters which were under the firmament, from the waters which were above the firmament; and it was so. And God called the firmament heaven: and the evening and the morning were the second day," v. 6–8.

This great act was the creation of the atmosphere. The firmament or expanse of the sky is the air. The event is described as it would have appeared to a spectator near the surface of the earth. As there was no atmosphere before, there was no general illumination of the space around the ocean, such as now takes place when the sun shines; but only such rays would have entered the eye of a spectator, as descended directly from the sun, or were reflected from the water, and no points of the surface of the ocean could have been visible, except those from which rays were directly reflected to the eye. To one looking on in any direction above the water, except immediately towards the sun, or a planet or star, the space would have appeared dark. The creation of the atmosphere, therefore, must have seemed, to a beholder, like the extension of a luminous expanse or arch overhead which instantly rendered the whole face of the deep, within the sphere of the eye, visible. A division of the waters followed as a natural consequence. The heat of the sun occasioning evaporation in a form lighter than the atmosphere, the vapor ascended in an invisible shape, probably, till it reached a height at which it was condensed, and assumed the form of clouds. That it was the atmosphere that was created, not a mere elevation of water in the form of mists or clouds, is seen also from the fact that God called the firmament heaven, which is the name of the upper regions of the air in which the clouds float, not of the clouds themselves; that it was the expanse in which the sun, moon, and stars seem to be, which is immediately above the clouds (v. 14, 15), and in which the fowls fly, which is below them (v. 20); and from the fact that it remained there permanently, not like the vapors and clouds that drift away, or fall in rain, and often wholly disappear. The supposition that it was anything less than the creation of the atmosphere; that it was a mere conversion of water into mist, and elevation of it into space at a distance from the abyss beneath, divests it of its character as a creative act, and reduces it to the level of an ordinary operation of nature. Besides, if the atmosphere had been created along with the earth and ocean, it would be inexplicable that some evaporation had not immediately taken place, and mists and clouds become in a measure diffused through the sky.

This great work was thus one of the most important in the series of creations, and was essential as a condition of those that followed. Air is necessary to vegetable and animal life, not only on the land, but beneath the ocean, which it pervades, and forms, it is estimated, one-fortieth part of its bulk. As it is the means of the illumination that is diffused by the sunlight over the surface of the earth, it is the instrument by which objects become visible, and display their forms and colors. Without it, even on the supposition that it were not necessary to our life, we could gain no idea by the eye of the shapes of things, and the beautiful hues by which they are adorned.

How, now, is this creation of the atmosphere on the second day to be reconciled with the geological theory, which asserts that the earth had existed through innumerable ages before, and been the scene of animal and vegetable life, and assumes, thereby, that it had been invested with an atmosphere? If that theory be true, that atmosphere, like the light which illuminated it, must have been annihilated:

and geologists, therefore, in order to verify their theory, must, on their own principles, produce proofs of that annihilation, and by the chemical and mechanical forces which they regard as the only agents that produce geological effects. What, then, are the explanations which they present of this stupendous catastrophe? Not a syllable is uttered by them on the subject! Not the slightest indication appears in their pages that they are aware that such an obstacle exists in the way of their theories! The supposition of a vast interval between the creation of heaven and earth announced in the first verse, and the wreck and submergence of the world, which they hold to be announced in the second, they regard as all that is necessary to the conciliation of their theory with the remaining narrative of the creation.* But that is a

* "There are two methods of conciliation, each of which will obviously *remove every appearance of discrepance* between the record of Genesis and our assumed geological periods. We may either, with Faber, consider the days as themselves, by a common figure of language, indicating such periods, or we may suppose an interval between the first and second verses of that record."—*Christian Observer*, May, 1834.

"A very unhappy conflict has been sometimes occasioned by comparing those results of geology which relate to periods left wholly undefined in the Scriptural narrative, with the successive works of creation which are in that narrative distinctly marked. If we take the first verse of Genesis as affirming the eternal superintendence of God over all the prior conditions of the world, from the epoch of its original creation until he saw fit to give it its present character, and to call into being its present races of man, animals, and plants, and

total mistake. They can no more assume the annihilation of an atmosphere at that imagined wreck of the world, without demonstrating its occurrence from the present condition of the earth, and by the forces of chemistry, fire, and water, than they can assume that wreck, and the extinction of light, which they treat as contemporaneous with it, without proof, and in contravention of the principles of their science. Here then is another stupendous postulate on which they tacitly proceed, that presents an insuperable obstacle to the reconciliation of their system with the Mosaic record. For how are they to demonstrate that such an annihilation of the air, as their scheme implies, took place, and through the agency of those

compare this with geological inferences relating to periods anterior to man, we shall find two conclusions inevitable: first, that there is *no word in the Scriptural narrative which limits in any way the inferences, or even the speculations of geology, with reference to these periods;* secondly, that nothing can ever be learned about these periods by human labor, except in the way of geological induction. This is sufficient for the purpose of the present inquiry, which relates to races of animals and plants, not only anterior to man, but even to the elevation of most parts of our continents from beneath the waters of the ocean."—*Phillips's Guide to Geol,* p. 63.

"This alleged disagreement *is chiefly chronological.* Moses represents the work of creation as completed in the space of six days, whereas the geologist asserts that the formation of the crust of the globe, with its numerous groups of extinct animals and plants, after the original production of the matter of the globe, must have occupied immense periods of time, whose duration we cannot estimate. Other minor discrepances between the *two records* are supposed to exist."—*Hitchcock's Geology and Revelation,* p. 17.

geological forces at the epoch to which they must refer it? The attempt were preposterous. If it had taken place, it is not conceivable that any traces of it would be found on the strata of the earth. But it is demonstrably impossible that it could have been produced by the chemical and mechanical agents to which they refer the formation of strata. The forces of chemistry, fire, and water, have not the slightest tendency to absorb, or annihilate the atmosphere. Though oxygen and nitrogen are continually absorbed by bodies, and disengaged from them in the processes that are going forward in the mineral, vegetable, and animal worlds, yet there is not the slightest reason to suppose that the volume of the atmosphere has undergone the least diminution since the moment of its creation. Such is the embarrassing position in which they have placed themselves. If they deny that there was an atmosphere during the innumerable ages which they affirm preceded the Mosaic creation, then they virtually deny the existence of plants and animals during that period, and overturn their theory. If they admit that an atmosphere then existed, and deny its annihilation anterior to the date of the creative act recorded in this passage, they then contradict the inspired record, and establish the antagonism—which they wish to escape—of their theory with the word of God. And if they admit its annihilation, then they equally contradict and confute themselves, because of the impossibility of their either proving or accounting for it on the principles of geology, or compatibly with the laws of matter. Their system is thus at as open war with the powers of nature as it is with the teachings of inspiration. No skill can ever bring it into harmony with either. No learning or philosophy can ever demonstrate it, or save it from the discredit of the grossest absurdity. Is it not singular that these men of science who display such admirable powers in the practical branches of their profession, should not have extended their inquiries far enough into this department to discover this fatal difficulty?

QUESTIONS.

How do geologists meet the contradiction to their own principles, and to the sacred text in which they are involved by supposing an annihilation of the light and the lands of a former world? Do they admit that light must on their theory have existed before the creation announced in the text? Did it not become Dr. Buckland, who makes that supposition, to offer, if in his power, some proof of its reality, and some intimation of the mode in which it is to be reconciled with the principles of geology? Is not his assumption wholly unscientific? Is it not absurd to attempt to reconcile the theory with the text, by an assumption that not only cannot be proved—but that directly contradicts both the sacred record and his own principles? Moreover, not having proved an annihilation of light, does not his admission that it existed during the life of the plants and animals that are buried in the strata, forbid the supposition that they existed anterior to the light, the creation of which is announced in the text, and thereby overturn the theory that they had their being in a prior age? By what method have other writers attempted to justify the supposition that a vast period intervened between the epochs of the first and the third verses? What is the first objection to that expedient? What is the second? What is the third? What does Dr. Buckland suppose was the mode of the extinction of light? How does that contradict the statement of the text, that light was then created; not caused by the dispersion of vapors, to shine on the earth? How does it contradict the text in respect to the day, which is said to have followed the creation of light? How does it affect the meaning of the other acts of creation? If the alleged creation of light was no creation, may not the creation of vegetables, animals, and man be with equal propriety held to be no creations? But how does Dr. Buckland's supposition consist with the fact that there was then no atmosphere by which vapor could have been diffused through the space above the earth, so as to intercept the light? And how does his supposition consist with the fourth geological axiom, which forbids the assumption of any geological events, that cannot be proved to have taken place, and to have been produced by the causes to which he refers all geological effects? What is Dr. Hitchcock's suggestion respecting the mode in which the light may have disappeared? What is the first objection to that hypothesis? What is the next objection to it? What is the third objection to it? Is it inconsistent with the laws of light, and of matter? Is it inconsistent with the third axiom of geology? Point out the absurdities of Dr. Hitchcock's fancy that the light which God called day, instead of emanating from the sun—was developed out of the matter of the earth in which it had become absorbed? Was day ever known to be produced in that manner? Are there any known chemical agents capable of developing a day from the matter of the earth? Has Dr. Hitchcock ever got up a day in Massachusetts by that process? Is the pretence of reconciling the theory with the text by such a supposition, worthy of a man of science, or only of an ignorant and presumptuous charlatan?

What is the sacred penman's history of the second day's creation?

What is meant by the firmament? Did an ascent of vapor, and a collection of water in the air in the form of clouds, follow as a natural consequence of the creation of the atmosphere? Was that the division of the waters of which the sacred text speaks? Can the geological theory be reconciled with this creation of the atmosphere on the second day? Why not? Do geologists evade this difficulty? Are they not bound however, to meet it? Is it not inconsistent with their own principles, as well as unphilosophical, to assume without proof, that an atmosphere which they assert had before existed, had been annihilated? Are not the chemical and mechanical forces to which they refer all the changes that have taken place on the earth, wholly inadequate to produce such an annihilation of the atmosphere? What is the dilemma then in which they place themselves?

CHAPTER VI.

Difficulties of geologists in respect to the elevation of Land from the Ocean on the Third, and the adjustment of the heavenly Bodies on the Fourth Day of the Creation.

THEIR scheme is equally irreconcilable with the creative acts of the third day.

"And God said, Let the waters under the heaven be gathered together into one place, and let the dry *land* appear: and it was so. And God called the dry *land* earth: and the gathering together of the waters called he Seas: and God saw that it was good. And God said, let the earth bring forth grass, and herb yielding seed, and the fruit-tree yielding fruit after his kind, whose seed is in itself, upon the earth: and it was so. And the earth brought forth grass, and herb yielding seed after his kind, and the tree yielding fruit, whose seed was in itself, after his kind: and God saw that it was good. And the evening and the morning were the third day," v. 9–13.

As the waters were now first collected into seas, and dry land made to appear, it is apparent that the ocean had continued up to this time to envelop it at every point; and thence, that it had as yet no mountains, nor even hills, unless of very moderate elevation. Its surface beneath the waters formed, probably, as even an outline as the ocean itself that reposed above it. The change that was wrought, accordingly, must have involved an alteration of the crust of the earth, either by an elevation of the whole body of the continents and islands above the level of the seas, and at such unequal heights as to form mountains, hills, slopes, and valleys; or by an elevation of the mountains and hills of the dry land, and a depression of the seat of the seas; or both combined. In either case, the event, as well as the language of the fiat, shows that it was produced by an act of omnipotence, and not by second causes. As the dry land immediately appeared and became the theatre of vegetable life, and in forms, doubtless, adapted to various climates, the waters cannot have been withdrawn by the mere force of gravity to which they owe their movement in streams and rivers. The descent of waters over slopes of several thousand miles, like those over which the Missouri, Mississippi, Amazon, Nile, and Ganges pass, instead of but a small part of twenty-four hours, would require several weeks, and perhaps months. In like manner the depression of the bed of the seas, and elevation of the continents and islands, and upheaving of their mountains and hills, must have been the work of omnipotence, not of mechanical force. Such a stupendous effect, wrought in an instant, or at most in a few hours, is infinitely beyond any of the volcanic powers, so far as we are able to estimate their energy, that have ever agitated the earth's surface. To attempt to explain it by the laws of matter, as far as we have a knowledge of them, is scarcely less unphilosophic than it were to ascribe to them the creation of the world. It was the fiat of the Almighty that wrought the change. "By the word of the Lord were the heavens made; and all the host of them by the breath of his mouth. He gathereth the waters of the sea together as an heap; he layeth up the depth in store-houses. Let all the earth fear the Lord; let all the inhabitants of the world stand in awe of him: for he spake and it was; he commanded, and it stood fast," Ps. xxxiii. 6–9.

As the earth was immediately fit for the support of vegetables and trees of all kinds, it is apparent that it was covered with a soil consisting of silica, alumine, lime, and other ingredients, which now enter into the composition of vegetables, and mixed in different places in the different proportions that are congenial to the several species of herbs and trees. What the extent was of the continents and islands we have no means of determining. They bore possibly a very different proportion to the seas, from that which subsists between the present lands and the waters of the globe.

The geological theory, which asserts the existence of the world through innumerable ages anterior to this epoch, is thus again in conflict with the sacred word; for that theory not only refers the upheaving of the mountains and elevation of the hills, as well as the formation of the strata in which the fossil relics of plants and animals are imbedded, to that distant age, but exhibits those strata themselves as formed mainly from the detritus of a preceding system of mountains and continents. Thus Dr. Macculloch says:—

"It is important to observe the exact resemblance between the present primary rocks and the still more ancient ones from the ruins of which they have been partly at least formed.

"Now, as the compounded rocks now forming are produced by the consolidation of materials carried *from the land* into the sea, it follows that before the formation of the present primary strata, and while they were all buried beneath the water in their germs, *there was a terraqueous globe*, an earth containing *land and water*, *mountains*, rivers, and seas. That earth, also, was formed of *rocks similar to those of the present primary strata;* and further, it is important to observe, of granite also, proving that this agent had then, as in later times, *been the cause of the elevation of the strata*."—*Geology*, vol. i. p. 464.

"The detritus of the *first* dry lands being drifted into the sea, and then spread out into extensive beds of mud, and sand, and gravel, would have for ever remained beneath the surface of the water, had not other forces been subsequently employed to raise them into dry land ; these forces appear to have been the same expansive powers of heat and vapor which, *having caused the elevation of the first raised portions of fundamental crystalline rocks*, continued their energies through all succeeding geological periods, and still exert them in producing the phenomena of active volcanoes."—*Buckland's Bridg. Tr.*, pp. 42, 43.

"One of the most interesting of the results to which the careful study of the elevation of mountains has conducted geologists, and at the same time one of the most certain, is the knowledge that the dry land is not all of the same antiquity ; in other words, that some mountain ranges and some large regions were raised above the sea long before the occurrence of the convulsions which affected the level of other countries, and *even before the production of the strata of these countries.* For instance, we have no doubt that the Grampian, Lammermuir, and Cumberland mountains were dry *long before* the Alps were raised from the sea, and while the greater part of Europe was occupied by the ancient ocean."—*Phillips's Guide*, p. 46.

As he holds not only that the lower strata of all countries, but that those which he regards as formed since the elevation of the Grampian and Cumberland mountains, were deposited innumerable ages ago ; he holds that those mountains, also, have existed through an incalculable period. This view is entertained also by Sir C. Lyell, who regards Etna as having existed through an immense series of ages anterior to the historical era; although, compared with the primary strata, he holds that it is of very modern date.

"There are no records within the historical era, which lead to the opinion that the altitude of Etna has materially varied within the last two thousand years. Of the eighty most conspicuous minor cones which adorn its flanks, only one of the largest has been produced within the times of authentic history. . . . The dimensions of these large cones appear to bear testimony to *paroxysms* of volcanic activity, after which we may conclude, from analogy, that the fires of Etna remained dormant for many years—since nearly a century of rest has sometimes followed a violent eruption in the historical era. . . .

"How many years, then, must we not suppose to have been expended in the formation of the eighty cones? It is difficult to imagine that a fourth part of them have originated during *the last thirty centuries.* But if we conjecture the whole of them to have been formed in *twelve thousand years, how inconsiderable an era would this portion of time constitute in the history of this volcano!* If we could strip off from Etna all the lateral monticules now visible, together with the scoriæ that have been poured out from them, and from the highest crater, during the period of their growth, the diminution of the mass would be extremely slight; Etna might lose, perhaps, several miles in diameter at its base, and some hundreds of feet in elevation; but it would still be the loftiest of Sicilian mountains. . . .

"On the grounds, therefore, already explained, we must

infer that a mass so many thousand feet in thickness must have required *an immense series of ages anterior to its historical periods for its growth; yet the whole must be regarded as the product of a modern portion of the tertiary epoch.*"—*Lyell's Principles*, pp. 404, 405.

These writers thus not only assert the existence of continents and mountains countless years anterior to the date of the creation recorded in Genesis, but they refer the present mountains of the earth, both such as are volcanic and those that consist mainly of granite, to that distant period. Their theory is, accordingly, in open antagonism to the inspired history of the third day's creation; and the contradiction which it offers to it is not slight, but as vast as the mountains themselves are that rear their rocky masses into the heavens, and the plains and vales that slope from their sides to the ocean. If their views are correct, the Mosaic record which exhibits the earth as submerged beneath the ocean till the morning of the third day, and its first dry land as then produced by the removal of the waters into seas, cannot be. No more palpable and irreconcilable contradiction between two statements can be conceived.

How now do the geological and theological writers who maintain the consistency of their theory with the account God has here given of the creation of the world, extricate themselves from this difficulty? Not a solitary allusion is made by them to it, so far as we are aware! They seem to have assumed, as in respect to the creation of the atmosphere, that if allowed to intercalate a vast tract of ages between the epoch of the first and of the second verses, their harmony with the narrative that follows is of course established. What a beautiful verification, again, of the claim which some of them put forth to an exclusive right and competence to treat of the subject! A more unfortunate position than that which they occupy cannot well be imagined. Let them interpose as many ages as they please betwixt the periods of the first and second verses, and it can contribute nothing towards reconciling their theory with the fact made known to us in this passage, that at the commencement of the third day there were no mountains or hills on the face of the earth, nor lands of any description above the level of the ocean. If all the mountains, hills, and dry lands of the present continents and islands were formed either then or since that epoch, as the record God has given of their origin testifies, then indisputably they cannot have been formed in the remote and indeterminable ages to which geologists refer them. It cannot be pretended that, after having existed through the vast periods ascribed to them, they were at the Mosaic epoch depressed beneath the ocean, and raised again to their former position on the third day. No intelligent geologist will venture on a supposition so wholly irreconcilable with the nature of the primitive masses of which the mountains consist, and the condition of the strata that are superposed on them. Such a movement would have dislocated and broken to fragments those of the latter, which now, although bent and contorted in many forms, are continuous, and conform in their curves to the outline of the primitive rocks on which they repose. The whole condition both of those primitive masses and the strata which they uphold, forbids the idea that they have undergone more than one elevation above the lands by which they are surrounded.

Here, then, we have again the most unanswerable proofs, and on the vastest scale, of the irreconcilableness of the geological theory and the history in Genesis of the creation of the world. No chemistry or mechanics can save the system from this dilemma. It were discreditable to attempt to reconcile representations so diametrically the opposites of each other. The supposition that the mountains of the earth were formed in the fabulous ages to which geologists refer them, must be renounced, or the inspiration and truth of the record God has given us of the origin of the world must be rejected.

Their theory is irreconcilable, also, with the creative acts of the fourth day.

"And God said, let there be lights in the firmament of the heaven, to divide the day from the night; and let them be for signs, and for seasons, and for days, and for years. And let them be for lights in the firmament of the heaven to give light upon the earth: and it was so. And God made two great lights; the greater light to rule the day, and the lesser light to rule the night; the stars also. And God set them in the firmament of the heaven to give light upon the earth, and to rule over the day and over the night, and to divide the light from the darkness: And God saw that it was good. And the evening and the morning were the fourth day," v. 14–19.

Writers on geology differ in their views of the import of this act. Some suppose that the light created on the first day, was either the ether, which is by many thought to be the medium of its perceptibility, or light that exists or is made perceptible independently of the sun, like that which is sometimes evolved from bodies by chemical action that produces combustion; and that the creative act *here* recorded was the investiture of the sun with its light-giving atmosphere. But that is inconsistent with the characteristics and offices of the light created on the first day. As that light constituted morning, and was followed by evening; as there was a division instituted between it and the night, that was the same as now subsists between day and night; and as the illumination which it caused was called day, and with the night that preceded it, occupied the period of a revolution of the earth on its axis, it is plain that it must have been the light that now constitutes day, and the light therefore of the sun.

Others suppose the effect of the divine fiat was merely the dispersion of vapors or clouds that had accumulated in the atmosphere, and obscured or hidden the sun. But that implies that the office to which the sun, moon, and stars were assigned, was to be exercised only in fair weather; as otherwise they must have filled it as fully before the fiat, as they could afterwards, when they were hidden by clouds. It is irreconcilable, also, with the representation that they were set for signs, and for seasons, and for days and for years; not for the mere periods in which they might happen to shine on the earth without obstruction. It was a great and permanent change that was wrought, not merely a purification of the atmosphere from exhalations that might have arisen from natural causes, and been immediately followed by fresh mists and clouds.

Others regard the fiat of the Creator as merely annunciatory of the office which the heavenly orbs were to fill towards the earth; not as causing a change of their relations to one another, or to the earth, or of the earth's relations to them.

That is equally inconsistent with the passage, which

exhibits the act of the Most High as creative, and as constituting the sun, moon, and stars, what they had not before been, the determiners to the earth of seasons, and days, and years. If it were not an omnipotent act accomplishing an important step in the completion of the system, then the work of the creation, instead of occupying six days, must have been confined to five.

The act, then, was almighty and creative; it was exerted, apparently at least, on the bodies of the solar system already in existence, and really so, or else on the earth, and perhaps on both, and its effect was an alteration of their relations or motions by which the sun, moon, and stars became the determiners to the earth of its seasons, days, and years. The plain sense of the fiat is, "Let the luminaries in the firmament of the heaven be to divide the day from the night; and let them be for signs, and for seasons, and for days, and for years." A change, therefore, was wrought in their adjustment and motions, which gave birth to seasons, and years, and the variations in the length of days. That may have been simply the inclination of the earth's axis—and the axes of the other planets, for the fiat may be considered as affecting them all—to the ecliptic, which is the reason that there is a diversity and succession of the seasons, that there is a variation in the length of the days and nights, and that the circle of changes through which they pass is completed in the compass of a year, and repeated in every answering period. If the earth's axis had previously been perpendicular to the ecliptic, and had continued so, there could have been no variation in the length of the days, no diversity and succession of seasons, and no obvious signs of the completion of the year. The last is now known, from the declination of the sun, and the consequent variation of the length of the days and nights, and succession of the seasons. It could then have been known only by observing the relation of the earth to the constellations of the zodiac. Such a change extended to the whole circle of the planets, all of which are inclined to the ecliptic—perhaps to the infinite crowd of similar orbs that are supposed to circle round the other suns of our star-system—and giving rise to such a train of important events in the economy of life, was worthy of the omnipotent fiat, and one of the sublimest of the creative acts.

It is possible, however, that it may have been of a still grander character. It may, besides that change, have embraced the communication to the earth and other planets of the projectile motion by which they are borne round in their orbits. It is conceivable that at their creation they received no other motion than that by which they revolve on their axes. Neither that nor their projectile motion is, like the force of gravity, inherent, but adventitious, and must be referred to an omnipotent fiat. As, however, they were subject to the gravitating power from the moment of their creation, the supposition that the force which drives them around their orbits was not imparted to them till the fourth day, implies that at their creation they were at a far greater distance both from the sun and from each other. The space which belongs to our system is, however, amply sufficient for the arrangement that would then have been required. Astronomers have estimated that the planet nearest the sun, if divested of its projectile force, and the centrifugal force also generated by its revolution on its axis, would not fall to the sun in less than fifteen days and a half; nor the moon to the the earth in less than about five days.*

It would be no difficult problem to determine what their respective distances from the sun must have been, that, falling under the force of gravity, they should at the end of 72 hours have reached the distances at which they are now stationed, when they received the projectile impulse that sends them around their orbits. The supposition implies, indeed,

* Mercury would fall to the sun in	15	days	13	hours.
Venus " " "	39	"	17	"
The Earth " " "	64	"	10	"
Mars " " "	121	"	0	"
Jupiter " " "	290	"	0	"
Saturn " " "	798	"	0	"
Georgium Sidus " "	5,406	"	0	"
The Moon would fall to the Earth in	4	"	21	"

that the momentum they had acquired was annihilated at those points, and may be thought to be improbable. Why should it be deemed more singular, however, than that the sun was created without the robe by which it fills its office as the luminary of its circle of revolving orbs? or that the earth was formed at first without mountains, hills, or dry land? As it would have given birth to a variation in the length of the days and nights and a succession of seasons and years, and meets, therefore, the conditions of the passage in even a more emphatic manner than the former, it may at least be considered as possibly the act God then exerted; and, if extended to all the planetary systems that revolve round the countless stars of our galaxy, was one of the vastest and most momentous of the whole series of the creative fiats.

Whichever of these is supposed to be the work of the fourth day—and one or the other undoubtedly must, as there is no other by which the sun, moon, and stars could be made to determine as they do, the length of the days, and the succession of seasons and years—it is, like the others, wholly irreconcilable with the geological theory. If the earth had already existed through an incalculable round of ages, and been the scene of vegetable and animal life, it must have revolved round the sun, and that orb and the moon and stars filled the office they now do, as determiners of the length of the days and nights, and the succession of seasons and years. It will be said, perhaps, that if the axis of the earth be supposed to have been perpendicular to the ecliptic during those ages, and to have received its present inclination on the fourth day of the creation, recorded by Moses, it will meet all the conditions of the text. That supposition, however, cannot be made by geologists; as their maxims forbid their assuming the occurrence of any event which is not demonstrated by the present condition of the earth, and was not caused by the forces to which they refer the facts of geology. But no traces exist in the crust of the globe, of such a change in the relation of the earth's axis to the ecliptic. It has been supposed, indeed, to have taken place at the deluge, and to have been the occasion of that catastrophe; but geologists treat it as wholly improbable. Some of them deny even that there are any evidences in the condition of the earth of the occurrence of the deluge itself. While many of them regard the fossil vegetables, and animals that are found in high latitudes, as decisive proofs that the temperature of those climes during their life must have been far higher than at present, they generally ascribe the superior warmth which is supposed then to have prevailed, to the influence of internal fires. They cannot, therefore, assume that the earth's axis received at the Mosaic epoch its present inclination, unless they previously assume that immediately before the six days' creation, when, according to them, the world was made a "wreck," it was raised from its inclination to a right angle to the ecliptic. But that were in contravention of their principles, both because there are no proofs in the present condition of the earth of such a change; and because, if it took place, it cannot have been caused by the chemical and mechanical forces to which alone they can refer such a change in the position of the globe. It were supremely absurd to suppose that chemistry, any volcanic action, or any movement of the ocean, can have thrown the axis of the earth from an angle, to a perpendicular to the ecliptic. In maintaining, therefore, that the earth had revolved round the sun through an immeasurable tract of years, with its present inclination to the ecliptic and diversity of days and seasons, they in effect assume either that at the close of that period it was made a "wreck," and lost its inclination to the ecliptic, or else that no such change was wrought in its condition on the fourth day of the Mosaic creation, as is related in this passage. If the latter, they offer a direct contradiction to the inspired record; if the former, they both contradict the announcement in the first four verses, and in Exodus xx. 3, that the earth itself, and the sun, moon, and stars, were created on the first of the six days; and contravene their own principles, which forbid them to assume the occurrence of any change of the earth's condition that was not produced by the chemical and mechanical agents to which they refer all geological effects. Of this difficulty, as they appear not to have been aware of its existence, they have not attempted a solution.

QUESTIONS.

Could there have been any mountains or high hills on the earth's surface while it continued to be covered by the ocean? What must have been the process by which the dry land was formed? Must the change have been rapid, if large continents and islands immediately became dry? Must the dry land have been covered with a soil fit for the support of vegetables? Is this narrative of the formation of mountains on the third day, reconcilable with the geological theory? To what epoch do geologists refer the elevation of the mountains? Do they hold that the soil of the present strata formed the surface of the earth which was elevated from the waters at this epoch; and that the materials of these strata were drawn from mountains and lands that had previously existed? State the opinions of Macculloch, Buckland, Phillips, and Lyell. Are not these opinions in the most open antagonism to the sacred text? To what expedient do geologists resort to extricate themselves from this difficulty? Is their omission to notice it adapted to confirm the claim they often put forth, to an exclusive competence to treat of the subject? Does the supposition on which they rely to save themselves from all difficulties—that a vast tract of ages intervened between the epoch of the first and second verses—relieve them in any measure from this contradiction to the sacred text? If continents and mountains had existed for ages before the era of the third day's creation, must not those mountains and continents have been got rid of and the earth reduced to a geological level, in order that a new set could be produced at the time and in the manner the text narrates? Can a more irreconcilable contradiction be conceived, than their theory thus forms to the inspired history?

What was the act of the fourth day's creation? What is the first of the views geologists entertain of this creative act? What is the objection to that view? What is the second construction they place on this act? What is the objection to that view of it? What is the third notion they entertain of it? Is that consistent with the language of the passage? What then was the true import of the creative fiat? What was the effect wrought by it? How may a change have been produced in the relations of the earth and other planets and the sun, that gave birth to seasons and years? What other change in their relations to each other may also have taken place? Is either of these effects reconcilable with the geological theory? Show how it is irreconcilable with the supposition that a change of the distances of the planets from each other and from the sun was wrought by the creative act. Show how it is inconsistent with the supposition that the effect wrought was the change of the earth's axis from a perpendicular to its present inclination to the ecliptic.

CHAPTER VII.

Difficulties of Geologists respecting the Creation of Animals and Man.

Their theory that the plants and animals whose relics are buried in the earth, had their life during the ages which they hold preceded the "wreck" and reconstruction of the globe six thousand years ago, is in like manner contradictory to the inspired history of the creative acts of the third, fifth, and sixth days.

"And God said, Let the waters bring forth abundantly the moving creature that hath life, and fowl that may fly above the earth in the open firmament of heaven. And God created great whales, and every living creature that moveth, which the waters brought forth abundantly after their kind, and every winged fowl after his kind. And God saw that it was good. And God blessed them, saying: Be fruitful and multiply, and fill the waters in the seas, and let fowl multiply in the earth. And the evening and the morning were the fifth day.

"And God said, Let the earth bring forth the living creature after his kind, cattle, and creeping thing, and beast of the earth after his kind: And it was so. And God made the beast of the earth after his kind, and cattle after their kind, and every thing that creepeth upon the earth after his kind. And God saw that it was good.

"And God said, Let us make man, in our image, after our likeness, and let them have dominion over the fish of the sea, and over the fowl of the air, and over the cattle, and over all the earth, and over every creeping thing that creepeth upon the earth. So God created man in his own image; in the image of God created he him; male and female created he them. And God blessed them. And God said unto them: Be fruitful, and multiply, and replenish the earth, and subdue it, and have dominion over the fish of the sea, and over the fowl of the air, and over every living thing that moveth upon the earth. And God said: Behold, I have given you every herb bearing seed, which is upon the face of all the earth, and every tree in which is the fruit of a tree yielding seed; to you it shall be for meat. And to every beast of the earth, and to every fowl of the air, and to every thing that creepeth upon the earth, wherein there is life, I have given every green herb for meat: and it was so. And God saw every thing that he had made, and behold, it was very good. And the evening and the morning were the sixth day."—Chap. i. 20–31.

"THUS *the heavens and the earth were finished, and all the host of them.* And on the seventh day God ended his work which he had made. And he rested on the seventh day from all his work which he had made. And God blessed the seventh day and sanctified it; because that in it he had rested from all his work, which God created and made.

"These are the generations of the heavens and of the earth when they were created, in the day that the Lord God made the earth and the heavens, and every plant and every herb of the field before it grew: for the Lord God had not caused it to rain upon the earth; and there was not a man to till the ground. But there went up a mist from the earth, and watered the whole face of the ground."—Chap. ii. 1–6.

The theory of a previous existence through innumerable ages of the heavens and earth, and the vegetables and animals that are buried in its strata, is thus in as marked antagonism with this part of the history as with the other. We are expressly told that these are the generations; that is, the origins, or modes of the first existence of the heavens and the earth when they were created; and that it was *thus*, that is in the manner related, that "the heavens and the earth were *finished*, and all the host of them." No language could more specifically declare that they were all called into being during the six days, or more effectually preclude the supposition of their previous existence. It is as unwarrantable a contradiction of the narrative to assert that plants and animals, the earth itself, and heavens, existed through countless ages before, as it were to assert that man lived through those ages. But geologists admit that man had no existence anterior to the date here assigned to his creation. Why then should they deny that the narrative exhibits the plants and animals also, and the earth itself as then first created? They unquestionably cannot, if governed in their views by the language of the history; and the fact, therefore, that they assert their previous existence, shows that the inspired record of the epoch and method of the creation not only is not the guide of their faith, but is not in reality of any authority with them in the determination of their system. It is accordingly admitted by some among them that this revealed history must be modified and forced to a metaphorical, or perhaps a mythical meaning, in order to remove its contradictions to their theory. It is directly claimed, indeed, that it is to be construed by that theory instead of its own language, in order to render its inspiration credible. While it is held to be true, its truth is equally held to depend on its being susceptible of a construction that admits the supposition of a previous existence of the earth and its vegetable and animal races through an incalculable series of ages. Thus Dr. Buckland:

"If the suggestions I shall venture to propose, require *some modification of the most commonly received and popular interpretation of the Mosaic narrative*, this admission neither involves any impeachment of the authenticity of the text, *nor of the judgment of those who have formerly interpreted it otherwise*, in the absence of information as to facts which have but recently been brought to light ; and if in this respect geology should seem to require some little concession from the literal interpretation of Scripture, it may fairly be held to afford ample compensation for this demand, by the large additions it has made to the evidences of natural religion, in a department where revelation was not designed to give information."—*Bridg. Treat.* p. 14.

It is thus unhesitatingly admitted that in order to exempt it from collision with the theory, the interpretation of the inspired record must be modified, and a meaning assigned it which, before the geological facts that have recently been brought to light were known, could not have been deduced by the laws of philology.*

* That Dr. Buckland penned the passage, however, with but a very inadequate consideration of its import, is apparent from the fancy he advances that such a violation of the narrative could be compensated by an addition to the evidences of natural religion. That an admission that that part of revelation, on the truth of which the veracity of all the rest depends, is shown by geology to be so false, as to make it necessary to put on it a forced and unphilological construction, can be counterbalanced by an addition to the evidences of theism, is truly a very extraordinary solecism, alike in hermeneutics and theology.

Dr. Hitchcock also asserts the necessity of construing the narrative by the facts of geology, in contravention of the laws of language.

"Moses represents the work of creation as completed in the space of six days; whereas the geologist asserts that the formation of the crust of the globe, with its numerous groups of extinct animals and plants, after the original production of the matter of the globe, must have occupied immense periods of time, whose duration we cannot estimate.

"We must decide whether geological facts can ever be permitted, as facts derived from civil history and astronomy are, to modify our interpretation of the sacred record. The Scriptures speak of the rising and setting of the sun; but astronomy shows us that they employ such language in accordance with optical, not physical truth. And the cases are too common to need particularizing, where the interpretation is essentially modified by civil history. Why should there be any question, then, whether geological facts ought to have the same influence in exposition? For so far as it bears on revelation, geology is nothing but a history of the globe anterior, for the most part, to the commencement of civil history. The only reason that has ever been alleged for refusing to use geological facts in this way, is that they are too uncertain. But although true half a century ago, the fundamental facts of this science may now be regarded as resting on as firm a foundation, and to be as well understood, as those of any science not strictly demonstrative. The principles of sound criticism, therefore, demand that they should be admitted equally with civil history and astronomy, as aids in the interpretation of the Bible."—*Geology and Revelation,* pp. 17, 23, 24.

The construction of the text, therefore, is not only to be modified by the facts of geology, but by his own concession completely reversed. No greater opposites can be conceived, than two representations of the creation, one of which assigns it to a date so distant that immense periods followed whose duration cannot be estimated, and the other fixes its epoch at about six thousand years ago, and exhibits it as accomplished in the space of six days. And what a singular tissue of errors and fallacies are employed to verify this assumption! In the first place, astronomy does not create any necessity of altering the interpretation of passages in which the sun is said to rise and set. No translator of the Bible rejects that form of representation, and substitutes the language in which it would be astronomically expressed. Such a change would be wholly unwarrantable. That description is as true to the senses, as the other is to the scientific intellect. It is not inaccurate, therefore, but expresses in that relation a genuine fact. There are many other forms of expression in which events are described in the same way, and with perfect truth. Thus, to say that one man sees another, expresses an absolute fact to the senses, although in reality he only sees by an image produced by rays of light at the bottom of the eye. In like manner, to say that one man hears another's voice expresses a fact to the senses, although, according to acoustics, he only perceives a vibration of the tympana of his own ears. Does Dr. H. consider it an inaccuracy to ascribe to objects colors, odors, tastes, and other qualities, which are mere effects, or forms of sensation? Is it not a fact to the senses, that snow and wool are white; that grass and the foliage of trees are green, and that the rainbow has the hues of the prism? Is it an inaccuracy to speak of seeing, and smelling, and painting a flower? This and all similar language of the senses is used on precisely the same principle as that which he quotes respecting the sun, and is employed as universally in conversation and every species of composition, scientific as well as that which relates to the ordinary affairs of life, as it is in the sacred writings. *Every single fact, indeed, throughout the domain of geology, and every one of its theoretical doctrines, is expressed in this language.* Is it not, then, to be interpreted as denoting identically what the facts which it expresses are to the senses? To deny it were at one blow to subvert the whole fabric of the science! For what are the facts of geology if they are not what they are to the senses? They have never been exhibited as anything else by any of those who have hitherto treated of them. But if this language is to be taken as denoting what the things which it expresses are to the senses, then how is its use in the instance he alleges to aid him in his argument? Does he regard the mode in which the Scriptures speak in respect to the sun, as parallel to the mode in which they exhibit the work of creation? Does he hold that that representation of the creation is to the facts of geology, optically considered, what the language of the Bible in respect to the motions of the sun is to the facts as they are to the senses? That were again to demolish his whole theory; for if the facts of geology are to the eye, in harmony with the account the Bible gives of the creation, then they present no visible indications of the earth's existence through an immeasurable period anterior to the epoch of that creation, but confirm the sacred narrative. If, however, there is no parallel between them, why does he quote that usage in respect to the creation? But he does not regard them as parallels. Instead, he holds that the facts of geology, optically considered, are irreconcilable with the representation of the sacred history, and the aim of the new element which he wishes to introduce into hermeneutics is, not to reconcile those facts to the inspired record by showing that they are what that record represents—not what they optically seem to be; but, instead, to show that that history does not teach what it literally means, but on the contrary, what the facts of geology optically indicate! The case which he alleges to illustrate what he wishes to accomplish, in place of presenting a resemblance, is thus a direct converse of it.*

He is equally unfortunate in the statement that "the cases are too common to need particularizing where the interpretation is essentially modified by civil history." Let him produce an example, if in his power. He may find instances in which, in one passage, a fact is related that is not mentioned in another that treats of the same subject; but none in which a fact is mentioned that renders it necessary to depart from the laws of philology in interpreting another.

But the great fallacy of his remarks lies in the representation that the facts of geology contradict the Mosaic record of the creation, and make it necessary to modify the interpretation of that record in order to bring them into harmony with each other. It is his *construction* of those facts, or *inferences* from them, not the facts themselves, that contravene the inspired

* The logic of his argument, seems, therefore, to be the following: —Inasmuch as the language of the Scriptures, of science, and of common life, used to express facts as they are to the senses, is *not* in accordance with the truth, philosophically considered; therefore, the record inscribed on the strata of the earth, as it appears to the senses of geologists, is to be considered as in harmony with the philosophical and absolute truth! This is no "airy hypothesis," it seems, but a "striking fact," and an "inference drawn according to the strictest rules of the Baconian philosophy."

account of the creation—things as distinct and as unlike as a false conclusion is from the premise from which it is drawn; as a creature's error is from the truth of God.

Geologists themselves, however, instead of adhering to this rule of interpretation, and applying it to the record, dismiss it on reaching the narrative of the creation of man, and assume that he was in fact first called into being at the epoch which that represents; and they accordingly allege the fact that no human bones are found fossilized in the lower or intermediate strata, as a proof that he did not exist till ages after the creation of vegetables and animals. But that is to desert their own principles. If they are justified in the construction they put on the history till they reach the narrative of his creation, they must, to be consistent, carry it through; and conclude, therefore, that the circumstance that no human skeletons have hitherto been discovered in the strata in which vegetables and animals are found, is no proof that they are not in fact imbedded in them, and will not be discovered in great numbers, when more extensive examinations are made. And should such discoveries be made, they will be compelled by their law of interpretation, not to relinquish their theory, but to apply it, in the light of that new fact of geology, to the history of the creation of man, and assume and assert his existence as well as that of vegetables and animals, through the immeasurable periods, whose duration we cannot estimate, anterior to the six days' creation. A single human skeleton, or fragment of one, found in the depths of the earth, amidst the relics of plants, fish, and land animals, which they refer to those fabulous periods, must drive them, by a logical necessity, to an instant rejection of the truth and inspiration of the whole of the history God has given us of the creation! Can a more decisive proof be asked of the total error of that system? According to them, the credibility of Genesis i. and ii., and thence of the rest of the Pentateuch, and consequently of all the other parts of the Old, and the whole of the New Testament, depends on the mere possibility that no fossil human bones are buried in the fossiliferous strata;—a possibility that not only cannot be proved, but that may be confuted any hour. A blow like this at the Christian system will hardly be regarded by prudent men as having an ample compensation "in the large addition" geology "has made to the evidences of natural religion."

In the next place, their theory of the existence of the earth with its fossil plants and animals through those imagined ages, is forbidden by their own principles, as well as by the divine word. In order to reconcile the creation of plants and animals recorded in Genesis with their theory, they suppose the races to which those buried in the strata belonged, to have been exterminated at the "wreck" of the world, which they regard as having immediately preceded the six days' creation. According to the axioms, however, by which they profess to be governed, they cannot assume such a stupendous occurrence and make it the basis of their theory, unless it can both be proved from the strata in which those relics are imbedded, and shown that it was produced by the chemical and mechanical forces to which they refer the geological facts on which they reason. But neither of these propositions can they prove. They do not undertake it. It were preposterous to attempt a demonstration from their nature, position, numbers, or any other consideration, that none of them descended from those that were created on the third, fifth, and sixth days of the Mosaic epoch. It were equally absurd to attempt to produce evidence that they were destroyed by chemical agents, volcanic fire, or the mechanical force of water. If it could be shown that those agents were adequate to their destruction, if brought in great force in contact with them, it is not possible to prove the fact of their contact. Here is thus another indispensable condition to the verification of their theory, that is taken for granted by them without evidence, and in contravention of their own principles, which prohibit their assuming the occurrence of any geological events that are not demonstrable from the earth's strata, and that are not the result of chemical and mechanical forces.

In the third place, there not only is no geological evidence that the animals that are fossilized were not either derived from those that were called into life in the six days of the Mosaic creation, or at a later epoch, but belonged to races of an anterior date; but there is positive and unanswerable proof to the contrary, in the fact that great numbers of those imbedded in the tertiary strata are of identically the species that now inhabit the seas and the earth. Thus Sir Charles Lyell says:

"M. Deshayes, of Paris, well known by his conchological works, at my request, drew up in a tabular form a list of all the shells known to him to occur both in some tertiary formation and in a living state, for the express purpose of ascertaining the proportional number of fossil species identical with the recent, which characterized successive groups; and this table, planned by us in common, was published by me in 1833. The number of tertiary fossil shells examined by M. Deshayes was about 3,000; and the recent species with which they had been compared, about 5,000. The result then arrived at was, that in the lower tertiary strata, or those of London and Paris, there were about 3½ per cent. of species identical with recent; and in the middle tertiary of the Loire and Gironde, about 17 per cent.; and in the upper tertiary or sub-alpine beds, from 35 to 50 per cent. In formations still more modern, some of which I had particularly studied in Sicily, where they attain a vast thickness and elevation above the sea, the number of species identical with those now living was believed to be from 90 to 95 per cent. . . .

"Since the year 1830, the progress of conchological science has been most rapid, and the number of living species obtained from different parts of the globe has been raised from about 5,000 to more than 10,000. New fossil species have also been added to our collections in great abundance; and at the same time a more copious supply of individuals, both of fossil and recent species, some of which were previously very rare, have been procured, affording more ample data for determining their specific character. . . .

"I have adopted the term post-pliocene for those strata which are sometimes called post-tertiary, or modern, and which are characterized by having all the imbedded fossil shells identical with species now living, whereas even the newer-pliocene, or newest of the tertiary deposits above alluded to, contain always some small proportion of shells of extinct species.

"These modern formations thus defined, comprehend not only those strata which can be shown to have originated since the earth was inhabited by man, but also deposits of far greater extent and thickness, in which no signs of man or his works can be detected. In some of those *of a date long anterior to the times of history and tradition, the bones of extinct quadrupeds* have been met with of species which probably *never co-existed with the human race,* as for example, the mammoth, mastodon, megatherium, and others, *and yet the shells are the same as those now living.*

"In Ischia, near Naples, . . . Dr. Phillipi collected in the stratified tuff and clay ninety-two species of shells of existing species. . . . In the centre of Ischia, on the lofty hill called Epomeo, at the height of about 2,000 feet, . . . I collected in 1828 many shells of species now inhabiting the neighboring gulf. It is clear, therefore, that the great mass of Epomeo was not only raised to its present height, but was also *formed* beneath the waters within the post-pliocene period.

"Such an upward movement has been proved to be in progress in Norway and Sweden throughout an area about 1,000 miles north and south, and for an unknown distance east and west. . . . Accordingly, we find near Stockholm, in Sweden, horizontal beds of sand loam and marl containing the same peculiar assemblage of testacea which now live in the brackish waters of the Baltic.

"On the opposite coast of Sweden, post-pliocene strata containing recent shells, . . . such as now live in the northern ocean, ascend to the height of 200 feet ; and beds of clay and sand of the same age attain an elevation of 300 and even 700 feet in Norway.

"Judging by the uniformity of climate now prevailing from century to century, and the insensible rate of variation in the organic world in our own times, we may presume that an extremely lengthened period was required even for so slight a modification of the molluscous fauna, as that of which the evidence is here brought to light. On the other hand, we have every reason for inferring, on independent grounds, namely, the rate of upheaval of land in modern times, that the antiquity of the deposits in question must be very great. For, if we assume that the mean rate of continuous vertical elevation has amounted to 2½ feet in a century, and this is probably a high average, it would require 27,500 years for the sea-coast to attain the height of 700 feet, without making allowance for any pauses, such as are now experienced in a large part of Norway, or for any oscillations of level." —*Manual of Geology*, pp. 110–115.

Species that are now living occur in great numbers in the newer pliocene strata, the upper of the tertiary.

"M. Murchison and De Verneuil found in 1840 that the flat country between St. Petersburgh and Archangel, for a distance of 600 miles, consists of horizontal strata, full of shells similar to those now inhabiting the Arctic Sea, on which rested the boulder formation.

"In Sweden in the neighborhood of Upsala, I observed in 1834 a ridge of stratified sand and gravel, in the midst of which is a layer of marl, evidently formed originally at the bottom of the Baltic, by the slow growth of mussel, cockle, and other marine shells, intermixed with some of the fresh-water species. The marine shells are all of dwarfish size, like those now inhabiting the brackish waters of the Baltic; and the marl in which myriads of them are imbedded is now more than 100 feet above the level of the Gulf of Bothnia. Upon the top of this ridge repose several huge erratics, consisting of gneiss, . . . which must have been brought into their present position since the time when the neighboring gulf was already characterized by its peculiar fauna. . . .

"The northern drift of the most southern latitudes is usually of the highest antiquity. In Scotland it rests on the older rocks, and is covered by stratified sand and clay, usually devoid of fossils, but in which at certain points . . . marine shells have been discovered. . . . Although a proportion of between 85 or 90 in 100 of the imbedded shells are of recent species, the remainder are unknown; and even many which are recent, now inhabit more northern seas, where we may, perhaps, hereafter find living representatives of some of the unknown fossils.

"The testaceous fauna of the boulder period in Scotland, England, and Ireland, has been shown by Prof. E. Forbes to contain a much smaller number of species than that now belonging to the British seas. . . . Yet the species are nearly all of them now living either in the British or more northern seas, the shells of more arctic latitudes being the most abundant, and the most wide-spread throughout the entire area of the drift from North to South."—*Lyell's Manual of Geol.* pp. 124—126.

"M. Deshayes and Mr. Lyell have recently proposed a fourfold division of the marine formations of the *tertiary series, founded on the proportions which their fossil shells bear to marine shells of* EXISTING SPECIES. To these divisions Mr. Lyell has applied the terms eocene, miocene, older-pliocene, and newer-pliocene, and has most ably illustrated their history in his Principles of Geology.

"The term eocene implies the commencement or *dawn* of

the existing state of the animal creation; the strata of this series containing a very small proportion of shells *referable to living species.* The calcaire grossier of Paris and the London clay are familiar examples of this *older tertiary,* or eocene formation.

"The term miocene implies that *a minority* of the fossil shells, in formations of this period, are of *recent species.* To this are referred the fossil shells of Bordeaux, Turin, and Vienna.

"In formations of the older and newer-pliocene taken together, *the majority* of the shells belong to *living species;* the recent species in the newer being much more abundant than in the older division.

"To the older pliocene belong the Sub-Appenine marine formations and the English Clay; and to the newer-pliocene the more recent marine deposits of Sicily, Ischia, and Tuscany."—*Dr. Buckland's Bridgewater Treatise,* pp. 78, 79.

A considerable number, also, of the fossil fish and land quadrupeds are of species that still exist. The tertiary strata which comprise all that are between the chalk formation and the diluvium, are of great depth, and are the depositories of by far the most important classes, especially of land animals.

"It appears that the animal kingdom was early established on the same general principles that now prevail; not only did the four present classes of vertebrata exist; and among mammalia, the orders pachydermata, carnivora, rodentia, and marsupialia, but many of the genera into which living families are distributed, were associated together in the same system of adaptations and relations which they hold to each other in the actual creation.

"The bones of all these animals found *in the earliest series of the tertiary deposits are accompanied by the remains of reptiles, such as now inhabit the fresh waters of warm countries,* e. g. the crocodile, emys, and tryonix.

"The second or miocene system of tertiary deposits contains an admixture of the extinct genera of lacustrine mammalia of the first or eocene series, *with the earliest forms of genera which exist at the present time.*

"The third and fourth of pliocene divisions of the tertiary fresh-water deposits, . . . abound in extinct species of pachydermata, e. g. elephant, rhinoceros, hippopotamus, and horse, together with the extinct genera mastodon. With them also occur the first abundant traces of the ruminantia, e. g. *oxen and deer.*

"The seas, also, of the miocene and pliocene periods were inhabited by marine mammalia, consisting of whales, dolphins, seals, walrus, and the lamantin, or manati, *whose existing species* are chiefly found near the coasts and mouths of rivers in the torrid zone.—*Buckland's Bridg. Treatise,* pp. 87–92.

"The largest, the most ferocious, and the least useful of the pliocene species have perished ; but the horse, the ass, the hog, probably the smaller wild ox, the goat, the red-deer, and roe, and many of the diminutive quadrupeds remain. . . . . . It is probable that the horse and ass are descendants of a species of pliocene antiquity in *Europe.* There is no anatomical character by which the present wild boar can be distinguished specifically from that which was contemporary with the mammoth. All the species of European pliocene Bovidæ come down to the historical period, and the aurochs and musk ox still exist. . . . There is evidence that the great *bos primigenius*, and the small *bos longifrons*, which date by fossils from the time of the mammoth, continued to exist in this island after it became inhabited by man. The small short-horned pliocene ox is most probably still preserved in the mountain varieties of our domestic cattle. The great urus seems never to have been tamed, but to have been finally extirpated in Scotland. Of the cervine tribe, the red-deer and the roebuck still exist in the mountainous districts of the north."—*R. Owen's Hist. Brit. Fossil Mammalia and Birds*, Introd. p. xxxii.

The period supposed by geologists to have intervened between the deposition of the eocene strata, in which a share of these fossils is found, and the epoch of the six days' creation, they regard as immense. Thus Prof. Owen says:

"With the last layer of the eocene deposits, we lose in this island every trace of the mammalia of that remote period. *The imagination strives in vain to form an idea* commensurate with the evidence of the intervening operations which continental geology teaches to have gradually and successively taken place—*of the length of time that elap-*

sed before the foundations of England were again sufficiently settled to serve as the theatre of life to another race of warm-blooded quadrupeds.

"In the endeavor to trace the origin of *our existing mammalia*, I have been led to view them as *descendants of a portion of a peculiar and extensive mammalian Fauna*, which overspread Europe and Asia at a period geologically recent, yet *incalculably remote, and long anterior to any evidence or record of the human race*."—*Hist. Brit. Fos.* pp. xxi–xxxv.

Sir C. Lyell refers the strata in which they are imbedded to an equally remote age.

"It would be rash to infer that these quadrupeds"—the mastodons, found in New Jersey and New York—"were mired in *modern* times, unless we use that term strictly in a geological sense. I have shown that there is a fluviatile deposit in the valley of the Niagara, containing shells of the genera Melania, Lymnea, Planorbis, Valvata, Cyclas, Unio, and Helix, &c., all of recent species, from which the bones of the great mastodon have been taken in a very perfect state. Yet the whole excavation of the ravine, for many miles below the Falls, has been slowly effected, since that fluviatile deposit was thrown down.

"Whether or not, in assigning a period of more than 30,000 years for the recession of the Falls from Queenstown to their present site, I have over or under estimated the time required for that operation, no one can doubt that *a vast number of centuries* must have elapsed before so great a series of geographical changes were brought about as have occurred since the entombment of this elephantine quadruped. The fresh-water gravel which encloses it, is decidedly of much more modern origin than the drift or boulder clay of the same region."—*Man. Geol.*, p. 138.

No demonstration could be more absolute than is presented by these facts that a large share of the present races of animals are derived from those that are fossilized, and had their origin, therefore, in the same creative fiat. There is no maxim more fundamental and indisputable in zoology than that all animals of the same species had a common parentage, or are to be traced to the same creation. To reject that axiom, would be to reject the tie that connects effects with their causes, and render it nugatory to reason on the subject. The supposition, therefore, that the fossilized races were wholly exterminated antecedently to the six days' creation, and that the present living races had an independent origin at that epoch, is shown to be erroneous. Those geologists who hold that the present races were called into being at that date, must, if they adhere to the maxims of zoology, admit that those that are entombed in the tertiary deposits had their origin also at the same era.

But the proof does not stop here. There is ample evidence that there never was an absolute break in the descent of certain classes of marine animals, from the date of the first that were fossilized down to the races that now inhabit the seas. For those in the tertiary strata of the genera and species that are now living, were contemporaneous with others now extinct that are fossilized in the strata of an earlier date; and they in their first periods were contemporaneous with other genera and species that were fossilized at a still earlier date, and these last were coeval with still other genera and species that appear in a still lower series of rocks; and so on to the lowest strata that contain fossil shells. An unbroken chain of coexisting genera and species can be made out from the date of the first to the races of the present hour.

"We find certain families of organic remains pervading strata of every age, under nearly the same generic forms which they present among existing organizations; *e. g.* the nautilus, echinus, terebratula, and various forms of corals; and among plants, the ferns, lycopodiaceæ, and palms. Other families, both of animals and vegetables, are limited to particular formations, there being certain points where entire groups ceased to exist, and were replaced by others of a different character."—*Dr. Buckland's Bridg. Treat.*, p. 100.

"By selecting genera and families, we may show through what ranges of strata, that is to say, through what geological periods, they existed, and at what periods they were the most numerous. Thus Trilobites existed during the primary and carboniferous epochs, but are never known in the more recent strata, nor do they exist at present ; Productæ pass through the primary and carboniferous epochs, and end in the saliferous ; Spiriferæ pass through all these epochs, and end in the oolites ; Ammonites pass through all these periods, and end in the chalk ; Terebratulæ* existed through all these periods, and also through the tertiary system, and *are still in being*. On the other hand, certain tribes began to exist at later periods, as the Belemites, many genera of Echini, &c., and ended their race before the dawn of the tertiary period."—*Phillips's Guide*, p. 75.

There are similar proofs also of the continuance of certain classes of vegetables from the period of the earliest strata to the present time.

"From the data hitherto obtained, the most eminent botanists consider that the Floras of the ancient world constitute three distinct epochs or eras.

"The first comprehends the earliest strata in which traces of vegetation appear, and includes the carboniferous. The plants of this epoch, as we have already shown, consist of fuci and other cellular tribes ; ferns of various kinds in great

* Thus of Terebratulæ there were—

In the Primary fossiliferous strata . . .	30 genera.
In the Carboniferous system	16 "
In the Saliferous system	14 "
In the Oolitic system	49 "
In the Cretaceous system	57 "
In the Tertiary strata	18 "

Phillips's Guide, p. 76.

abundance ; coniferous trees related to species of warm climates ; of palms and other monocotyledons, gigantic lycopodia, and trees (Sigillaria) in great abundance, whose precise relations to known forms are not accurately determined. In this Flora the tree ferns predominate, constituting nearly two-thirds of the whole known species ; and the general type of the vegetation is *analogous to that of the islands and archipelagoes of intertropical climates.*

"The second epoch extends from the New Red or Saliferous strata to the Chalk inclusive, and is characterized by the appearance of many species of Cycadeæ, Zamiæ, and other Coniferæ, while *the proportion of ferns is much less than in the preceding period;* and the *lycopodiaceous tribes*, Calamites, &c., of the carboniferous strata are absent. *A Flora of this nature is analogous to that of the coasts and maritime districts of New Holland and the Cape of Good Hope.*

"The third epoch is that of the tertiary, in which dicotyledonous tribes appear in great numbers, the Cycadeæ are very rare, *the ferns in diminished numbers*, and the Coniferæ more numerous. Palms and other intertropicals are found associated with the existing European forest trees, as the elm, ash, willow, poplar, &c., presenting, in short, the general features of our continental Flora."—*Mantell's Medals of Creation*, vol. i., pp. 200, 201.

These facts thus completely confute the assumption that an extermination of the vegetables and animals took place between the fossilization of those that are imbedded in the strata and those that were called into life at the epoch of the six days' creation. The chain of coexistence is shown, by the discoveries geologists have already made, to have extended without an interval from the first to the last; and the proofs of the uninterruptedness of the line will be augmented at every step in the progress of the science. The examinations have hitherto been confined to comparatively a few sites, chiefly in Europe. When they shall have been made on a greater scale there, and extended to western, northern, and eastern Asia, Africa, North and South America, and the islands of the Pacific and Indian oceans, the evidences of the unbroken continuance of vegetable and animal life through the whole series of the strata to the present hour, will undoubtedly accumulate to an indisputableness and vastness that must for ever set aside the fancy of their extermination at any point in the succession.

And finally, their theory is equally inconsistent with the history of the deluge. The sacred writer relates that "the waters prevailed exceedingly upon the earth, and all the high hills that were under the whole heaven were covered. Fifteen cubits and upward did the water prevail; and the mountains were covered." And as a consequence, "all flesh died that moved upon the earth, both of fowl, and of cattle, and of beast, and of every creeping thing that creepeth upon the earth, and every man. All in whose nostrils was the breath of life, of all that was on the dry land died," Genesis vii. 19–22. As the waters of the globe were wholly inadequate to cover its whole surface to such a depth, if the hills and mountains continued to maintain their elevation, it is manifest that they must have been depressed to near the general line of the lands, and the whole body of the continents and islands carried down to a level with the bottom of the seas; or else the surfaces on which the seas rested must have been elevated to the line of the continents and islands. Whether the hills and mountains of the antediluvian globe equalled in height those that now stud the surface of the earth, we have no means of knowing.* The present system of mountains and hills must indisputably, therefore, have received at least their main upheaval since the flood reached its height; and probably most of them, at the period when the continents and islands on which they rise were elevated to their present position, and the waters of the deluge again thrown back into the seas and oceans which now surround them.

The advocates of the geological theory, however, assign our present mountains and hills a far earlier date, and assert that many of them at least have

* "If we suppose the elevation of one part to be compensated by the depression of another, the ocean level will vary merely as the quantity of land above its surface. If we suppose all the dry land to sink till it be submerged, it will cause the ocean to rise about 250 feet."—*Phillips's Guide to Geol.* p. 49.

existed through a vast series of ages. The supposition that they were thrown up from the sea at so late an epoch as the deluge, they reject as little better than a solecism. They are thus again in conflict with the sacred record. No hypothesis can reconcile them; no artifice—if the theory is held to be true—can shield the text from the discredit of a consummate error.

Such are the proofs that this great doctrine of modern speculative geology presents, at every step, the most direct and absolute contradiction to the history God has given us of the creation and deluge. If that doctrine be true, the record in Genesis cannot be. They are at an infinite distance from each other in respect to each of the acts by which God accomplished the six days' work. The sacred record ascribes the creation of the heavens and earth to the first of the six days. The theory asserts that they had then existed through an immeasurable round of ages. The inspired history assigns the creation of light to the first day. The theory affirms that the sun had then existed and shone on the earth through an incalculable series of years. The Bible testifies that God created the atmosphere on the second day. The theory asserts that it had before enveloped the globe through periods whose duration we cannot estimate. The sacred history relates that the seas were first formed, and dry land made to appear on the third day after the creation of the earth. The theory declares that they had existed through innumerable ages anterior to that epoch. The sacred history teaches that on the fourth day the earth first received that adjustment to the sun, moon, and stars, by which they determine the succession of seasons and years, and the variations of the days and nights. The geological theory assigns that arrangement to an immeasurably earlier date. The inspired record refers the creation of plants to the third day, the creation of fish and fowls to the fifth, and the creation of land animals to the sixth. The theory declares that record to be contradicted by the relics that lie buried in the strata of the earth, and affirms that they were created at an epoch incalculably earlier, and flourished through a vast tract of ages that intervened, to the time of the six days' creation. And finally, the Bible represents that at the deluge the whole earth was overspread by the ocean, which implies that the mountains and hills were depressed, and near a level produced between the bed of the ocean and the continents and islands. The geological theory controverts that representation, and maintains that the present mountains and hills were formed at an epoch immeasurably more remote. They are thus, on all these subjects, in the most open and undisguised antagonism. Had it been the object of its authors to devise a theory, in conflict in every element with the inspired history, they could not have formed one more conspicuously and absolutely of that character. Strauss's hypothesis respecting the facts of Christ's birth, ministry, miracles, death, and resurrection, is not more at antipodes with the gospel narrative, than this is with the record God has given of the creation and deluge. The great postulates on which it proceeds—that the earth anterior to the six days' creation was reduced to a "wreck," mountains and hills obliterated from its bosom, the light of the sun extinguished, the atmosphere annihilated, the earth deprived of its inclination to the ecliptic, and races of vegetables and animals that had inhabited it exterminated—are equally inconsistent with the axioms of the science. Like Buffon's hypothesis respecting the origin of the solar system, and Whiston's theory of the cause of the deluge, they are at war alike with the principles of geology and the laws of nature, and could never have been entertained, had their advocates duly considered the assumptions which they involve, and the embarrassments in which they entangle them.

The fancy, then, that the theory has been reconciled, or is reconcilable with the Mosaic record, must be abandoned. The verification of their postulates, which is necessary in order that they may proceed on them as facts, they can never accomplish. They might as well attempt, by chemistry and mechanics, to bring the antipodes into our hemisphere, as to bring their fancied record of the rocks into unison with that of Genesis. They might as well undertake to compress the universe into the dimensions of the earth, as to attempt to shrink their fabulous ages into harmony with the six days of the creation.

There is no consistent medium, therefore, between the rejection of their theory and the rejection of the Bible. Geologists and their disciples must, indeed, on their principles, abandon the hypothesis on which they have proceeded, and discard the inference of a prior existence of the vegetables and animals, which they have mistaken for a scientific deduction—as they are as inconsistent with the maxims of geology as they are with allegiance to the volume of inspiration.

On the other hand, the believers in revelation, and expositors of the sacred word especially, must adhere, in the interpretation of the inspired history, to the laws of philology, and receive and maintain the narrative of the creation as of absolute truth and authority; and they surely cannot need more ample means than are furnished by the foregoing considerations to shield it from the imputations which have been cast on it by the geological theory.

QUESTIONS.

What were the creative acts of the fifth and sixth days? Are not these irreconcilable with the geological theory, which affirms that the animals and vegetables that are buried in the strata, existed innumerable ages before this epoch? Do not geologists admit that man had no being anterior to the sixth day? Does not the sacred narrative teach with equal clearness, that the beasts of the earth had no existence before that day, nor fish nor fowls before the fifth day, nor vegetables before the third? Is it not as contradictory to the text, to assert that animals and vegetables had existed millions of years anterior to the six days' creation, as it would be to assert that man had? Do not geologists indeed admit that the sacred narrative, according to the literal import of its language, is at open war with their theory? By what means then do they attempt to bring them into harmony? State Dr. Buckland's expedient. State Dr. Hitchcock's. Is not this an explicit admission that the declarations of the sacred text are to be deliberately set aside, in defiance of the laws of language, and the doctrine of the geological theory substituted in their place? Is such an undisguised elevation of the hypotheses of geologists to a higher authority than the word of God, entitled to be dignified with the name of science? Is it anything else than an attempt to fix the brand of falsehood on His word, because it contradicts their speculations? Is not Dr. Hitchcock mistaken in imagining that the language of the history of the creation and other parts of the Scriptures is inconsistent with the real nature of the facts which they respect? Is it not as literally true and proper to say that the sun rises and sets, as it is to say that the earth turns on its axis, so as to produce that apparent motion of the sun? Are not mankind accustomed to express themselves in that manner in regard to all the facts which they perceive by the senses? Give examples. Do not geologists themselves use similar language in the description of the facts of geology? If the principle of interpretation for which Dr. Hitchcock contends in respect to the language of the senses is applied to the terms and phraseology of geology, will it not strike the whole of its facts from existence, as effectually as it would those of the sacred text which it is employed to annihilate? Do geologists adhere to their method of interpreting the history of the six days, when they come to the creation of man? Would not consistency reqnire them to? Were human skeletons found intermixed with the fossil animals and vegetables that are imbedded in the strata, which they refer to ages that preceded the creation narrated in Genesis, would not consistency oblige them to assert that man had existed many ages before the creation of Adam and Eve? Is not their theory of the existence of plants and animals ages before the creation recorded by Moses, unwarrantable by their own principles, as well as contradictory to the sacred word? Show how it is forbidden by their axioms. But is not their theory confuted by the fact that many of the plants and animals that now subsist, are of the same species as those that are buried in the strata, and which geologists affirm had their existence anterior to the creation of the present races? In what great division of the strata are these fossils principally found? What species of animal relics are the most numerous? In what countries are they found? Are fossil fish and land quadrupeds also found in those strata? Specify some of the quadrupeds which are still common. Do geologists refer the formation of the strata in which these animals are buried, to ages long anterior to the Mosaic epoch of the creation? What language does Prof. Owen employ to express his views of their antiquity? To how remote a period does Sir C. Lyell refer bones of the Mastodon found near Niagara? But beyond this, are there not evidences that certain classes of animals that now exist, have existed at every period from the first strata in which fossils are found? Does not that prove that there has never been an absolute extinction of those races from the period in which they first appear in the strata, to the present time; and confute the pretence therefore, that the present races of animals are of a wholly different creation, from those that are buried in the strata? Are there not classes of plants also now existing, that have existed through every period during which the fossilized strata were forming? Does not that prove that no extermination of vegetables took place between the fossilization of those that are buried in the strata, and the creation of those that now spring from the soil? Is not their theory irreconcilable also with the deluge? Point out the manner in which it contradicts it. Is it not clear then, that this doctrine of geology, is in the most palpable contradiction to the sacred history of the creation and deluge? State the principal points on which they contravene each other. Is there any consistent medium then, between either rejecting their theory, or rejecting the inspiration of the Bible?

CHAPTER VIII.

The false Theories of Geologists respecting the Sources of the Materials of which the Strata were formed.

It was the object of the preceding chapters, to show that the theory of the vast age of the world is irreconcilable with the inspired history of the creation; and that the great postulates on which it proceeds, respecting a chaotic condition of the earth, an extinction of light, an annihilation of an atmosphere, an erosion of mountains, a change of the earth's axis in relation to the ecliptic, and an extermination of vegetables and animals, are unauthorized and incompatible with the principles of geology. We now proceed to show that the theories respecting the mode in which the strata of the earth were formed and brought into the condition in which they now subsist, which geologists make a principal ground of their inference that immense periods must have been occupied in the process, are in like manner mistaken, and inconsistent both with the facts and with the maxims of the science.

That deduction they found—not directly on the strata themselves, but—mainly, first, on an assumption respecting the sources whence the materials of which they consist were derived; next, on an hypothesis respecting the forces by which those materials were transported to the places of their deposition, arranged in their several combinations, and thrown into the conditions in which they now exist; and thirdly—which holds but a very subordinate place in their reasonings—on a theory respecting the production and destruction of the vegetables and animals, the relics of which are imbedded in the strata.* As the facts themselves of the science are not the basis directly of their deduction of the period which they assign to the formation of the strata, but hypotheses respecting the causes and processes to which they

* "The whole period occupied in the deposition of the fossiliferous rocks must have been immensely long. There must have been time for water to have made depositions more than six miles in thickness, by *materials worn from previous rocks,* and more or less comminuted; time enough, also, to allow of hundreds of changes in the materials deposited, such changes as now require a long period for the production of one of them; time enough to allow of the growth and dissolution of animals and plants often of microscopic littleness, sufficient to constitute almost entire mountains of their remains; time enough to produce, by an extremely slow *change of climate,* the destruction of several nearly entire groups of organic beings; for although sudden catastrophes may have sometimes been the immediate cause of their extinction, there is reason to believe those catastrophes did not usually happen till such a change had taken place in the physical condition of the globe as to render it no longer a comfortable habitation for beings of their organization. *We must judge of the time requisite for these deposits by similar operations now in progress; and those are in general extremely slow.*"—*Hitchcock's Geology of Massachusetts,* p. 773.

owe their existence, those facts themselves do not demonstrate that deduction. In order to sustain it, they must *prove* that the materials of the strata were drawn from the sources to which they refer them; that they were borne to their respective places, arranged in their combinations, and subjected to the modifications which they have undergone, by the forces to which they ascribe those processes. If they cannot verify these hypotheses, if they are inconsistent with the facts of the science and the laws themselves of matter, then their deduction from them of the vast age of the world falls to the ground. On the other hand, the claims of that inference to be regarded as a scientific deduction will be confuted, if we simply show that the postulates from which it is drawn are merely supposititious, not demonstrated. If, in addition to that, we prove also that they are altogether irreconcilable with the facts and principles of the science, and the laws of nature, and infinitely self-contradictory, we shall furnish all the evidence that can be required to overthrow their theory; and that we propose to do.

Of the two great postulates on which they mainly found their deduction of the great age of the world, that which relates to the geological agents is, as stated in a former chapter, that the forces by which the strata of the earth were originally formed and subsequently modified, were those of chemistry, fire, and water, which are now acting on the globe, and producing somewhat similar effects ; and that the energy with which they are now exerting their powers, and the scale on which they are giving birth to changes in the earth's surface, are to be taken as the measure of their intensity, and the rapidity with which they wrought their several effects in the formation of the strata. There is, indeed, some diversity of opinion among them in respect to this branch of the hypothesis. Thus Sir H. T. De la Beche says:

"The two prevailing theories of the present time are—1st, That which attributes all geological phenomena to such effects [operations] of existing causes as we now witness ; and 2d, That which considers them referable to a series of catastrophes, or sudden revolutions. The difference in the two theories is not in reality very great ; the question being merely one of intensity of forces, so that probably by uniting the two we should approximate nearer to the truth."—*Manual of Geology*, p. 32.

He accordingly, and all others who regard the formation of the strata as having occupied immense periods, hold that though at some few stages—as in the elevation of mountains, the dislocation of the strata, and their subsequent denudation—volcanic fires and the waters of the ocean must have acted with far greater energy than ordinarily; yet that, in the main, the rate at which they are now giving birth to their several effects is to be taken as the measure of their past agency. The mode in which this theory is advanced by them was exemplified in a former chapter, by a variety of passages from the leading writers. We add a few others:

"It is only by carefully considering the combined action of all the causes of change *now in operation*, whether in the animate or inanimate world, that we can hope to explain such complicated appearances as are exhibited in the general arrangement of mineral masses."—*Lyell's Principles*, vol. ii., p. 210.

"The geologist must on no account think it out of the bounds of his legitimate province to examine with care and interest into the history of the processes *now performed in the ocean and on land; for it is only by discrimination and generalization of these* that we can hope to draw satisfactory inferences concerning *the force and direction of the agencies formerly exerted in earlier oceans, and on earlier continents.*" —*Phillips's Guide*, p. 102.

"It is presumed that the reader will . . . be convinced that *the forces formerly employed to remodel the crust of the earth, were the same in kind and energy as those now acting;* or at least he will perceive that the opposite hypothesis is very questionable."—*Lyell's Principles*, pref. xi.

"Moving water is the only agent known to us capable of carrying away the great collective mass of rock"—that has been swept from the mountains and hills. "In order, therefore, to form a just conception of *the time and conditions* required to produce the effects observed, we should carefully examine the latter, and estimate the transporting powers of those waters which now exist among the mountains themselves, and which transport detrital matter from the central parts outwards."—*Sir H. T. De la Beche's Theoretical Geology*, p 147.

"The immense period requisite to wear away such a mass of rock as this theory supposes to have once occupied the whole valley of the Connecticut, will seem to most minds the strongest objection to its adoption ; I mean, *supposing it to have been effected by such causes as are operating at present.* But this is not a solitary example, in which geological phenomena indicate the operation of existing causes through periods of duration inconceivably long. We may in this case, indeed, suppose the occurrence of other agencies in the earlier periods of our globe. Still even with this aid the work must have been immensely protracted. And why should we hesitate to admit the existence of our globe through periods as long as geological researches require?" —*Hitchcock's Geology of Massachusetts*, p. 339.

These views are advanced by a crowd of other writers. There is no element of their speculations in which they more generally agree, than that the causes to which the strata owe their origin and modifications, were those now in activity on the globe, and that they produced their effects by agencies in the main of only their present energy.

Their other great postulate is, that the stratified portions of the crust of the earth were formed mainly from the detritus of rocky continents and islands, and borne down to the ocean by rivers, or beat off by waves from the shores, and distributed over the bottom of the sea by tides and currents. Thus Dr. Buckland:—

"Beneath the whole series of stratified rocks that appear on the surface of the globe, there probably exists a foundation of unstratified crystalline rocks, bearing an irregular surface, from the detritus of which *the materials* of stratified rocks have in great measure been derived, either directly by the accumulation of the ingredients of disintegrated granitic rocks, or indirectly by the repeated destruction of different classes of stratified rocks, the materials of which had, by prior operations, been derived from unstratified formations, amounting to a thickness of many miles. This is indeed but a small depth in comparison with the diameter of the globe; but small as it is, it affords certain evidence of a long series of changes and revolutions, affecting not only the mineral condition of the nascent surface of the earth, but attended also by important alterations in animal and vegetable life.

"The detritus of the first dry lands being drifted into the sea and there spread out into extensive beds of mud and sand and gravel, would for ever have remained beneath the surface of the water, had not other forces been subsequently employed to raise them into dry land.

"Wherever solid matter arose above the water, it became exposed to destruction by atmospheric agents ; by rains, torrents, and inundations, at that time probably acting with intense violence, and washing down and spreading forth in the form of mud and sand and gravel upon the bottom of the then existing seas, the materials of primary stratified rocks, which by subsequent exposure to various degrees of subterranean heat, became converted into beds of gneiss, and mica slate, and hornblende slate, and clay slate. In the detritus thus swept from the early lands into the most ancient seas, we view the commencement of that enormous series of derivative strata which by long continued repetition of similar processes have been accumulated to a thickness of many miles."—*Bridgewater Treatise*, pp. 42, 50, 51.

"Thus the origin of strata is derived from depositions of the materials of the dry land under the waters of the sea, and, in some cases, of great inland lakes intermixed with the spoils of animals that have lived and died through a long succession of ages. If the daily causes of waste pulverize the solid mountains, and the rivers transport their ruins to the sea, so other causes acting more extensively and powerfully, must be allowed a share in producing and depositing the materials to which we owe our present stratified rocks. The extent and nature of those operations will be fully examined in its proper place, *as they are now in progress,* or are past ; and *as they include the geology which relates to the present surface of the earth. In the ruins of an ancient earth we find the materials which formed the present ;* as in the destruction of the land which we now inhabit nature seems to be preparing habitations for future races of animated beings.

"But though I have here said that causes operating more extensively and powerfully than the slow actions of waste and transportation may have aided in preparing the materials of the strata, we must beware of allowing more effect than they were capable of producing, as has been done by those who object to certain geological claims on indefinite time, and who seek for solutions in transitory diluvian powers. The effects of such torrents must have been to deposit mixed materials of various sizes in a confused manner ; and they could therefore have prepared *the germs of the conglomerated strata only.* The strata formed of finer materials must have been the consequences of tedious actions, analogous to those which we daily witness ; while their separation into distinct rocks, into alternations of clay and sand, producing schist and sandstone, must have equally been the work of a slow process beneath the water."—*Macculloch's Geology,* vol. i. pp. 81, 82.

"Denudation is the removal of solid matter by running water, whether by a river or marine current, and the consequent laying bare of some inferior rock. Geologists have, perhaps, been seldom in the habit of reflecting that this operation has exerted an influence on the structure of the earth's crust as universal and important *as sedimentary deposition itself;* for denudation is the inseparable accompaniment of the production of all new strata of mechanical origin. The formation of every new deposit by the transport of sediment and pebbles necessarily implies that there has been somewhere else *a grinding down of rocks into rounded fragments, sand, or mud, equal in quantity to the new strata.* All depositions, therefore, except in the case of a shower of volcanic ashes, is the sign of superficial waste going on contemporaneously, and to an equal amount elsewhere. The gain at one point is no more than sufficient to balance the loss at some other.

"If then *the entire mass of stratified deposits* in the earth's crust is at once *the monument and measure of the denudation which has taken place,* on how stupendous a scale ought we to find the signs of this removal of transported materials in past ages?

"Professor Ramsay has shown that the missing beds removed from the summit of the Mendips must have been nearly a mile in thickness, and he has pointed out considerable areas in South Wales and some of the adjacent counties of England where a series of palæozoic strata not less than 11,000 feet in thickness have been stripped off. All these materials have of course been transported to new regions, and have entered into the composition of more modern formations. On the other hand, it is shown by observations in the same 'Survey,' that the palæozoic strata are from 20,000 to 30,000 feet thick. It is clear that such rocks, formed of mud and sand, now for the most part consolidated, are the monuments of denuding operations, which

took place at a very remote period in the earth's history."
—*Lyell's Manual*, pp. 66–68.

"The strata are accumulations of consolidated sand and other detritus, the sedimentary deposits of rivers and seas, combined with the durable remains of animals and plants.

"From the first moment that dry land appeared on the earth's surface, whatever may have been the material of which it was composed, the disintegrating effects of atmospheric agents and of water in motion must have commenced. The detritus thus produced transported to the tranquil depths of the ocean, would then subside in successive layers, and a series of sedimentary strata be gradually formed; and after the creation of living things, the durable remains of animals and vegetables must have become intermingled with the detritus of the land, and imbedded in the deposits then in progress.

"If the land were sterile, destitute of vegetation, and untenanted by any species of animals, the relics of the inhabitants of the sea would alone be imbedded; on the contrary, if the sediments were produced by the action of streams and rivers flowing through a country covered with forests, and swarming with animal life, the strata accumulated in lakes and inland bays would teem with the remains of terrestrial and fluviatile animals and plants."—*Mantell's Geological Principles, in his Excursion round the Isle of Wight*, pp. 56–58.

"It is universally admitted that the materials of the sedimentary strata . . . are derived from the disintegration, decomposition, and abrasion of older rocks, and from animal and vegetable secretions."—*Mather's Geology of the first Geological District of New York*, p. 273.

They thus universally exhibit the strata as formed from detritus borne down by streams and rivers from pre-existing continents and islands and distributed over the bed of the sea.

The surface of that imagined primitive earth, instead of loose soils and strata that are easily disintegrated and borne by torrents and rivers to the sea, consisted, according to these writers, exclusively of granite, one of the most solid and indestructible of the rocks.

"Assuming that the whole materials of the globe may have once been in a fluid or even a nebular state, from the presence of intense heat, the passage of the first consolidated portions of this fluid or nebulous matter to a solid state may have been produced by the radiation of heat from its surface into space; the gradual abstraction of such heat would allow the particles of matter to approximate and crystallize; and the first result of this crystallization might have been the formation of a shell or crust, composed of oxidated metals and metalloids, *constituting various rocks of the granitic series*, around an incandescent nucleus of melted matter heavier than granite."—*Buckland's Bridgewater Treatise*, p. 40.

"That granite has in reality furnished a very large part

of the materials of the recent strata, is proved by their constitution. Quartz, felspar, mica, and hornblende are the chief materials of the sandstone, shales, and clays ; nay, the very fragments of that rock are found everywhere. Even in our recent alluvial soils they abound ; and it is a question worth considering whether the granite boulders, of which the immediate origin has so often been vainly traced, are not rather the portions of decomposed conglomerate strata, or the more durable remains of the alluvial soils on which they now repose."—*Macculloch's Geology*, vol. i., p. 155.

"He who shall divest the present surface of all but its rocks, who shall exterminate from our maps the great alluvial plains and deltas of the globe, with the countless interior tracts of the same nature, will produce a sketch *of the original earth* in no small degree interesting. It is through decomposition and disintegration, aided by mechanical power, that these changes have been produced."—*Macculloch's Geology*, vol. ii. p. 2.

We shall have occasion in the course of the discussion to cite other passages in which the same views are presented. According to the theory, then, the continents from which the vast materials of the sedimentary strata were originally drawn, consisted throughout their whole mass of granite, and it was by the slow process of disintegration by the action of the atmosphere, heat, moisture, frost, rains, torrents, and rivers, that that generally hard and almost unyielding substance was reduced to fragments and minute particles, and transported to the sea.

The question now is, whether they have demonstrated these great postulates. It is not enough to authorize the stupendous inference they have grounded on them respecting the age of the world, and invest it with the character of a scientific deduction according "to the strictest rules of the Baconian philosophy," to show that they are possibly or even probably true. They must be established by the most unanswerable evidence, in order that they can serve as a foundation for the vast fabric which is attempted to be erected on them. If they are mere suppositions, or gratuitous assumptions—if, instead of being demonstrated, they involve gross self-contradictions, and are irreconcilable alike with the laws of matter and the principles of geology, then the lofty structure which has been reared on them must be equally unsubstantial; and such we shall now proceed to show is their character.

The question which first requires consideration respects the sources from which the materials of the strata were drawn. And we remark in the first place that it is a mere hypothesis, not a demonstrated fact, that they were derived from continents, islands, or mountains that consisted exclusively of granite. These writers have not proved it. They do not even claim to have demonstrated it. They have taken it for granted, or advanced it simply as a supposition that furnishes in their judgment a more probable explanation than any other of the formation of the primary crust of the earth, and of the origin of the materials of the strata that were subsequently imposed on the primitive rocks. Thus Dr. Buckland says:—

"As the materials of the stratified rocks are in great degree derived directly or indirectly from those which are unstratified, it will be premature to enter upon the consideration of derivative strata until we have considered briefly the history of the primitive formations. We therefore commence our inquiry at that most ancient period, *when there is much evidence to render it* PROBABLE that the entire materials of the globe were in a fluid state, and that the cause of this fluidity was heat. . . . . ASSUMING that the whole materials of the globe *may have once been* in a fluid state, from the presence of intense heat, the passage of the first consolidated portion of this fluid to a solid state *may have been* produced by the radiation of heat from the surface into space; the gradual abstraction of such heat would allow the particles of matter to approximate and crystallize; and the first result of this crystallization *might have been* the formation of a shell or crust, ... constituting various rocks of the granitic series."—*Bridgewater Treat.*, pp. 39, 40.

"Whence came the materials of the great mass of deposits which rest upon the primary gneiss and mica schist? *Probably* the true answer to this, *though we cannot now give adequate proof of it,* is that *the disintegration of granite and other igneous rocks,* to which—on what seem good grounds—we have already ascribed the origin of gneiss and mica schist, has been *the prolific source of all these sedimentary strata.* Analysis of the principal rocks of the slaty systems does certainly not contradict this view; which neither those who admit with Leibnitz the first solid covering of the globe to have been a mass of rocks cooled from fusion, or with Lyell that strata added above are melted and reabsorbed into granite below, have any reason to deny."—*Phillips's Geology,* vol. i. p. 150.

This view of the primitive earth, which they make the basis of their theory of the formation of the strata and inference of the immense age of the world, is thus merely supposititious. It is not advanced as an ascertained and indubitable fact. It is not even held to be susceptible of demonstration. An attempt to verify it by "the strictest rules of the Baconian philosophy" would be regarded by geologists themselves as an extravagance. In its highest character it is only a conjecture. This consideration overturns, therefore, the deduction that is founded on it respecting the long existence of the world. That conclusion cannot be established on a mere hypothesis. It cannot rise any higher in certainty than the premise from which it is drawn. To build it, moreover, on such a basis, is as inconsistent with the principles of geology, as it is with the laws of logic; as they—as was shown in a former chapter—forbid the assumption of any geological effect or condition of the earth as a ground of induction, that cannot be proved to have actually existed. The whole fancy, accordingly, of a scientific confutation by it of the inspired history of the creation, and demonstration that the earth has subsisted through a vast round of ages, is mistaken. The circumstance that the sacred narrative is at variance with an undemonstrated and undemonstrable *supposition*, is no proof that it is not consistent with fact.

In the next place, their theory of the formation of the granitic world, from which they represent the materials of the strata as derived, is altogether gratuitous also, and in contravention of the laws of matter. That theory is, as stated by Dr. Buckland in the passage already quoted from him, that the matter of the earth was, when created, "in a fluid" or "nebulous state;" that is, in the form of gas, "from the presence of intense heat;" and that it was by "the radiation of that heat into space" that "the particles" were allowed to approximate and crystallize. Mr. Macculloch also entertains the same view.

"The first condition of the earth which has been inferred, is that of a gaseous sphere; while it is my business to state that *the only evidence for this is derived from* THE ANALOGY OF COMETS, *itself rather more inferential than proved,* as far as the study of these bodies has hitherto proceeded. But it must also be said, as corroborative of such an inference, that the laws of the radiation of heat, and those of chemical combination, *do permit the needful inference* that such a sphere *might or must* finally become a fluid ; or at least a fluid globe surrounded by an atmosphere.

"This, then, is the second *presumed* condition. And the evidence for such a fluid globe is found, first in its statical figure, and secondly in the various geological facts already reviewed, and founded primarily on the phenomena of volcanoes, which prove that the interior of the earth, beyond a certain depth, is at present in a fluid condition from the heat which was once sufficient for the preceding more extensive effects.*

"And here terminates that which is of most difficult investigation in the theory of the earth, and which *by many will still be held with* HYPOTHESES. The evidence, *such as it is*, is given ; what a rational philosophy will pronounce on it, will always deserve attention. . . .

"I know of no mode in which the surface of a fluid globe could be consolidated, but by the radiation of heat ; while of the necessity of such a process I need not again speak. The immediate result of this must have been the formation of rocks on that surface : and if the interior fluid does now produce the several unstratified rocks, the first that were formed must have resembled these, if not all. We may not unsafely infer that they were granite, perceiving that sub-

* An assumption not only without proof and against the laws of matter, but rejected by a large body of the most eminent geologists themselves.

stances of this character have been produced wherever the cooling appears to have been most gradual. *The first apparently solid globe was therefore a globe of granite,* or of those rocks which bear the nearest crystalline analogies to it."—*Geology,* vol. ii., pp. 416, 417.

Essentially the same views are advanced by Sir H. T. De la Beche.

But this hypothesis is altogether unphilosophical. The fusion of matter, or its existence in a gaseous form, "*from the presence of intense heat,*" which is the necessary condition of its assuming that shape, is not a natural but an artificial state. It is the result of chemical action, and implies therefore *a previous existence of the matter in a different form.* The supposition that the earth was *created* in that state is a self-contradiction, therefore, and at war with the laws of matter. It might as well be supposed that the world was created with thunderstorms and earthquakes in progress, which imply a previous existence of the globe and atmosphere in a different state; or with animals on the point of giving birth to offspring, which implies their previous existence. Moreover, as the heat that is evolved in the action of chemical agents on each other is always previously latent in those agents, the supposition of the fusion of the matter of the globe by the presence of intense heat, implies that that heat had previously existed in the matter of the globe in a latent state; and that again implies that anterior to the development of that heat, that matter existed in a different form. It assumes also that an immeasurably greater quantity of latent heat existed in the matter of the globe in its original condition than now subsists in it; and it is implied also in the supposition, that beyond that which is now latent in the earth, a quantity as much greater as would raise the whole of the substances of the globe to the most intense fusion and convert them into gas, has passed off from it by radiation into the realms of space. But that is not only wholly gratuitous and infinitely improbable, but is in contravention of the principles of geology also, which forbid the assumption of any geological condition of the earth as a basis of induction, that cannot be proved to have actually existed; or any geological effect that cannot have resulted from the chemical and mechanical forces that are now giving birth to changes in the materials of the globe. But what can transcend the extravagance of the fancy that these forces, acting with even thousands of times their present intensity, can have held all the materials of the globe in a state of fusion; or that all the chemical agents which it contains, in any combination that is possible, are adequate to such a stupendous effect? By the supposition, caloric, the grand agent of the imagined fusion, has in a great degree radiated from the earth into space, so that it no longer exists here in the force that is requisite to that effect. A splendid combination of solecisms for the basis of a philosophical theory! A magnificent platform for a scientific confutation of the record God has given of the work of creation! How is it that these writers have overlooked a consideration so obvious, and that indicates so decisively the untenableness of their theory?

QUESTIONS.

What is the object of the discussion commenced in this chapter? Do geologists deduce their inference of the age of the world from the strata themselves, or from some *theory* respecting them? What is the first ground on which they found it? What is the second? What is the third? If the facts of geology are not the basis of that inference, is it not clear that those facts do not prove it? In order to sustain it, must they not prove, not merely assume or suppose the ground from which they deduce it? Will then, proving that the postulates from which it is drawn, are mere suppositions, be to confute its claim to be regarded as a truth scientifically demonstrated? Will showing that their hypotheses are irreconcilable with the facts and principles of the science, and the laws of nature, be still more effectually to overthrow it? What is the first postulate on which they found their deduction of the great age of the world? State some of the forms in which they express their belief that the forces by which the strata were constructed, were the same in kind and energy, as those which are now acting on the surface of the earth. Are they generally agreed on this point? What is their other postulate? What principal writers maintain that proposition? State the form in which Dr. Buckland expresses it. In what language is it asserted by Mr. Macculloch? How is it taught by Sir C. Lyell? How by Mr. Mantell? Are geologists generally agreed in this doctrine? Of what did the surface of the primitive earth consist, according to these writers? By what do they hold those supposed granite continents were disintegrated? By what were the particles to which it is held they were reduced, borne off to the ocean? What must geologists do, to demonstrate their theory? Must they prove that it rests on indubitable facts? Or is it enough that it rests on mere hypotheses? What then is the first objection to their theory respecting the sources from which the materials of the strata were drawn? Do not geologists attempt to prove their theory? State the language in which they present it as a supposition, or hypothesis. But if the derivation of the materials of the strata from such continents, is merely hypothetical, must not the inference that a vast series of ages was occupied in disintegrating those continents, transporting their detritus to the ocean, and forming the strata from them, be merely hypothetical also? Can an inference from a mere imagined fact, have any more reality, or be any more entitled to be considered as a demonstrated truth, than the merely imagined fact itself is? If there is no certainty that the strata were drawn from such a source, how can the *supposition* that they had such a derivation, *prove* that infinite ages were occupied in their formation? Ought not these philosophers who claim that they, alone, are competent to treat the subject scientifically, to be able to answer this question plainly and demonstratively?

What is the next objection to their theory of the formation of such granite continents? What is the language in which Dr. Buckland teaches that the world was created in the form of gas? What is the language in which Mr. Macculloch represents it as originally existing in that shape? Is this proved by them, or merely assumed or supposed? What is the first objection to it? State some other absurd supposition that is parallel to it. Does the supposition that the world was created in the form of gas, contradict itself? By implying what? What unauthorized assumption does it involve respecting the quantity of heat in the globe? Is that in contradiction to the principles of geology, as well as assumed without authority?

CHAPTER IX.

The False Theories of Geologists respecting the Sources of the Materials of which the Strata were formed.

But geologists are not only forbidden by the laws of matter from assuming the existence of such granitic continents, islands, and mountains as they suppose, anterior to the formation of the strata, but they are without any certainty that there were any mountains, islands, or continents whatever, that could have furnished materials in any considerable measure for such vast deposits. This is admitted by Professor Phillips.

"Whether at the time when all our continents were beneath the sea, there were other continents raised above it, is a matter which it is difficult to bring fairly within the scope of inductive science, except in a very limited form, and upon rather doubtful assumptions. *The only clear and certain evidence* of the existence of the land in other situations than where it now appears, is to be sought in the history of terrestrial organic exuviæ imbedded in the earth; the only reasonable presumptive evidence in favor of such a doctrine must be founded on mechanical considerations connected with the mass and depth of the waters of the ocean. To conclude that because continents were raised in one quarter, others *must* have been depressed elsewhere in a certain proportion, is inadmissible, because it requires us to admit what is perhaps false, viz. that the spaces occupied by the solid and liquid parts of the mass of the globe have always been exactly and invariably in the same proportion to each other as at present. Who can assure us of the truth, or even the probability of such a law ?"—*Guide to Geology*, p. 38.

Such is undoubtedly the fact. The only certain evidence which the strata themselves can furnish of the existence of dry land at the period of their formation, is the presence in them of fossilized animals and vegetables, to the existence of which dry land was necessary. The mere fact that the strata were formed beneath the waters of the ocean is no proof that the materials of which they consist were derived from continents and mountains, any more than it is that they were not. Nor is the fact that a portion of their materials were probably or certainly drawn from such a source, any proof that they all were, any more than the fact that some of the waters of the ocean have run from mountains and continents is a proof that they all originally descended from those sources.

Mr. Lyell makes the same admission.

"If asked where the continent was placed, from the ruins

of which the Wealden strata were derived, we might be almost tempted to speculate on the former existence of the Atlantis of Plato as true in geology, although fabulous as an historical event. We know that *the present European lands have come into existence almost entirely since the deposition of the chalk;* and the same period may have sufficed for the disappearance of a continent of equal magnitude situated farther west."—*Lyell's Principles,* vol. ii., p. 458.

Mr. Macculloch held that the mountains and continents from which the materials of the strata were *originally* derived, preceded those that directly furnished the elements of the present series.

"That this system had a beginning we are certain; *where that may be, we know not;* but for us it is placed beyond that era at which we can no longer trace the marks of a change of order of the destruction and renovation of its form. It is from this point that a theory of the earth must at present commence.

. . . .

"Hence, then, I have drawn the conclusion that there was one terraqueous globe, one earth divided into sea and land, even *prior to that last named;* containing mountains to furnish and an ocean to receive those materials which formed *the second set of mountains,* whose fragments are *now* imbedded in *our primary strata, or in those of a third order.* Geologists may perhaps be startled at conclusions which they have hitherto overlooked, obvious as they are, and clear as the reasoning is: how they should not have been seen by those who have shown such anxiety to maintain the antiquity of the globe, it is not for me to explain."—*Geology*, vol. i., pp. 462, 464–466.

Yet notwithstanding this fancied proof of the existence of at least two sets of mountains and continents that were the sources, in succession, of the materials of "our primary strata," he yet acknowledges himself unable to decide whether or not those first mountains were, in a measure at least, identical with those that now exist on the globe.

"In this state of the earth the present primary strata occupied horizontal positions beneath this ocean; *though we are uncertain whether certain parts of those which we now esteem such might not have been the very mountains whence they were formed.* This is probably the fact, however incapable we yet are of proving it, owing to our imperfect observations, and the still more imperfect views which geologists have hitherto taken of a theory of the earth. We cannot conceive that all the supra-marine land which produced the primary strata should have been mouldered and transferred to the sea before these underwent their first disturbance; nor that it should have all been depressed beneath the sea while the new-formed rocks were elevated."—Vol. i., p. 468.

This extraordinary induction scarcely merits a formal confutation. A more dim and uncertain argument could hardly be made the ground of the vast train of consequences he deduces from it. The point on which he builds his inference is altogether assumed by him, inasmuch as the existence in the strata of the fragments of other rocks, is not of itself a proof that those fragments were derived from mountains, unless it is first established that the materials of such rocks cannot have been drawn from any other source; which is the precise point he was to demonstrate. This whole imagined induction, indeed from the processes that are now taking place, is, as we shall hereafter show, a fallacy; inasmuch as the fact that minute particles and sands are borne down to the sea from the present mountains and plains, which consist in a large degree of loose soils, or sedimentary rocks that are easily disintegrated, is no evidence that similar materials and on much the same scale would have been carried down from mountains and plains that consisted exclusively of granite. The supposition is a solecism, as it implies that the same causes, though acting on different materials and in different conditions, would nevertheless produce precisely the same effects.

Other writers regard the mountains and continents from which the strata were derived as no longer in existence.

"However incomprehensible it may appear to those who

have not studied the subject, geologists entertain no doubt that all our present mountains, *composed of sedimentary matter*, were accumulated *beneath the sea* during countless ages; and, if so, other continents must have existed to furnish materials, though no traces of such lands now remain."—*Sir R. I. Murchison's Silurian System*, p. 573.

"It is universally acknowledged among geologists that these immense sedimentary deposits could only have accumulated beneath the waters of the ocean during an incalculable period of time, long anterior to the present condition of the surface. Now, in order to furnish materials for such formations *we must conceive of the existence of continents where no vestige of them now remains; from the abrasion and destruction of these*, and from the transporting power of river and ocean currents, the materials composing them were reduced to the state of pebbles, sand, and finely comminuted mud, which were widely diffused, and gradually or rapidly precipitated upon the ocean bed."—*Hall's Geology of Western New York*, p. 521.

If no trace of those continents now remains, it is plainly impossible, from the mere strata themselves, to demonstrate that they were in such positions and consisted of such elements, that they can have furnished the materials from which the strata were formed. It is only by assuming the point to be proved, that all sedimentary strata must have been formed of materials derived from pre-existing mountains and dry land, that such a conclusion can be obtained. Discard that assumption, and let the question to be determined be, whether the materials of stratified rocks must necessarily be derived by disintegration and transportation from granitic continents and mountains, and the error of their argument is apparent; as it is on the assumption that that must be their origin that their whole theory is founded.

Some geologists seem to suppose that a large share at least of those materials were derived from the mountains that now subsist on the globe. But it is shown to be erroneous by the fact that all the great ranges, and most of every subordinate class, have been thrown up from beneath the ocean since the formation of the tertiary, the last great division of the strata.*

"If we admit that the primary, the transition, the secondary, and the tertiary classes of rock were formed at

*"If we date the age of granite from the period of the elevation of granite mountains we must admit that some granite mountains are comparatively recent, for they have been elevated since the deposition of the secondary strata. I have shown this to be the case with the Bernese and Savoy Alps in my Travels published in 1827. In the edition of the present work in 1828, I have shown also, by a description and sections, that the elevation of the granite of Savoy is more recent than that of the central part of England. M. Elie de Beaumont has since adopted the same views, and has extended them to other mountain ranges. Professor Sedgwick and Mr. Murchison have further proved that a part of the Tyrolean and Bavarian Alps was elevated since the deposition of tertiary strata; for these strata are filled up with them to the height of several thousand feet."—*Bakewell's Geology*, p. 101.

different successive epochs, and that the lower beds in each of these classes are more ancient than the beds that rest upon them, it follows as a necessary consequence that the elevation of any of these rocks must be dated from a later epoch than the period of their formation. The elevation of a range of primary or transition mountains, if they are not covered by any secondary or tertiary formations, may indeed be dated either from an epoch coeval with their consolidation, or from any subsequent epoch; but if they are partly covered by secondary or tertiary beds which are tilted up with them, we have direct evidence that the date of their elevation was posterior to the secondary or tertiary epoch."—*Bakewell's Geology*, p. 101.

"It is a general law, confirmed by most ample evidence, that the interior parts of mountainous regions consist of granite and other pyrogenous rocks rising from below all the strata, and bearing them up to their present elevations. From these elevated points and lines, both the subjacent igneous and the superior stratified rocks descend at various angles towards the plains and more level regions, beneath which they sink and pass at various distances until they again emerge in some other mountain group having similar characters. In consequence of this arrangement, it happens generally that the oldest strata, those which sink deepest under the plains, rise highest against the mountain slopes. . . . . The most constant of all the facts connected with this part of the subject, is the development of granitic or some other pyrogenous rocks about the centres of the elevated groups from beneath all the strata there occurring."—*Phillips's Guide*, p. 31.

"Etna would appear to have been the seat of volcanic action through *a long series of ages, commencing with the supercretaceous rocks*, on which much of the igneous mass is now based.

"In central France, amid the extinct volcanoes which there constitute such a remarkable feature in the physical geography of the country, we certainly *approach* relative dates in some instances. Thus the volcanic mass of the Plomb du Cantal appears to have burst through, to have upset, and to have fractured the fresh water limestones of the Cantal, which, according to Messrs. Lyell and Murchison, may be equivalent to the fresh-water deposits of the Paris basin, and to those of Hampshire and the Isle of Wight.

"With regard to the igneous rocks of Auvergne, MM. Croiset and Jobert consider that there are about thirty beds above the fresh-water limestone, which may be divided into four alternations of *alluvial* detritus and basaltic deposits. Among the beds there are three which contain organic remains ; two belong to the third of the ancient alluvions, that which succeeded the second epoch of volcanic eruptions ; the third fossiliferous deposit being referable to the last epoch of ancient alluvion.

"The principal ossiferous bed is about nine or ten feet thick, and can be traced a considerable distance. . . . The fossil species, according to MM. C. and J., are very numerous, consisting of Elephant, Mastodon, Hippopotamus, Rhinoceros, Tapir, Boar, Felis, Hyæna, Bear, Canis, Castor, Hare, Water Rat, Deer, and Ox."—*H. T. De la Beche's Manual*, pp. 241, 242.

"The same phenomena are exhibited in the Alps on a much grander scale ; those mountains being composed, in some even of their higher regions, of newer secondary formations, while they are encircled by a great zone of tertiary rocks of different ages, both on the southern flanks towards the plains of the Po, and on the side of Switzerland and Austria, and at their eastern termination towards Styria and Hungary. This tertiary zone marks the position of former seas or gulfs, like the Adriatic, which were many thousand feet deep, and wherein masses of strata accumulated, some single groups of which seem scarcely inferior in thickness to the whole of our secondary formations in England. These marine tertiary strata have been raised to the height of from 2,000 to 4,000 feet, and consist of formations of different ages, characterized by different assemblages of organized fossils. *The older tertiary groups generally rise to the greatest heights, and form interior* zones nearest to the central ridges of the Alps. Although we have not yet ascertained the number of different periods at which the Alps gained accessions to their height and width, yet we can affirm that the last series of movements occurred when the seas were inhabited by *many existing species of animals.*

"The Pyrenees also have acquired the whole of their present altitude, which in Mount Perdu exceeds 11,000 feet, since the deposition of some of the newer or cretaceous members of our secondary series."—*Lyell's Principles,* vol. i., p. 139.

There are similar proofs, also, of the elevation from

the ocean of the other great ranges of Europe and Asia since the formation of the secondary strata.

The great mountains of this continent, also, the Appalachians and Andes, are now universally regarded as having been thrown up from the ocean since the period of the secondary formations. The Appalachians bear on their tops or sustain on their sides the main members of the great series from the Potsdam sandstone, the lowest of the fossiliferous rocks on this continent, up to the upper division of the carboniferous group. Deposits of equally late date are found also in the lofty ranges of the Andes.

"I will give a brief sketch of the geology of the several parallel lines forming the Cordilleras. Of these lines there are two considerably higher than the others ; namely, on the Chilian side, the Peuquenes ridge, which, where the road crosses it, is 13,210 feet above the sea ; and the Portillo ridge on the Mendoza side, which is 14,305 feet. The lower beds of the Peuquenes ridge, and of the several great lines to the westward of it, are composed of a vast pile many thousand feet in thickness of porphyries, which have flowed as submarine lava, alternating with angular and rounded fragments of the same rocks, thrown out of the submarine craters. These alternating masses are covered in the central parts by a great thickness of *red sandstone, conglomerate, and calcareous clay slate*, associated with and passing into prodigious beds of *gypsum*. In these upper beds *shells are tolerably frequent ;* and they belong to about the period of *the lower chalk of Europe.* It is an old story, but not the less wonderful, to hear of shells which were once crawling in the bottom of the sea, now standing nearly 14,000 feet above its level. The lower beds in this great pile of strata have been dislocated, baked, crystallized, and almost blended together, through the agency of mountain masses of a peculiar white soda-granitic rock.

"The other main line, namely, that of the Portillo, is of a totally different formation; it consists chiefly of grand bare pinnacles of a red potash-granite, which low down on the western flank are covered by *a sandstone,* converted by the former heat into quartz-rock. On the quartz there rest beds of a *conglomerate* several thousand feet in thickness, which have been upheaved by the red granite, and dip at an angle of 45° towards the Peuquenes line. I was astonished to find that this conglomerate was partly composed of pebbles derived from the rocks, with *their fossil shells* of the Peuquenes range, and partly of red potash-granite, like that of Portillo. Hence we must conclude that both the Peuquenes and Portillo ranges were partially upheaved and exposed to wear and tear, when the conglomerate was forming. . . .

"Looking at its earliest origin, the red granite seems to have been injected on an ancient pre-existing line of white granite and mica slate. In most parts, perhaps in all parts of the Cordilleras, it may be concluded that each line has been formed by repeated upheavals and injections; and that the several parallel lines are of different ages. Only thus can we gain time at all sufficient to explain the truly astonishing amount of denudation which these great, *though comparatively with most other ranges recent, mountains* have suffered.

"The shells in the Peuquenes, or oldest ridge, prove, as before remarked, that it has been upraised 14,000 feet since a *secondary period,* which in Europe we are accustomed to consider as *far from ancient;* but since these shells lived in a moderately deep sea, it can be shown that the area now occupied by the Cordillera must have subsided several thousand feet—in northern Chili as much as 6,000 feet—so as to have allowed that amount of submarine strata to have been heaped up on the bed on which the shells lived."—*Darwin's Voyage of the Beagle,* pp. 319–321.

"The Uspallata range is separated from the main Cordillera by a long narrow plain, or basin, like those so often mentioned in Chili, but higher, being six thousand feet above the sea. This range has nearly the same geographical position with respect to the Cordillera which the gigantic Portillo line has, but it is of a totally different origin; it consists of various kinds of submarine lava, alternating with volcanic sandstones and other remarkable sedimentary deposits; the whole having a very close resemblance to some of *the tertiary beds on the shores of the Pacific.* From this resemblance I expected to find *silicified wood,* which is generally *characteristic of those formations.* I was gratified in a very extraordinary manner. In the central part of the range, at an elevation of about 7,000 feet, I observed on a bare slope some snow-white projecting columns; these were petrified trees, eleven being silicified, and from thirty to forty converted into coarsely-crystallized white calcareous spar. They were abruptly broken off, the upright stumps projecting a few feet above the ground. The trunks measured from three to five feet each in circumference. They stood a little way apart from each other, but the whole formed one group. Mr. R. Brown, who has examined the wood, says it belongs to the fir tribe, partaking of the character of the Araucanian family, but with some curious points of affinity with the yew. The volcanic sandstone in which the trees were imbedded, and from the lower part of which they must have sprung, had accumulated in successive thin layers around their trunks ; and the stone yet retained the impression of the bark."—*Darwin's Voyage of the Beagle*, pp. 331, 332.

All the great ranges are thus of recent origin, and there are mountains—generally of inferior height, and consisting mainly of granite—that were elevated at an earlier period, yet none are known that can, with any probability, be regarded as having emerged from the ocean anterior to the formation of the lower groups of the strata.

"No truth is more certain or important in geological reasoning, than the formation of all our continents and islands by causes acting below the sea. As far as relates to the stratified rocks this is obvious ; but it is not the less certain for the unstratified rocks, *those having undoubtedly been uplifted to our view from beneath the strata. It is possible* there may yet be found *some* granite rocks which were raised above the general spherical surface before the production ot *any* deposits from water, and which therefore may be presumed to form an exception to this general rule ; but such truly primitive rocks have nowhere been seen, nor is there any ground of expectation that they will be discovered."—*Phillips's Geology*, vol. ii., p. 248.

As the most ancient of our present mountains are thus of later date than the primary strata, and all the principal ranges—like the Alps, the Himalaya, and the Andes—were elevated subsequently to the deposition of the secondary, and even portions of the tertiary formations, we have the most decisive evidence that they were not the sources of the materials from which the strata were formed. If their materials were derived from mountains and continents, it must have been from a different set, of which neither any traces remain, nor any indications of the positions which they occupied.

This consideration is thus again fatal to their theory. No condition can be more indispensable to its establishment, than that it should be shown that contemporaneously with the deposition of the strata, there were continents and mountains in existence that might have furnished materials for their formation; and in order to that, their position should be determined and their dimensions and elevation proved to be such as rendered them adequate to the office that is assigned them. To admit that no vestiges of them remain, and that there are no means even of determining where they were stationed, is to admit that the induction that is founded on them is supposititious also and without authority. This branch of their scheme is thus inconsistent also with the principles of geology, which prohibit the assumption of any condition of the earth as a basis of induction, which cannot be proved to have truly existed.

Let us, however, suppose that precisely such continents as they contemplate were in existence, and situated in positions the most favorable for the office they assign them; and in place of relieving their theory from embarrassment, it only renders its error more apparent.

The average elevation of the present continents and islands above the ocean is but a few hundred feet. Lake Superior is estimated to be about six hundred and forty feet only above that level. Were all those portions therefore of the mountains and high lands of the continent north of the equator that are above the surface of that lake, removed and spread over those parts that are below it, they would undoubtedly be altogether inadequate to raise them to the same height above the sea. On the other hand, the strata of the continents are estimated by geologists to be on an average not less than six, eight, and perhaps even a greater number of miles in depth.

Were they removed therefore and thrown into the ocean, the granitic basis on which they now rest, would be on an average at almost an equal depth beneath the surface of the sea. It is implied accordingly that the imagined continents from which the materials of those strata are supposed to have been drawn, were elevated a corresponding height above the ocean. This is distinctly indicated by Macculloch.

"The immense deposits of materials which now form the alluvial tracts of the globe, the enormous masses of secondary strata which have been produced by ancient materials of the same nature, all prove *the magnitude of the destruction which mountains have formerly experienced*, which they are now daily undergoing. Let imagination replace the plains of Hindostan on the Himalaya, or rebuild the mountains which furnished the secondary strata of England, and it needs not be asked what is the extent of ruin, modern or ancient. In this ruin the highest rocks participate most largely ; so largely that we can scarcely hope to find one portion of that surface which was once most elevated above the waters. If in the progress of such extensive destruction, thus probably acting on the primary rocks at two distinct periods, every vestige of overflowing granite has disappeared, it is assuredly an event not calculated to excite surprise."—*Geology*, vol. i. p. 154.

He here speaks as though those deposits were

drawn from the present mountains of the globe; that, however, is inconsistent with the views we have quoted from him on another page, and is erroneous; as is shown by the proofs we have adduced, that the elevation of our present mountains took place mainly since the formation of the principal strata. His exemplification, nevertheless, serves to indicate the extraordinary height which the theory ascribes to those imagined continents. The super-position upon England of a mass of granite mountains in height as many miles within a fraction above the present surface, as the under surface of the lowest of its stratified rocks is below that line, which is reckoned at an average of seven, eight, or even ten miles, would give the elevation which the corresponding portion of the supposed granite continent or island must have possessed in order to have furnished the materials of those strata. The only deduction required is that of the average of the present surface above the level of the ocean, which is but a few hundred feet. The height of the imagined continent or island must accordingly have been far greater than of the loftiest present mountains of the earth, or at least six, seven, or eight miles.

On the other hand, on the supposition on which he here seems to proceed, that the materials of the strata were derived from the present mountains, the bases of which they surround, then the super-position on the Himalaya and the table lands on which they rest, of an equal area of the strata of the plains of Hindostan, would give the height which those mountains must, according to the theory, originally have possessed; which, if those strata are on an average like those of England, six, seven, or eight miles in depth, would raise that mountain range to the height of eleven, twelve, or thirteen miles.

Making the most moderate estimate, therefore, of those supposed continents and islands, they must have soared to a height immensely above the loftiest summits of those that are now on the earth. Their existence is, accordingly wholly incredible, and would have altogether precluded the effect which they are employed to explain. For their whole surface must have towered to such a distance within the regions of perpetual congelation as to have been buried to a vast depth in snow, on the supposition that sufficient vapor to form snow ascended to such a height in the atmosphere, and rendered it impossible that any considerable streams should have flowed from them to bear their loosened particles and broken fragments into the surrounding sea; and if no vapor ascended to that height, then no water or snow could have fallen on them, and thence no rivers could have run from them and borne their detritus to the ocean. No condition can be imagined presenting a more absolute barrier to their disintegration and transference to a distant scene. No animals or vegetables could have lived on such frozen lands; and probably no such warmth could have been communicated by the sun to the sea as to have fitted it for the existence af animals like those that are buried in the strata. What an extraordinary conception of the methods taken by the Almighty Creator to prepare the world for the residence of man! Where in the annals of crude and thoughtless speculation can a more absurd and monstrous extravagance be found?

Not to insist, however, on this embarrassing condition of their theory; let us suppose that those fabulous continents and islands were not of such an incredible and fatal elevation, but only of the height of our present continents, and were diversified like them in their surfaces; and they must still have been wholly unsuited to the purpose for which geologists invent them; for, consisting exclusively of granite, there could not have been any permanent rivers on them like those of the present earth, by which their detritus could have been borne down to the ocean. No matter how much rain fell, no springs like those that form our rivers could have risen from their surface; inasmuch as a soil that is permeable by water, strata, and strata that are at an angle with the horizon, are indispensable conditions to the existence of such springs. The supposition of water rising through unstratified rocks by the force of gravity is a solecism. It is only by volcanic forces that water is thrown up from beneath the unstratified rocks. Without soils and strata, therefore, by which rains could be absorbed as they fell, and thence gradually drained again, there could be no permanent rivers like those which now bear a tide of earthy and vegetable matter from the hills and plains to the seas. From such a vast floor of impermeable granite the waters, wherever there was a descent, would have run as they fell, and the rivulets and streams to which they gave rise, vanished on the discontinuance of rain. The rains of a monsoon on ranges like the Andes, the Himalaya, or the mountains of Abyssinia, instead of saturating the surface with a mass of water, which, slowly emerging again, should supply permanent streams like the Amazon and Orinoco, the Ganges and Indus, the Nile and Niger, that roll without intermission to the sea, would have swept to the ocean with the rapidity of torrents, and immediately left their channels dry, till renewed by the return of another season of storms. But such torrents and floods acting on the surface only at intervals, or during a few days of the year, could never have disintegrated such granitic masses and borne their ruins to the ocean on a scale at all commensurate to the representations of the theory. Myriads of ages would have been almost as inadequate to such a process as so many days or hours. The cause, through whatever period continued, would have been wholly unequal to the effect. This consideration, which again evinces the error of their views, has been altogether overlooked by geologists. Notwithstanding they so expressly represent the continents to which they refer the materials of the strata as consisting exclusively of granite, they in fact treat them, in most of their reasonings, as though they were covered, like the present mountains and plains, with vast masses of loose earth and easily disintegrated strata, that were everywhere moistened by rains and traversed by streams and rivers, and they found their estimate of the rates at which the strata were deposited *on the quantities of matter that are now borne down the great rivers to the sea*, and deposited in the deltas at their mouths.

But the present action of rain and rivers on the soil and strata can only be taken as a measure of their agency at former periods on surfaces of the same kinds. It is no criterion of the action of similar volumes of water on continents composed exclusively of granite, from which the strata of the present are held to be derived. To reason thus, from one world to another of a wholly different nature, is an extraordinary method of establishing a scientific induction according to "the strictest rules of the Baconian philosophy." Nearly the whole of their reasoning, accordingly, on this topic is irrelevant and deceptive.

They have thus had the misfortune to unite a singular complication of impracticable conditions in their theory; first selecting as the only source from which the materials of the strata were derived, continents and islands of granite that, from its solid and impervious nature, is generally almost insusceptible of disintegration by the most powerful agents that act on it; next, elevating those indestructible mountains to such a stupendous height that if vapor ever reached them, not a drop could descend on them, except in a state of the intensest congelation, nor a particle of the vast masses of snow, in which they must have become enveloped, ever melted, so as to exert its disintegrating power on their surface; and finally, employing only occasional and insufficient agents to exert a destroying force on their unyielding masses, and only occasional and transient agents to bear the slight spoils that might have been drawn from them to the distant sea! Admirable architects truly of the world! Who can wonder at the haughty disdain with which so many of them are accustomed to repel the criticism of their theory by any except of their own profession, as an infringement of their rights and an impeachment of their infallibility!

QUESTIONS.

Have geologists any certainty of the existence of granite continents, like those from which they represent the materials of the strata as having been derived? Does Professor Phillips admit that their existence is merely conjectural, or assumed? Does the fact that the strata were formed beneath the ocean, prove that the materials of which they were constructed were drawn from granite continents? Does Sir C. Lyell indicate that he cannot tell where the continent was situated from which he supposes some of the strata of Great Britain were formed? Does Mr. Macculloch make a similar admission? How many sets of continents and mountains does he hold have existed on the earth? Do other writers maintain that no traces now remain of the continents from which they hold the materials of the strata were derived? If no traces of them now remain, is it not clear that there are no evidences of their once having existed? If there are no traces of such continents, is it not possible that the strata were derived from some other source? And if they may have been drawn from some other quarter, is it not to beg the question to assume that they were derived from them? Do some geologists seem to suppose that a large part of the materials of the strata were derived from the present mountains of the globe? What fact proves that supposition to be erroneous? Are most of the present mountains covered in a measure with the tertiary or latest great division of the strata? Is that universally admitted by geologists? Is it true of the Alps, and other mountains of Europe? Cite the proofs of it from Bakewell, Phillips, De la Beche, and Lyell. Is it true of the Appalachians and Andes of this country? Cite the proofs of it. Are these great ranges of recent origin, compared with the older strata? Is it held by geologists that the ranges of granite instead of being older than the main groups of the strata, have been thrown up since the strata were deposited, and reached the surface by being driven through them? Cite the testimony of Professor Phillips to that fact. Is it true also of the great mountains of Asia as well as of this continent and Europe? Is not the fact that these mountains were not in existence when the strata were formed, sufficient proof that the strata were not constructed of detritus drawn from them? Is not this consideration fatal to their theory? Is not the assumption of the existence of continents and mountains of which they have no proof, against their fourth axiom, also, which prohibits their assuming any geological facts, the reality of which they are not able to demonstrate?

But let it be supposed that such continents as they imagine, existed, would it in any measure relieve the advocates of the theory from their difficulties? Would the height of those mountains be an obstacle to their furnishing materials for the strata? How is it apparent that they would have been of an immense height? Must they not have continued as long as rivers ran from them and carried down materials for the strata, to be at as great an elevation above the ocean as the present continents and mountains are? How else could rivers have run from them with sufficient force to carry any amount of detritus to the ocean? If then the present strata were drawn from them, must they not originally have been as much higher than our present continents, as a quantity of materials equal to those of the strata, superimposed on them would make them? As then the strata are eight or ten miles in thickness, must not those continents and mountains have been eight, ten, twelve, or more miles in elevation? But could mountains of such a height have furnished materials for the formation of the strata? Is it sure that vapors would have ascended to such a height as to have fallen on them in rain or snow? If snow fell on them, would not the cold that would have reigned there have kept them bound in perpetual frost, and prevented the disintegration of their surface, and the descent from them of rivers? Could any species of either animals or vegetables have subsisted on them? Can a grosser contradiction to the laws of matter and of life be imagined, than that the materials of the strata which abound with animals and vegetables that were inhabitants of temperate climes, were drawn from such frozen regions?

"Let it be supposed, however, that those imagined continents and mountains were no higher than those of the present earth, could they then have filled the office which geologists assign them? Why could there be no permanent springs and rivers there? Is there any reason to believe that the mere action of the air—changes of temperature and occasional moisture, would ever disintegrate whole continents of solid granite, as hard and impermeable as most of the rocks of that kind are which rise to the surface of the earth? If such granite continents could not have been disintegrated, and no permanent rivers could have run from them to bear off their detritus, is it not clear that they never could have furnished the materials of which the strata were formed? Have geologists noticed these difficulties in framing their theory? Have they proceeded in their calculations on the assumption that their fancied continents, instead of consisting exclusively of granite, were covered with loose soil, like the present lands of the globe, and were traversed by numerous permanent streams and rivers? Is that legitimate? Does the fact that some measure of mud, sand, and vegetable matter is borne to the sea by the continually running rivers of the present globe, which is covered by a deep layer of loose earth, and annually shoots up a vast growth of vegetables, prove that an equal quantity of similar matter would annually be borne to the sea from mere granite continents, which had neither any loose earth nor vegetable matter on their surface—nor any rivers to bear such materials, if they existed, to the ocean? Recapitulate the several impracticable positions they have thus incorporated in their theory of the origin of the strata.

CHAPTER X.

The false Theories of Geologists respecting the Sources of the Materials of which the Strata were formed.

But let us suppose that the chemical and mechanical agents that may be presumed to have acted on those rocky continents would have rapidly disintegrated their surface, and reduced them on a vast scale to such minute particles as could have been transported by streams to the sea; and their theory still continues embarrassed with equally insurmountable difficulties. For they proceed in it on the assumption, first, that their whole mass would, during the progress of the process, be converted into detritus; and next, that every particle of the detritus produced from them would be borne to the sea, and enter into the composition of the strata; as otherwise they must have been of a still more enormous height than that which is assigned to them. As the bulk, which we have indicated as ascribed to them by the theory, is only equal to that of the strata which are held to have been formed from them, if but one third, one half, or three quarters of their mass is supposed to have been transferred to the sea, then they must have been of a still greater bulk, in order that that proportion may correspond to the dimensions of the strata that are held to have been built out of their ruins. But neither of those conditions is consistent with the laws that govern the disintegration of mountains and the transportation of their detritus to the ocean. Let us, in the first place, suppose the surface of those imagined continents to have become disintegrated to such a depth that the fragments and levigated particles, if spread out on the bottom of the ocean, would have formed a stratum of several feet in thickness; and yet no known or conceivable agency of streams, torrents, and rivers could have ever conveyed the whole, or any considerable portion of them, to the sea. The supposition is as inadmissible and preposterous as the fancy were that the rivulets and streams now running, can ever bear to the ocean all the comminuted dust, sand, and gravel with which our present continents and islands are overspread. So far from achieving such a stupendous result, they would never have made any more appreciable progress towards it than our present rivers have made in reducing the elevation of the continents and diminishing the quantity of dry land. If they were shaped, like the continents of this hemisphere, with a vast range of mountains running through their whole length along their western verge, so that no rains could have fallen on their western slope to bear their debris on that side to the ocean; and if from the foot of that range on the east they were spread out like the vast regions of South America, that are traversed by the La Plata, the Amazon, and the Orinoco, and the immense plains and prairies drained in this division of the continent by the Mississippi, the St. Lawrence, and the Mackenzie, it is obvious that their detritus could never in any great quantity have been transported to the ocean. Ninety-nine parts out of a hundred—probably nine hundred and ninety-nine out of a thousand—would for ever have remained where they fell, as the materials that constitute the surface of our present continents have continued where they were first formed. The rivulets and rivers that are of sufficient force to bear particles of earth and sand from their places towards the sea, probably do not come in contact even with one particle in millions of those that constitute the soils and debris that are spread on the surface. They act only on the narrow line of their channels, which, compared to the whole area, are but what the lines of longitude marked on an artificial globe are to the spaces that lie between them. If the supposed continents were formed like Europe, with a few lofty ranges, from the bases of which vast plains extended like those of the Po, the Rhine, and the Danube, or immense levels like those that stretch from the Baltic to the Ural Mountains, and the steppes of northern Asia, then also a great share of their detritus must for ever have remained where it originated; and that would have been still more emphatically the fact, if, like Australia, their interior through vast spaces was depressed below the level of their coasts, so that the waters falling on them could have no outlet to the ocean. Whatever might have been their forms, therefore, if they corresponded in any considerable measure to those of our present continents, the transportation of any large quantity of detritus from their general surface by torrents and rivers must have been wholly impossible. We have in the vast experiment that has been made on our present continents for four thousand years, the most ample demonstration that streams and rivers are altogether inadequate to such an effect. Were all the detrital matter that has in that period been borne by them from the dry land, and now lies buried beneath the seas, restored to the places from which it was removed, the largest portion of it would undoubtedly be lodged along the line of the streams. The share that nine tenths of the surface would receive would scarcely be appreciable.

And next, the conversion of the whole mass of those granite continents into detritus—the other condition of their theory—would be equally impossible. For the rate of disintegration and the area on which it took place, instead of advancing or continuing the same, would continually decrease in proportion as the detritus accumulated on the surface and protected it from the action of destructive chemical and mechanical agents. A thin layer of loam, sand, or gravel, would have been a shield against the decrystallizing action of the atmosphere and erosion by water. This is shown by the fact that granite rocks that have been cut and scored by the passage over them, as it is supposed, of icebergs armed with boulders, and afterwards buried by drift, on the removal of the soil with which they have been covered, exhibit no indications of having undergone disintegration after they had received those marks. Many of those, indeed, that have been exposed to the action of the elements appear unaltered. The grooves ploughed across them are as smooth and well defined as they can be believed to have been when first made.

It is shown also by the failure of the most powerful streams to produce any important change on the height or form of the granite rocks over which they have run for thousands of years. Let any one examine the granite rocks that in many places lie at the bottom of the rapid streams of New England, and form the dykes over which they fall, and he will find them generally free from any marks of disintegration or erosion by the grinding of sand, pebbles, or ice. The cavities that are cut where the water rushes down rapids or over falls, are caused by the whirl of gravel and pebbles in depressions, not by the mere passage of the stream. This is indicated by Humboldt in respect to the great cataracts of the Orinoco, formed by granite dykes, that have not been worn away, he represents, in any perceptible measure by the rush of that vast volume of water.

"When seated on the bank of the Oroonoko, our eyes are fixed on those rocky dykes, the mind inquires whether, in the lapse of ages, the falls change their form or height. I am not much inclined to believe in such effects of the shock of water against blocks of granite and in the erosion of silicious matter. The holes narrowed towards the bottom, the funnels that are discovered in the *raudales*, as well as near so many other cascades in Europe, are owing only to the friction of the sand and the movement of quartz pebbles. . . . .

"We will not deny the action of rivers and running waters when they furrow friable ground covered with secondary formations. But the granite rocks of Elephantine have probably no more changed their absolute height during thousands of years than the summits of Mont Blanc and of Canigou. When you have closely inspected the great scenes of nature in different climates, it is impossible not to admit that those deep clefts, those strata raised on end, those scattered blocks, those traces of a general convulsion, are the results of extraordinary causes, very different from those which act slowly on the surface of the globe in its present state of tranquillity and repose. What the waters carry away from the granite by erosion, what the humid atmosphere destroys by its contact with hard and undecomposed rocks, almost wholly escapes our perception; and I cannot believe, as some geologists admit, that the granitic summits of the Alps and the Pyrenees lower in proportion to the accumulation of pebbles in the gullies at the foot of the mountains. In the Nile, as well as in the Oroonoko, the rapids may diminish their fall, without the rocky dykes being perceptibly altered."—*Humboldt's Narrative*, vol. v. pp. 62, 64, 65.

The supposition, then, that such granitic continents could ever be disintegrated and transported to the ocean by the chemical and mechanical agents that are now acting on the surface of the earth, is altogether untenable. Such indestructible masses stretched along the line of the ancient seas could no more have furnished the materials of our strata than though they had been stationed in another world. Geologists themselves could never have advanced such an hypothesis had they properly considered the impracticable conditions it involves.

Admitting, however, that those imagined continents of granite could have been disintegrated by the chemical and mechanical agents to which they would have been subjected, and the theory is still embarrassed by the equally fatal objection, that they would not even then have furnished the materials of the stratified rocks; inasmuch as some of the most important of the mineral substances that enter into their composition are not constituents of granite, except in quantities almost too slight to be appreciable.

Granite is composed either of quartz, felspar, and mica, or quartz, felspar, and hornblende; and usually in the proportion of two parts of quartz, two or three of felspar, and one of mica, or hornblende; and consists, when mica is an element, of 74 to 75 per cent. of silica, 13 to 14 of alumine, 8 or 9 of potash; and four or five other ingredients, amounting together to the remaining four or five per cent. The quantity of lime is less than half of one per cent., and of iron, less than two. When hornblende is an element, the potash is diminished one half, the lime increases to near five per cent., and the iron to near three; and these elements are not promiscuously blended, but the quartz, felspar, and mica, or hornblende, are separately crystallized and united in that form in a compact mass.* On the supposition, then, that such mountains and continents of granite could have been decrystallized and transferred to the bed of the ocean, they could not have contributed to the formation of any strata except those of which silica and alumine are the constituents; that is, gneiss, quartz rock, sandstones, shales, and sand and gravel. They could have furnished nothing, except on a scale too insig-

* Phillips's Geology, vol. ii., pp. 65, 66.

nificant to merit consideration, towards the structure of the vast beds of limestone, iron, chalk, salt, and several other important deposits.

The theory thus fails again to fill the office for which it is devised, and on a vast scale. Grant them all that it can yield, exhaust its utmost resources, and instead of supplying, as it professes, the whole of the materials of which the strata are constituted, it can only furnish from one-half to two-thirds. How fatal to their system this defect is, is seen from the fact that limestone, to the formation of which it could contribute nothing, occurs among the lowest of the stratified rocks, and alternates either with sandstones, shales, or coal, throughout the whole series of the primary, secondary, and tertiary groups, extends over immense areas, and is often of great depth.

"One of the most remarkable geological features of this continent is the vast extent of the carboniferous limestone. I have traced its eastern border—conforming to the course of the other mineral formations east of the Mississippi—more than one thousand miles running to the west of south, from the State of New York to the thirty-fifth degree of north latitude in the State of Alabama ; the course is there changed, and lies to the north of west, leaving Little Rock on the Arkansas about thirty miles to the south, and disappearing between five and six hundred miles from the Rocky Mountains. This deposit extends uninterruptedly a geographical distance of at least 1,500 miles from east to west ;

underlying portions of the states of New York, Pennsylvania, Ohio, Indiana, Illinois, Missouri, and the territory of Arkansas on that line. In Tennessee, Kentucky, Virginia, and Maryland, it is bounded by a line of which the Cumberland Mountains form a part. In the plains through which the Mississippi flows, and which include the Illinois prairies, it appears like a continuous floor, forming an almost unvarying flat."—*Featherstonhaugh's Geological Report*, 1835, pp. 27, 28.

Of the aggregate of the several layers in the carboniferous group, the following section of the upper coal series in Western Virginia may be taken as an example:

"First or lower bed,	. . .	12 feet	0 inches.
Second, "	. . .	6 "	4 "
Third, "	. . .	3 "	0 "
Fourth, "	. . .	1 "	6 "
Fifth, "	. . .	6 "	6 "
Sixth, "	. . .	2 "	0 "
Seventh, "	. . .	7 "	6 "
Eighth, "	. . .	7 "	0 "
Ninth, "	. . .	5 "	0 "
		50 "	10 "

Making a total thickness of limestone in this group along the line of section of fifty feet; adding to these twenty-four in the lower shale and sandstone group, and three in the lower coal group, and we have in the whole extent of the coal measures embraced in the section, a thickness of about seventy-seven feet of limestone."—*Rodgers's Report on the Geology of Virginia*, 1839, p. 93.

The inadequacy of their theory to account for this important portion of the strata, though seen and acknowledged by geologists, has not led them either to abandon or modify it. Some candidly confess themselves unable to give a satisfactory explanation of its origin; while Macculloch, Phillips, and some others, maintain, as the most probable hypothesis, that it was formed of the exuviæ of testaceous animals, and was drawn originally by them from the waters of the sea. But that, besides being a mere conjecture and infinitely improbable, furnishes no indication of its original source; as it implies either that the lime was previously held in solution in the waters of the sea—which was impossible, as the quantity is such as would have thickened all the waters of the globe to a paste—or else that it was gradually introduced into them from some unknown source, which is no explanation whatever of its origin. Instead, therefore, of demonstrating their hypothesis that the whole of the materials of the strata were drawn from their fabled mountains of granite, by their own concession that large portion of them that consists of limestone was of a different derivation. Those vast formations, accordingly, interspersed through the whole mass of the strata, are so many monuments of the error of their theory.

Iron, also, which enters very largely into the composition of many of the strata, especially of the carboniferous groups, cannot have resulted from the decomposition of granite, but must have been altogether drawn from some other source. Besides, indeed, those rocks which imbed it in masses and derive from it their principal character, it exists in ordinary sandstones, and shales consisting mainly, like granite, of silica and alumine, in far greater portions than in that rock.

So, also—to say nothing of chalk—of the vast beds of salt. The nature of that mineral forbids the supposition that it can have resulted from the disintegration of granite; as there is no such element in its composition.

The theory thus fails to make any provision for the formation of at least one-third of the strata for which it professes to account by a scientific induction according to "the strictest rules of the Baconian philosophy." Can higher evidence be asked of its utter erroneousness? Yet its authors, though aware that it is thus incommensurate to the vast task which they assign to it, seem not to regard its failure on so immense a scale as a proof of its inaccuracy, or reason for its abandonment. They continue to make it the basis of their arguments for the vast age of the world, and treat the inference they found on it as a scientific induction.

Unfortunately, however, for the theory, this defect does not terminate at that point. It, in fact, fails as entirely to account for those strata of which silicious sand is the principal element, as for those which consist of limestone, iron, and salt; for though the main materials of sandstone are those of which granite consists, silica and alumine, yet the form in which they now exist demonstrates that they cannot have been derived from that rock. In granite those elements, with a slight mixture of potash, iron, and lime, are combined in three different proportions in *crystals* of quartz, felspar, and mica, or hornblende; but in sandstone they are not in the form of quartz, felspar, and hornblende, or mica crystals, as the first three would undoubtedly have been, at least in a chief degree, had they been drawn from granite. Nor are they crystallized; but instead, are, at least mainly, of a mere granular structure, or formed by an aggregation of particles by a law essentially unlike that of crystallization. The nature and importance of the distinction in structure and form that exists between them—the crystals of granite being geometric, though imperfect, but the particles of sandstone generally simple grains or comminuted mud—may be seen from the following passage:

"Quartz is *crystallized* in *double six-sided pyramids* in the substance of granitic, porphyritic, and other igneous rocks; in *six-sided prisms* terminated by *six-sided pyramids* in mineral *veins and in cavities* in granite; *compact* in veins; *nodular* in amygdaloidal traps; *rolled masses in old red conglomerate* millstone grit, and grauwacke; *worn grains in sandstones, clays, certain quartz rocks, and coarse clay slates.*

"Felspar; primary *rhomboidal crystals* in granite, porphyry, trachyte, and basalt; composite crystals in cavities of granite and veins; *disturbed* crystals in gneiss; *rolled* crystals in conglomerate; *decomposed or porcelain clay* in some granites and *sandstones.*

"Mica, *crystallized* in *hexagonal plates* in granite, porphyry, lava, and primary limestone; *disturbed* crystals in gneiss and mica schist; *fragmentary scales* in *sandstone, sand, shale, and clay.*

"Hornblende, crystallized with felspar in granite, greenstone, basalt, and lava, also in hornblende slate."—*Phillips's Guide*, p. 79.

In granite, quartz has thus a geometric shape, but in sandstone it is in the form of minute particles or grains. The Potsdam Calciferous and Medina sandstones, for example, of this State, generally exhibit no traces in any of their parts of a crystalline structure, but are formed by a mere aggregation of minute particles, and, on being broken, are easily reduced to the most attenuated granules or dust. They are nevertheless usually represented by geologists as drawn wholly from granite, and as owing their new shape to the fracture, rolling, or abrasure of the crystals, of which they originally formed a part.

"Take for example the very common rock sandstone; its component *grains* of quartz, felspar, and mica, are more or less *rolled* or *fragmented* crystals of these substances, derived from rocks like gneiss, mica, schist, &c., which are also composed of grains of the same kinds, less affected by mechanical processes; or from granite, porphyry, &c., which are purely crystalline rocks. Such derivative sandstones are formed at this day from such crystallized granite and other rocks."—*Phillips's Geology*, vol. i. p. 31.

"In a general sense, the red sandstone must be considered as formed of *fragments*, more or less minute, of preceding rocks or minerals. When these are of the usual size of sand, the finer sandstones are produced; when larger, the results are coarser gritstones and conglomerates, or breccias. The term sandstone is, however, equally applied to the whole, although rather in a geological than in a mineralogical sense."—*Macculloch's G. C. of Rocks*, p. 402.

In the first place, however, this transformation from crystals to grains is not demonstrated. The mere fact that the particles of sandstone consist of the same elements as the quartz crystals of granite, is no proof that they were derived from that rock, any more than the fact that the elements of granite are essentially the same as gneiss and the primary shales and sandstones is proof that that rock was—

according to the hypothesis proposed by Sir C. Lyell —formed from them. Yet the theory has no other ground for its support than the mere similarity of their elements.

In the next place, it is inexplicable, on the supposition that they had their origin in granite, that no traces remain in them of the crystals from which they were drawn. Crystallized quartz, even in the state in which it usually exists in granite, is an extremely hard, and under the action of the chemical and mechanical agents to which it is ordinarily exposed, almost indestructible mineral. That vast mountains, that whole continents towering several miles into the atmosphere, and consisting largely of that element, should have been dissolved and reduced in a great measure to the most comminuted particles by the mere chemical and mechanical forces that are now acting on the surface of the globe, may justly be pronounced a physical impossibility. No effect can be conceived more obviously and absolutely beyond the powers of those agents.

No mode of the production of such a change can be suggested that does not leave the theory embarrassed with this insuperable objection. To suppose the quartz and other crystals in granite to have been subjected to a chemical solution, were first to assume that there were chemical forces then in activity of immeasurably greater energy, and operating on a far wider area, than there now are on the globe. But that is prohibited by the maxims of geology, which require that if the solution of granite mountains and continents is to be accounted for, it should be by forces the same in kind and intensity as those that are now exerting their powers on the earth. Next, if they are supposed to have undergone a solution, then their assumption of their present granular form must have been the effect of a different and peculiar chemical agency. But that is again forbidden by the principles of geology. As no chemical agents are now in activity that generate such silicious grains and aggregations of grains as those that constitute the Potsdam, Calciferous, Medina, and other sandstones, it cannot, according to the maxims of the science, be assumed that they existed and acted at a former period.

The supposition that they were reduced from crystals to their present granular forms—spherical, irregularly rounded, and angular—by mechanical forces, abrading or fracturing them, is embarrassed by equally formidable difficulties. It is altogether incredible that any mechanical force—as of the waves of the ocean, or the current of rivers—should have acted on every point of vast mountains and continents so as to have broken, worn, and disintegrated their whole mass. It is equally incredible that such agents, acting wherever they might, should have reduced the silicious elements universally of the masses with which they came in contact, to grains of such a minute and uniform size. No result can be conceived more wholly without the limits of possibility than that such causes acting with indefinitely varying forces on rocks differing widely in their solidity, should give birth to such extraordinary effects, and in such unvarying uniformity. No such results spring from their present action. The supposition is, therefore, as absolutely prohibited as the others, by the principles of geology.

We might extend this argument to arenaceous shales, granular quartz, the conglomerates of which silicious pebbles are a principal element, and ordinary sand and gravel. Instead of crystals, they are aggregates of grains, or concretions of minute particles by a law wholly unlike that of geometric crystallization. The theory thus fails as entirely to account for these vast formations as for those that consist of ingredients wholly unlike those of granite.

These considerations thus furnish the most resistless demonstration of its error. Whatever else may be thought to have been susceptible of derivation from such continents of granite,—the vast beds of gravel, sand, salt, chalk, limestone, and sandstone, cannot have been drawn from that source. Their nature, or the forms in which they exist, make the supposition a paradox. The most indisputable proofs are graven on their fronts that that was not their origin. But withdrawing these, there is nothing left through the whole mass of the fossiliferous rocks—even granting that all the other insuperable obstacles to the theory could be overcome—which its advocates can refer to those fabulous continents, except certain conglomerates and those shales and clays of which alumine is a chief ingredient; a slender basis truly, could they verify their hypothesis in respect to them, on which to erect a demonstration of the immeasurable age of the world! Can a more unfortunate predicament be imagined of writers who have indulged so confident a persuasion that they had established their system by evidence scarcely inferior in certainty to that of mathematics?

Passing over, however, all these insurmountable objections to their theory, let us suppose their imagined continents reduced in any requisite measure to disintegration, transformed into sand, gravel, and pebbles, and traversed by streams and rivers of sufficient size and force to bear such materials to the sea; and there still would be no agent by which they could be spread out on the bottom of the deep over the vast spaces that are occupied by many of the strata. The larger streams, like the Ganges, Indus, Nile, Niger, Amazon, Mississippi, and St. Lawrence, would carry no gravel or sand whatever to the ocean. These great rivers deposit all the heavier particles with which they are charged, in their first stages, hundreds of miles before they reach their mouths, and bear nothing to the ocean but comminuted mud and vegetable matter that is held in solution; and that they throw down almost immediately on reaching the sea. No portion of it, probably, is carried beyond the lines at which their currents are arrested by the resistance of the waters of the ocean: and that is within a very narrow circle, compared to the vast spaces that lie beyond. The result accordingly of their transporting agency is, simply, at first slowly to diminish the depth of the ocean at their mouths, and finally, gradually to extend the dry land at those points into the sea. Their influence is exhausted in the formation of their deltas. The main bed of the ocean is as completely unaffected by them as though they were not in existence. Their limited power and the narrow sphere within which their agency is circumscribed, forbid the supposition that such rivers can have been the instruments of conveying to the ocean the materials of which the strata are constituted. The area over which many of the strata extend is immense. Gneiss is generally considered as one of the most universal of the rocks, and lies very generally, it is held, between the granite which is the fundamental rock, and the fossiliferous strata. The fossiliferous strata in some of their divisions exist everywhere, except in the narrow spaces in which either granite, or some of the lowest orders of the stratified rocks, rise to the surface. In this country the New York or Silurian system, extending from the lowest of the fossiliferous rocks up to the old red sandstone, and comprising a vast series of sandstones, limestones, and shales, spreads in some of its divisions from the eastern range of the Appalachians to Lake Superior, and from Lake Champlain to the Rocky Mountains, and forming a bed on an average many thousand feet, and in places probably several miles in thickness. The fancy that that vast mass of matter can have been borne there, and distributed in so equable a manner by rivers, is an extravagance at which common sense revolts. It is only matched in its disregard of probability, by the hypothesis that the limestone and chalk formations are the product of testaceous animals elaborated by them from other matter, of which lime is not in any appreciable measure a constituent. The effect, in the conditions that are supposed, lies wholly out of the sphere of possibility. It might as well be imagined that the granite mountains themselves that rise from beneath these strata and rear their naked summits into the sky, were floated in solid masses by streams or tides from those fabled continents, and planted in their present positions. The cause is infinitely disproportioned to the task that is assigned it. It has none of the qualities that are requisite to the production of such an effect.

Sir C. Lyell, however, notwithstanding he admits

that all the heavy matter borne down by a river must fall to the bottom almost immediately on its entering the sea, still maintains that the stream naturally advances the line of its deposits further into the deep, and that the change of the area, by that cause, on which its sediment is thrown down, and a transferrence of the river itself to a new line and point of debouchure by the elevation or inclination of the continent from which it descends, will sufficiently account for the distribution of the detritus out of which he holds the strata were formed, over the area which they occupy.

"It is only by carefully considering the combined action of all the causes of change now in operation, whether in the animate or inanimate world, that we can hope to explain such complicated appearances as are exhibited in the general arrangement of mineral masses.

"The surface of the terraqueous globe may be divided into two parts, one of which is undergoing repairs, while the other, constituting, at any one period, by far the larger portion of the whole, is either suffering degradation, or remaining stationary without loss or increment. The dry land is for the most part wasting by the action of rain, rivers, and torrents; and part of the bed of the sea is exposed to the excavating action of currents, while *the greater part, remote from continents and islands, receives no new deposits. For as a turbid river throws down all its sediment into the first lake which it traverses,* so currents flowing from land or from shoals purge themselves from foreign ingredients *in the first deep basin which they enter, and beyond this the blue waters of the ocean may for ages remain clear to the greatest depths.*

"The other part of the terraqueous surface is the receptacle of new deposits, and in this portion alone the remains of plants and animals become fossilized. *Now the position of this area, where new formations are in progress,* and where alone any memorials of the state of organic life are preserved, *is always varying, and must for ever continue to vary;* and for the same reason *that portion of the terraqueous globe, which is undergoing waste also shifts its position*; and those fluctuations depend partly on the action of aqueous and partly on igneous causes.

"In illustration of these positions I now observe that the sediment of the Rhone, which is thrown into the Lake of Geneva, is now conveyed to a spot a mile and a half distant from that where it accumulated in the tenth century, and six miles from the point where the Delta began originally to form. We may look forward to the period when the Lake will be filled up, and then a sudden change will take place in the distribution of the transported matter; for the mud and sand brought down from the Alps will thenceforth be carried nearly two hundred miles southwards, where the Rhone enters the Mediterranean."—*Principles of Geology,* vol. ii. pp. 210, 211.

No river, however, nor rivers could ever, by that process, spread a layer of pebbles, sand, or the most comminuted mud over the whole bed of a spacious sea; nor bear any appreciable quantity of matter more than a very short distance within the deep. The current of a river on entering the sea, whether the waters of the deep are stationary, or in motion on a line that is transverse to that current, must meet a resistance that instantly checks its rapidity, and soon puts an end to its progress. All the matter accordingly borne forward by its impulse, or held in solution, must necessarily be deposited in the area within which it is circumscribed. Not a particle can ever be carried out of that limit, except by a movement of the waters of the sea that is independent of the river. It is demonstrable, therefore, that the detritus carried down by a river cannot be spread over the whole of the bed of an ocean, or spacious sea; inasmuch as it would require that the current of the river should extend over the whole of the area, and displace the whole mass of the waters of the ocean, or sea, which is as much out of the circle of possibility as it is that it should transport the solid strata themselves by its current. This part of Sir C. Lyell's theory, therefore, furnishes no solution of the diffusion over the bed of the ocean of the materials of which the strata are formed.

His supposition that it could be produced by a change of the position of the continents from which it is supposed to be drawn, causing a transferrence of the rivers to new lines and points of debouchure, is equally untenable.

"On the other band, if a current charged with sediment vary its course—a circumstance which must happen to all of them in the lapse of ages—the accumulation of transported matter will at once cease in one region, and commence in another.

"Although the causes which occasion the transferrence of the places of sedimentary depositions are continually in action in every region, yet they are particularly influential where subterranean movements alter from time to time the levels of land; and their effect must be very great during the successive elevations and depressions which must be supposed to accompany the rise of a great continent from the deep. A trifling change of level may sometimes throw a current into a new direction, or alter the course of a considerable river. Some tracts will be submerged and laid dry by subterranean movements; in one place a shoal will be formed, whereby the waters will drift matter over spaces where they once threw down their burden, and new cavities will elsewhere be produced both marine and lacustrine which will intercept the waters bearing sediment, and thereby stop the supply once carried to some distant basin.

"Without entering into more detailed explanations, the reader will perceive that according to the laws *now governing* the aqueous and igneous causes, distinct deposits must at different periods be thrown down on various parts of the earth's surface, and that in the course of ages the same area may be again and again the receptacle of such dissimilar sets of strata."—*Principles of Geology*, vol. ii. p. 212.

But this does not account any more than the other for the diffusion of the materials of any one of the strata over the whole bed of the ocean; it only indicates a mode in which the points where rivers enter the sea may be changed from time to time so as to produce a change of the areas at the margin of the ocean, where the sediment borne down by them shall be deposited. It leaves all the other parts of the bottom of the sea as unprovided as they were before, with materials for the formation of new strata. In order to explain their deposition over the whole bed of the ocean by such a cause, it would be necessary to suppose, not only that the continents from which the materials of the strata were derived, but that small divisions of the bottom of the sea itself, also, were successively elevated, so that the river should in succession enter it at as many points as would be requisite, in order to the deposition of a stratum over its whole area. That, however, cannot have happened; inasmuch as the elevation and depression of the surface in detached parts that must then have taken place at the formation of each layer of the system, would have broken their whole mass into fragments, and reduced them to a promiscuous heap of ruins. But they have suffered no such violence. The New York or Silurian groups which underlie the whole country from the Alleghanies far into the Canadas, and from Vermont beyond the Mississippi, are but slightly dislocated. Throughout a large part of their immense area they lie at a dead level, or moderate inclination, and have never been seriously disturbed in any of their members since their deposition. It is clear then beyond debate, that their materials were never transported to their several places by the action of rivers. The supposition is indeed so palpably at war with the laws that govern their agency, and so absurd and enormous an extravagance, as to render it surprising that considerate persons should have ever entertained it, and made it the basis of an argument for the immeasurable age of the world.

And finally, in addition to all these evidences of the error of their theory, the distribution of the elements, silex, alumine, and lime, of which the formations chiefly consist, into separate strata, is an equally decisive proof that they cannot have been drawn from such pre-existing continents, nor been borne to their several places and arranged in their positions by the agency of streams, rivers, and currents. The detritus that is wafted down by rivers to the sea, is not separated, on its deposition, according to the species of which it consists, and its different ingredients thrown down on different areas. Instead, they fall together and form a promiscuous mass. The only separation that takes place, is of the heavier from the lighter grains and particles—gravel falling first, sand next, then comminuted mud, and last, light vegetable particles; and as their fall takes place by the force of gravity, the points at which they severally descend are determined by their weight, not by the material of which they consist.

The strata, however, were not formed in that manner, but their great elements were distributed into separate layers; sandstone, sand, and gravel, of which silex is the chief ingredient, being arranged by themselves; slate, marl, and clay, which owe their principal character to alumine, forming a different set of layers; and limestone and chalk, of which lime is the great ingredient, constituting beds and masses by themselves. The sand, gravel, and pebbles, moreover, that enter into the composition of many of their layers, instead of being sorted according to size and weight so that they regularly decrease in dimensions in one direction, and increase in the other, as in the deltas of rivers, are distributed indiscriminately throughout the spaces—sometimes of vast extent—which they occupy. Thus the sandstones of the New York system stretching, there is reason to believe, from Vermont to the Rocky Mountains, and from the Appalachians far into the Canadas, do not vary in the coarseness of their grains and pebbles in any ratio to their distance from their eastern, western, southern, or northern edges, or from any interior points in the area over which they are spread. Nor do those of the carboniferous system, which extend from the Alleghanies through the western parts of Pennsylvania and Virginia, the southern part of Ohio, and a large share of Kentucky, Indiana, and Illinois. Their variations, if they vary, are obviously from chemical, not from mechanical or geographical reasons.

These facts form, therefore, the most unanswerable demonstration, in the first place, that the materials of the strata were not derived, as the theory represents, from disintegrated continents of granite—as they could not then have been assorted as they are, and their several elements arranged in layers by themselves; and in the next place, that the distribution throughout their whole extent, of the sand and gravel that enter into the composition of sandstones and other strata, were not transported in their present form from a distance to their places, by the action of streams and currents.

Such are the proofs of the error of this extraordinary theory, which refers the materials of the stratified rocks to anterior continents and islands of granite. There is not a solitary step in the process which it contemplates at which it is not confuted by a palpable contradiction to the laws of the physical world, and the principles of geology. The supposition with which it commences of the creation of the earth in a state of gaseous fusion, is a paradox. There are no indications where the continents and mountains were stationed, from the ruins of which it is held the strata were formed. Had there been such continents and mountains as the hypothesis implies, they must have been of such an elevation as to have been protected by congelation from being disintegrated and transported to the sea by the action of water. Had they been depressed into a temperate region, still no springs could have emerged from their surface, nor permanent streams and rivers descended from them to the sea. Had they been disintegrated and traversed by streams and rivers, they could never have borne more than an inconsiderable portion of their detritus to the ocean. Had their detritus been transported to the sea, it could not have been transformed into sand, gravel, and pebbles: it could not have been spread over the bed of the ocean: it could not have been assorted according to the materials of which it consists, and formed into separate layers of sandstone, limestone, and shale. There is not one of these processes through which the theory represents the materials of the strata as having passed, that is not in contradiction to the laws of the physical world, and an infinite impossibility. The demonstration is absolute, therefore, that the strata cannot have been formed by these processes, and that the whole theory is groundless and mistaken. The inference accordingly that is founded on it of the vast age of the world, is equally unphilosophical and false.

QUESTIONS.

Suppose that chemical agents could have acted on those continents, and produced a rapid disintegration, is it credible that it could have gone to the extent the theory assumes? What are the two conditions which that implies? Is either of them consistent with the laws of matter? If those continents became covered with a soil, is it not as incredible that streams should have borne it all to the ocean, as it is that the streams of the present continents should bear all the earth and gravel of the regions from which they run to the sea? Is there any reason to suppose that a millionth part of the detritus of the Andes ever reaches the ocean? Does it not, with the exception of comparatively few particles, lodge near the foot of the ranges from which it is disintegrated? Does not all but the merest fraction of the debris of the Rocky Mountains remain where, or near where, it first falls? Could the other condition which they assume have been realized? Give the first reason that it could not. Give the second reason. What does Humboldt state in regard to the inadequacy of rivers to wear away the rocks over which they pass? Is it clear then that continents of granite could never have been converted into sand and dust, and transported to the ocean by the chemical and mechanical agents that are now acting on the earth's surface?

But could those granite continents have been reduced to dust, would they have furnished the various substances of which the strata consist? Of what is granite composed? What are the proportions in which these elements exist in it? What are the only strata that might have been formed out of those elements? What other strata are there of which they could not have furnished the principal ingredient? What proportion of the strata then must have been derived from some other source? By what formation is this exemplified in this country? Is limestone spread over vast regions? What aggregate thickness do its several beds in a single group sometimes attain? Are geologists aware that these immense deposits of lime cannot be accounted for on their theory? What other substances are there that enter into the composition of the strata, that cannot have been derived from granite? Do these facts confute their theory? Does it fail also to account for those strata, such as sandstone, that consist of substances that exist in granite? State the reason. What is the difference of the form of quartz in granite and sandstone? Is the assumption of geologists that the crystals of granite have been changed into the granules of sandstone, admissible? What is the first reason against it? What is the second? Can such a change have been produced by chemical agents? Can it by mechanical forces? What other classes of strata are there that cannot, for the same reason, have been derived from granite? Does the theory then fail to account for all but an inconsiderable portion of the strata?

Suppose, however, those difficulties were overcome, and that rivers could have borne down a large quantity of detritus to the sea; could they have spread it over vast areas of the bottom of the ocean? Do the great rivers of the present earth carry the earthy matter with which they are charged more than a short distance into the sea? Is it not a law that of the matter borne down by a river, that which is of greater specific gravity than the water itself, sinks as soon as the force of the current ceases to bear it forward? Is it not certain that no river of the globe continues its current more than a few miles after it enters the ocean? Is it not impossible then that rivers can have diffused their detritus over the whole bottom of the ocean? Are not the strata, however, spread over vast areas? Give examples. What can be more clear than that these strata can never have been formed over such immense spaces by the agency of rivers? What is Sir C. Lyell's theory of the agency of rivers in the formation of strata? Could a river ever by that process form a layer of pebbles or sand over more than a very limited space? State the reason that it could not. What is his theory in respect to a change of the points at which rivers enter the ocean? Could such changes ever enable them to spread their earthy and vegetable matter over the whole bottom of a spacious sea?

And finally, is not the distribution of the chief elements of the strata into separate layers inexplicable on their theory? What are those elements? How are the different earthy elements borne down by rivers usually deposited? Are they sorted, or thrown down promiscuously? What is the manner in which the elements of the strata were distributed? Specify the elements of the leading groups. Recapitulate these various proofs of the error of the theory.

CHAPTER XI.

False Theories of Geologists respecting the Formation of the Strata.

THAT branch of their theory which relates to the sources whence the materials of the strata were derived, and the agents by which they were conveyed to their place of deposition being thus confuted, the next inquiry respects their other great postulate, that the original formation of the strata and the modifications to which they have been subjected, were the work of the chemical and mechanical forces that are now producing changes in the earth's surface, and were the result of agencies, in the main, of only their present measure of intensity. If this postulate, on which they found the most of their reasonings, is shown to be gratuitously assumed also, inconsistent with the most important characteristics of the strata, and in contravention of the principles of the science, then the second main ground of their inference of the great age of the world will also be overthrown: and such is undoubtedly its character.

As it is apparent from the preceding discussion that streams and rivers have had no important agency in the conveyance of the materials of the strata to the points of their deposition, they are in the main excluded from the question. There are no traces of their influence until a large part of the depositions were formed, and whatever effects they may have produced towards the close of the secondary and during the tertiary periods, they must, from the resistance currents from the land meet on entering the ocean, have been confined to the vicinity of the points of their debouchure. The question, therefore, as far as all the most extensive and important effects are concerned, relates only to the chemical and volcanic forces, and the mechanical agencies of the ocean under which the strata were formed, and subsequently thrown into their present conditions.

And in the first place, the assumption that all these great effects are the result of the causes that are now in activity, and arose gradually from agencies of essentially the intensity they are now exerting, is based on altogether inadequate and mistaken ground. It certainly is not a self-evident proposition. There is nothing in the nature of the strata themselves that shows directly that they must have been formed exclusively by causes like these, acting with only their present energy. If that is made a principle or postulate of the science, it must first, like other facts, be established by appropriate evidence. But no such demonstration of it is furnished by geologists.

It is either assumed without any attempt at its verification, or founded on vague and imaginary analogies. Thus Sir Charles Lyell, for example, who in the construction and support of his theory reasons altogether from the present to the past, takes for granted at every step of his argument, the point on which its validity depends;* namely, not only that the causes now producing geological effects on the globe are the same in kind as those to which the stratified rocks owe their existence and modifications, but that the scale on which they are now acting, and the rate at which they are giving birth to their several effects, are the measure of the energy with

* "Now the principal source from whence we are enabled to draw such conclusions respecting the nature of the solid materials of the earth, and the changes which they have undergone, is a comparison of geological phenomena with the effects previously known to have been produced in modern times by running water and subterranean heat. Hence the utility of one of the preceding treatises on aqueous and igneous causes, in which it was shown that strata are at present in the course of formation by rivers and marine currents; both in seas and lakes; and that in several parts of the world rocks have been rent, tilted, and broken, by sudden earthquakes; or have been heaved up above, or let down below their former level; also that volcanic eruptions have given rise to mountain masses made up of scoriæ, and of stone both porous and solid. . . . .

"From these remarks it will be seen that a study of systematic treatises on the recent changes of the organic and inorganic world, affords a good preliminary exercise for those who desire to interpret geological movements. They are thus enabled to proceed from the known to the unknown, or from *the observed effects of causes now in action to the analogous effects of the* SAME *or* SIMILAR CAUSES *which have acted at remote periods.*"—*Lyell's Principles, Preface*, pp. xiii., xiv.

which they acted, and the rapidity with which they wrought their results, in the formation of the strata. For he offers nothing but the effects themselves that are now in the process of production, the strength of the agents that are bringing them into existence, and the rapidity with which they are wrought as proofs that all the geological effects of ancient times which it is his aim to explain, were wrought, by the same agents at the same rate; and thence makes the ground of his inference that the periods occupied in their production must have been of the immeasurable length which he ascribes to them. But the effects that are now taking place plainly yield no verification of his inference, unless it is either self-evident, or is shown by extraneous proof, that all the geological effects in question must necessarily have been produced by the same cause, acting, uniformly with the same energy. But that, instead of proving, he takes for granted. His argument, accordingly, expressed syllogistically, is nothing more than the following:

All the geological changes that have been produced on the globe have been the work of causes identically the same in kind, energy, and the rapidity with which they produced their effects.

But the causes that are now giving birth to geological changes are feeble, and advance at a very slow rate in the production of their effects.

Therefore, the causes under which the formation of the stratified rocks took place, must have been similarly feeble, and advanced at a similarly slow rate in the production of their effects.

And again:

The energy with which geological causes act, and the rate at which they give birth to their effects, are uniformly the same at all periods.

But the energy of the causes that are now working changes on the earth is slight, and long periods are occupied in the completion of their effects.

Therefore, the causes by which the strata of the earth were produced were equally slight in their energy, and periods equally long in proportion to the magnitude of the effects they produced, were occupied in their completion.

The whole point to be established, is thus assumed in the premise from which it is deduced. He proceeds throughout his discussion on a mistaken view of the real question in debate—which is, what the causes were by which the stratified rocks were formed, and what the mode was of their agency and the rapidity with which they wrought their effects—which is to be determined by the nature of the effects; not—which is the position he employs himself in endeavoring to evince—whether, on the supposition that the causes that are giving birth to geological effects, are in nature, strength, and rate of production, identically like those by which all former effects were produced, immeasurably long periods must not have been occupied in their completion. In the one case, those ancient effects are made the measure of their causes; in the other, modern effects, which are wholly inferior in magnitude, and in a large degree of a different nature, are made their measure. His whole system is thus built on the assumption of the premise from which it is deduced. He accordingly does not generally attempt directly and absolutely to demonstrate the solutions he suggests of the phenomena, real or presumed, which he endeavors to explain; but presents them simply as suppositions which—admitting the postulate on which he proceeds—furnish possible or probable explanations of them. Thus it is by such a mere hypothesis that he endeavors to account for the great variations in the temperature of the globe, which he assumes have taken place.

"I shall now proceed to speculate on the vicissitudes of climate which must attend those endless variations in the geographical features of our planet, which are contemplated in geology. That our speculations may be confined within the strict limits of analogy, I shall assume, 1st, That the proportion of dry land to sea continues always the same; 2dly, That the volume of the land rising above the level of the sea is a constant quantity; and not only that its mean, but that its extreme height, are liable only to trifling variations; 3dly, That both the mean and extreme depth of the sea are invariable; and 4thly, It may be consistent with due caution to assume that the grouping together of the land in great continents is a necessary part of the economy of nature; for it is possible that the laws which govern the subterranean forces, and which act simultaneously along certain lines, cannot but produce at every epoch continuous mountain chains, so that the subdivision of the whole land into innumerable islands may be precluded.

"If it be objected that the maximum of elevation of land and depth of sea are *probably* not constant, nor the gathering together of all the land in certain parts, nor even *perhaps* the relative extent of land and water: I reply, that the arguments about to be adduced will be strengthened, if in these peculiarities of surface there be considerable deviations from the present type. If, for example, all other circumstances being the same, the land is at any one time more divided into islands than another, a greater uniformity of climate might be produced, the mean temperature remaining unaltered; or if at another era there were mountains higher than the Himalaya, these, when placed in high latitudes, would cause a greater excess of cold. Or if we suppose that at certain periods no chain of hills in the world rose beyond a height of 10,000 feet, a greater heat might then have prevailed than is compatible with the existence of mountains thrice that elevation.

"However constant may be the relative proportion of sea and land, we know that there is annually some small variation in their respective geographical positions, and that in every century the land is in some parts raised, and in others depressed by earthquakes, and so likewise is the bed of the sea. By these and other ceaseless changes, the configuration of the earth's surface has been remodelled again and again since it was the habitation of organic beings, and the bed of the ocean has been lifted up to the height of some of the loftiest mountains. . . . . .

"If we now proceed to consider the circumstances required for a *general* change of temperature, it will appear from the facts and principles already laid down, that whenever a greater extent of high land is collected in the polar regions, the cold will augment ; and the same result will be produced when there is more sea between or near the tropics ; while, on the contrary, so often as the above conditions are reversed, the heat will be greater. *If this be admitted*, it will follow, that unless the superficial inequalities of the earth be fixed and permanent, there must be never-ending fluctuations in the mean temperature of every zone ; and that *the climate of our era can no more be the type of every other*, than one of our four seasons of all the rest.

"To simplify our view of the various changes in climate which different combinations of geographical circumstances may produce, we shall first consider the conditions necessary for bringing about the extreme of cold, or what may be termed the winter of the 'great year,' or geological cycle, and afterwards the conditions requisite to produce the maximum of heat, or the summer of the same year.

"To begin with the northern hemisphere, let us suppose

those hills of the Italian peninsula and of Sicily, which are of comparatively modern origin, and contain fossil shells identical with living species, to subside again into the sea from which they have been raised, and that an extent of land of equal area and height, varying from one to three thousand feet, should rise up in the Arctic ocean, between Siberia and the north pole. In speaking of such changes I shall not allude to the manner in which I conceive it possible they may be brought about, nor to the time required for their accomplishment—reserving for a future occasion not only the proof that revolutions of equal magnitude have taken place, but that analogous operations are still in gradual progress. The alteration now supposed in the physical geography of the northern regions would cause additional snow and ice to accumulate where now there is usually an open sea; and the temperature of the greater part of Europe would be somewhat lowered, so as to resemble more nearly that of corresponding latitudes of North America; or, in other words, it might be necessary to travel about 10° further south to meet with the same climate which we now enjoy. No compensation would be derived from the disappearance of land in the Mediterranean countries; but the contrary, since the mean heat of the soil in those latitudes is probably far above those which would belong to the sea, by which we imagine it to be replaced.

"But let the configuration of the surface be still further varied, and let some large district within or near the tropics, such as Mexico, with its mountains rising to the height of twelve thousand feet and upwards, be converted into sea, while lands of equal elevation and extent rise up in the arctic circle. From this change there would, in the first place, result a sensible diminution of temperature near the tropic, for the soil of Mexico would no longer be heated by the sun, so that the atmosphere would be less warm, as also the neighboring Atlantic. On the other hand, the whole of Europe, Northern Asia, and North America would be chilled by the enormous quantity of ice and snow, thus generated on vast heights on the new arctic continent. If, as we have already seen, there are now some points in the Southern hemisphere where snow is perpetual down to the level of the sea, in latitudes as low as central England, such might assuredly be the case throughout a great part of Europe, under the change of circumstances above supposed ; and if at present the extreme range of drifted icebergs is the Azores, they might easily reach the equator after the assumed alteration. But to pursue the subject still further —let the Himalaya mountains, with the whole of Hindostan, sink down, and their place be occupied by the Indian Ocean, while an equal extent of territory and mountains of the same vast height rise up between North Greenland and the Orkney Islands. It seems difficult to exaggerate the amount to which the climate of the Northern hemisphere would then be cooled. . . . .

"Let us now turn from the contemplation of the winter of the 'great year,' and consider the opposite train of circumstances which would bring on the spring and summer. To imagine all the lands to be collected together in equatorial latitudes, and a few promontories only to project beyond the thirtieth parallel, would be undoubtedly to suppose an extreme result of geological change. But if we consider a mere approximation to such a state of things, it would be sufficient to cause a general elevation of temperature. Nor can it be regarded as a visionary idea that amidst the revolutions of the earth's surface, *the quantity of land* should, at certain periods, have been *simultaneously lessened* in the vicinity of both the poles, and increased within the tropics. We must recollect that even now it is necessary to ascend to the height of fifteen thousand feet in the Andes under the line, and in the Himalaya mountains which are without the tropic, to seventeen thousand feet, before we reach the limits of perpetual snow. On the northern slope, indeed, of the Himalaya range, where the heat radiated from a great continent moderates the cold, there are meadows and cultivated land at an elevation equal to the height of Mont Blanc. If, then, there were no arctic lands to chill the atmosphere and freeze the sea, and if the loftiest chains were near the line, it seems reasonable to imagine that the highest mountains might be clothed with a rich vegetation to their summits, and that nearly all signs of frost would disappear from the earth.

"When the absorption of the solar rays was in no region impeded, even in winter, by a coat of snow, the mean heat of the earth's crust would augment to a considerable depth; and springs, which we know in general to be an index of the mean temperature of the climate, would be warmer in all latitudes. The waters of lakes, therefore, and rivers, would be much hotter in winter, and would never be chilled in summer by melted snow and ice. A remarkable uniformity of climate would prevail amid the archipelagoes of the temperate and polar oceans, where the tepid waters of equatorial currents would freely circulate. . . . .

"We might expect, therefore, in the summer of the 'great year,' which we are now considering, that there would be a predominance of tree-ferns and plants allied to palms and arborescent grasses in the islands of the wide ocean, while the dicotyledonous plants and other forms now most common in temperate regions would almost disappear from the earth. Then might those genera of animals return, of which the memorials are preserved in the ancient rocks of our continents. The huge iguanodon might reappear in the woods, and the ichthyosaur in the sea, while the pterodactyle might flit again through umbrageous groves of tree-ferns. Coral reefs might be prolonged once more beyond the arctic circle, where the whale and the narwal now abound ; and droves of turtles might wander again through regions now tenanted by the walrus and the seal.

"But not to indulge too far in these speculations, I may observe, in conclusion, that however great during the lapse of ages may be the vicissitudes of temperature in every zone, it accords with this theory that the general climate should not experience any sensible change in the course of a few thousand years, because that period is insufficient to affect the leading features of the physical geography of the globe." —*Principles*, Book i., chap. vii., pp. 121–131.

This is perhaps the most ingenious and elaborate

theory presented by Sir Charles Lyell in the whole course of his speculations to account for the geological conditions which he supposes to have once existed; and were the reality of those conditions admitted, it would in some respects form a plausible solution of the effects he refers to them. Instead, however, of being established by a scientific induction, it is a mere *supposition.* Not a pretence is made of demonstrating it by direct and indubitable evidence. Every one of its propositions that is made the basis of the inference he aims to sustain by it, is preceded by an IF, tall

> "As the mast
> Of some great admiral."

The only consideration he offers to support it is, that if the conditions and processes he supposes *are admitted*, they seemingly furnish a natural and adequate explanation of the variations of temperature and peculiar forms of vegetable and animal life, which he holds characterized the earth at certain stages of its ancient history. It contributes nothing, therefore, towards the verification of his general theory respecting the force by which the strata were formed, and the vast series of ages their deposition occupied. To treat it as a fact; to exalt it to the rank of a positive proof of that great hypothesis; to make it the basis of a rejection and confutation of the testimony of the Scriptures respecting the date of the creation of the earth, is truly an extraordinary misjudgment. The fact that it apparently presents an explication of the conditions and events it is invented to explain is no evidence of its truth. To admit the validity of such a method of establishing a system, would be at a blow to annihilate every fact of experience, and overthrow every truth of science. The theory of Buffon, of Burnet, of Whiston, of La Place, respecting the origin and laws of the world, might, by such a process, be as effectually established as that of Newton.

Its want of pertinence to the immediate purpose for which he employs it is not, however, its only disqualification for the support of his system; as he deserts in it the great postulate on which he professedly proceeds, that the forces that are producing changes in the earth's surface act without intermission and with a uniform energy; and tacitly assumes that those forces at certain crises operate with thousands of times their ordinary intensity, and give birth to changes immeasurably above the usual range of their effects; as it is inconsistent with the conditions he prescribes to himself, to suppose that under such a process, "the general climate should not experience any sensible change in the course of a few thousand years; because that period is insufficient to affect the leading features of the physical geography of the globe," which he supposes to be so wholly revolutionized. It would be impossible that such an elevation of a continent with lofty mountains in one part of the ocean, should take place simultaneously with a depression of an equal area of land with mountains of the same height in another; and yet at the same time, "the proportion of dry land to sea continue the same; the volume of the land rising above the sea be a constant quantity; and not only its mean but its extreme height be liable only to trifling variations; and both the mean and extreme depths of the sea be invariable," unless the change took place instantaneously, or at least was completed in so brief a space that the period occupied in it would not be of any geological consideration. For on no other condition could the proportion of dry land to sea, the volume of land above the level of the sea, and both the mean and extreme height of the mountains, continue the same. If the elevation, for example, of the supposed continent in the sea between Greenland and the Orkneys, took place at the same rate as the depression of the Himalaya mountains and Hindostan, and advanced so gradually as to be prolonged through a vast round of ages, it is manifest that Hindostan would descend beneath it thousands of years before the corresponding part of the arctic continent could emerge from its bosom. The submersion of Hindostan would take place in the early stages of the revolution; the ascent of the other at its close. During the vast period therefore that intervened, the proportion of dry land to sea, and of the volume of land rising above the level of the sea, instead of remaining constant, would, to that extent, be altered; and consequently an equal change would be produced in the mean and extreme depth of the ocean. Moreover, as there are great inequalities in the surface of Hindostan, a large part consisting of low plains, part of high table lands and elevated valleys, and part rising into lofty mountain ranges— other subordinate variations in the proportion of land to sea would take place while the submersion was in progress. A depression of two to three hundred feet would carry beneath the waters all the lower plain of the Ganges and a wide tract along the eastern coast of the peninsula, probably together equal to one third of the whole. A further descent of five hundred feet would leave nothing above the waves except the mountains, the table lands, and the high valleys that lie between the ranges or heights of the Himalaya. The table lands that slope from the Ghauts on the western side of the peninsula to the opposite coast on the bay of Bengal, rise from 1700 to 2800 or 3000 feet above the level of the ocean; and the lower of the high valleys of the Himalaya, 2000 feet. They would be submerged therefore by an additional descent of 1200 to 2200 feet. A further depression of 1200 to 1500 feet would carry beneath the waters other valleys of the Himalaya, that are at an elevation of 4000 to 4500 feet. There would then remain south of the Himalaya only the Vindhyan range of mountains, running across the peninsula, north of the Nerbudda to the western coast, and the western and eastern Ghauts, the former of which rise from 6000 to near 9000 feet.* There would thus be five or six stages in the submersion, at which great changes would take place in the proportion of the land to the sea, and of the volume of land rising above the water. Equal variations also in the opposite direction would result from the emergence from the ocean of those parts of the supposed arctic continent, that would correspond to these divisions of Hindostan.

It is physically impossible, therefore, that the changes he contemplates should take place without producing repeated and great variations in the average of the extent and the volume of dry land, and of the depth of the sea, unless they were wrought with such rapidity that the time which they occupied should be of no consideration. But to be accomplished with such rapidity would require an intensity of volcanic forces immeasurably transcending those that are ordinarily exerted in the modification of the earth's surface. The effects also would boundlessly surpass in magni-

* Macculloch's Geographical Dictionary; Articles Himalaya and Hindostan. Guyot's Earth and Man, p. 66.

tude any that are now in progress, or that have happened for many ages. Such a depression of one continent and elevation of another would produce movements of the ocean also, on a scale and of a violence immensely beyond those of ordinary disturbances of its bed by earthquakes. Wide-spreading deluges, and the wreck of islands and continents generally, would inevitably result from them.

He thus in his hypothesis completely deserts the theory of the uniform force and activity of geological agents, on which he founds his system; and tacitly raises those of fire and water to so vast an energy, and exhibits them as acting on so stupendous a scale, and dispatching their effects with such celerity, as to discountenance and set aside the grounds on which he builds his inference, that long periods have been employed in the deposition and modification of the strata. Of this purely supposititious character are many of the other solutions which he presents of the phenomena he attempts to explain; and such are the speculations also generally of those who maintain that the stratified rocks were formed by the geological agents that are now in activity, and at a rate essentially the same as that at which they produced their present

* We may indicate as examples, their theories respecting the production of gneiss, the origin of lime and chalk, the formation of salt and coal, the causes of denudation, the sources of drift, the deposition of alluvia, the periods at which different classes of animals began to exist, and a crowd of others.

effects.* They are mere conjectures or suppositions, not demonstrated facts, and present, therefore, no basis for a scientific induction of the inference they found on them of the great age of the world.

QUESTIONS.

What is their second postulate which is examined in this chapter? Is it clear from what has already been shown, that rivers had no important agency in the formation of the strata? What then are the agents by which, according to the theory, the strata must have been formed? What is the first objection to the theory that the strata are the work of such causes in kind and energy as are now in activity on the earth's surface? Ought it not to be demonstrated, instead of gratuitously assumed? Have geologists verified it by proofs? What course does Sir C. Lyell pursue in regard to it? What is the only consideration which he offers to prove it? But what points ought he to establish, in order that that consideration may demonstrate that which he alleges it as proving? Does he establish that point, or does he take it for granted? State his argument in a syllogistic form: first, in which all changes are affirmed to be the effects of the same causes; and next, in which all causes are affirmed to act with the same energy. Is it clear from these that he assumes in his premise the whole point which he affects to prove? What is the question which he should have debated? What is the question which he in fact debates? Does he thus try the question by a false measure? Does he pursue this course generally in his attempts to account for particular effects? State his mode of explaining the changes in the temperature of the earth. Does he establish this by a scientific induction, or does he merely affirm, that if the conditions he *supposes* are *admitted*, then the results for which he contends would follow? Is it not wholly unphilosophical thus to substitute hypotheses for facts; assumptions for proof? Might not the theories of Buffon, Whiston, La Place, and the author of the Vestiges of Creation, be established by that process, as well as his theory of the changes for which he attempts to account? Does he not also desert in it the postulate on which he professedly proceeds, that the forces that are producing changes on the earth act uninterruptedly, and with the same energy? State the mistake into which he falls in the representation that if Hindostan with the Himalaya mountains were slowly to sink beneath the ocean, and a continent of equal dimensions, a similar general surface, and like mountains, were at the same time to rise at the same rate from the ocean between the Orkneys and Greenland, the quantity of land that would rise above the ocean would, at any stage of the process, precisely equal that which would descend beneath it. Exemplify the error of that assumption. If two pyramids of equal dimensions were to pass through such a change of positions, is it not clear that the twenty feet of the base of the pyramid that sunk beneath the water, while twenty feet of the apex of the other rose out of it, would comprise hundreds and thousands of times as many cubic feet as the apex comprised? Are many of the solutions of facts which geologists offer as confirmations of their theory, of the same supposititious character, and contradictory to their own principles?

CHAPTER XII.

False Theories of Geologists respecting the Formation of the Strata.

BUT this great postulate of their system is not only merely hypothetical and unsupported by evidence; it is confuted, and shown to be wholly groundless, by the fact that many of the most extensive and important of the geological effects which it professes to explain, are not now in the process of production, nor the causes to which they owed their existence any longer in activity. If the assumption were correct that the forces by which geological effects are produced are in the main at all periods identically the same, act uniformly with the same energy, and generate the changes to which they give birth at the same rate, then every class of effects that has ever resulted from their agency would continue to be wrought by them at the present time, and on a scale as vast as at any former period. Nothing, however, is more certain than that many of the most important species of those effects are no longer taking place, and thence that the causes in which they originated are no longer in activity, at least in the conditions and forms in which they give rise to such products.

Such is the formation of granite. That rock is more extensive, exists in greater volume, and fills and has filled a more important office in respect to the sedimentary strata, than any other in the series. It is far the greatest and the most significant of the effects that are the subject of geological inquiry. It wraps, it is generally believed, the whole circle of the globe, and is the basis on which all the other formations rest; and it has come into existence, or received its present form, at least to a vast extent, since the formation of large portions of the rocks which now repose on it. Those masses of it indisputably which rise above the original level of the sedimentary rocks, and form the centres of the great mountain ranges, were formed and elevated into their present positions after the deposition of the strata that lie on their summits, or rest on their sides, and they are now accordingly referred by geologists generally to the close of the secondary, or to the tertiary period.

But no granite, so far as is known, is produced at the present time, nor has been since the formation of the masses that constitute the main element of the great mountain ranges, and were the instrument by which the sedimentary strata that clothe their sides, and rest on many of their heights, were thrown up. There is not the slightest proof, or probability even, that a particle of it has been crystallized for ages. What the conditions are, indeed, that are essential to its formation, are not fully known. It is generally held to be the result of fusion; but what the precise combination of causes is, or what the circumstances are in which they must act in order to unite the ingredients of which it consists in the proportions and forms that constitute its peculiarities, there are no means in the present state of the science of determining.

The greatest and most important geological process that has ever taken place on the earth's surface, and that was wrought on its greatest scale at a late period in the formation of the sedimentary strata, is thus wholly unlike any that is now in progress, or has been for ages, and confutes therefore the theory that the forces by which the crust of the earth was formed and modified, exist and operate with the same energy, and give birth to the same species of effects, and on the same scale, at all periods.

Gneiss, also micaceous, chlorite, and argillaceous schist, quartz rock, and other species that belong to the first series of the stratified formations, are not now in the process of deposition, and have not been for ages, nor are there any indications that the causes from which they sprang are any longer in activity. These also, though not universal, like granite, are very extensive. They underlie very generally, as far as is known, the secondary formation, and are, in many localities, of immense depth. They constitute proofs, therefore, as vast as they themselves are, that the geological forces by which the strata have been formed, do not act without intermission, and with an unvarying energy, and give birth to their effects at the same rate at all periods. If that were their law, these rocks, instead of being confined to the primary formation, would have been intermixed with the whole secondary and tertiary series, and would now be generating on as great a scale as they were in their own proper age. Can a more emphatic confutation be asked of the doctrine, that geological causes act at all periods with an unvarying energy?

Serpentine, greenstone, basalt, and nearly the whole series of trap rocks, also came into existence exclusively, so far as is known, at a period long past. They were first thrown up, it is generally held, after the completion of the primary series, and their epoch appears to have closed near the commencement of the tertiary. They were as manifestly the product of a limited period, and owed their existence to a condition of the globe that no longer exists, as the formation of granite, gneiss, quartz rock, old red sandstone, or any other rock, the production of which has ceased. To assume, as a self-evident proposition, that the causes by which these immense masses were thrown up from the unfathomable depths of the earth, through the vast series of crystalline, primary, and secondary rocks, are still in uninterrupted activity, and giving birth on an unvarying scale to the same effects, and make that postulate the basis of a theory of the whole series of formations, is to offer a contradiction to fact that is not often exceeded in boldness and extravagance.

Sand, gravel, and pebbles, are still more important elements of the earth's crust, that owe their existence to causes that are no longer in activity. They not only form, in a great measure, the loose unstratified mass that lies on the surface of the globe, but enter very largely into the composition of the principal layers in every group of strata throughout the secondary and tertiary formations—sandstones of every class, many conglomerates, and the arenaceous forms of shale and limestone—and constitute not improbably one-third of the whole mass from the lowest to the last of the fossiliferous beds. And they were all formed undoubtedly by chemical forces at the points and at the time of their deposition from the ocean; as there are no known agents by which, had they originated elsewhere, they could have been distributed over such vast spaces, and immixed so equably in the strata in which they are imbedded. Had the materials of which they consist been originally derived, as geologists maintain, from granite continents, and borne down to the sea by rivers, they still must have received their present form after their diffusion through the waters from which they were precipitated ; as their structure is not now crystalline like that of the quartz, felspar, mica, and hornblende of granite, but granular and concretionary, and the product therefore of a wholly different chemical agency. Their formation is, accordingly, one of the greatest and most peculiar of which the surface of the earth has been the theatre. The number of particles, grains, pebbles, and stones of larger size, that belong to this class in single layers of moderate extent, transcends immeasurably our powers of enumeration, and can be grasped only by Omniscience. How infinite then is the multitude that constitute their whole mass! Many of the strata of which they are the principal ingredient, are spread over vast areas, and of great depth. Groups of the old red sandstone are in some localities three or four thousand feet in thickness. Yet every one of those grains and pebbles, small or large, is of itself a proof of the error of the doctrine that the causes by which they were produced are still in activity, and perpetually giving birth to similar formations. Not a particle of sand or gravel, not a solitary pebble or mass of larger size, like those which are imbedded in conglomerates, has been brought into existence for ages. The supposition is, as we have already shown, inconsistent with the conditions that are requisite to such concretions. The silex that is now deposited on the earth's surface, is deposited from waters that are raised to an intense heat, and instead of uniting to form sand or gravel, takes the shape of incrustations on stems, leaves, and other objects on which it happens to be thrown down. As absolute proof as the lapse of many ages, without a solitary addition to their countless throng, can form, exists therefore, that neither the chemical agents are now in activity, nor the waters of the ocean in the conditions that are requisite to their production. The fancy that they are, is as palpably against the fact, and as irreconcilable with the laws that now govern the modifications of matter, as it were to imagine that new suns are forming in our firmament, or new moons generating to revolve with ours around our earth.

Such is the fact, also, with lime. No deposits of that mineral now take place on the surface, except such as is thrown up by springs, and is derived therefore from the strata over which those waters run : and that, on its deposition, forms a loose porous mass, essentially unlike the limestones from which it is drawn. Not a grain is added by the process to the general mass of the mineral. There is only a transference of particles from earlier formations that lie at a considerable depth, and union of them again at the surface in a new form. But if the causes that originally gave birth to the vast beds of limestone that occur throughout the whole series, from the earliest to the latest of the stratified rocks, are still in uninterrupted activity, and generating new deposits on as great a scale as at former periods, why is it that none of these new formations are noticed or discovered? Why is it that not a particle can be shown to be added to the aggregate? What can be more unscientific than thus to maintain the continued activity and undiminished energy of causes that once operated on so immense a scale and generated such massive products, though no fruits whatever are seen of their present agency; though the most indisputable proofs of their discontinuance for ages are presented in the fact, that through that long period they have not given birth to any of their proper effects?

Chalk was, in like manner, the product of peculiar causes acting in peculiar circumstances for a limited period. It is not, like limestone, sandstone, and shales, distributed in frequent beds throughout the whole series of the strata, but occurs only in a single group near the close of the secondary formation. Nor is it generally diffused like many of the earlier and later deposits, or found in all the localities where the other members of the group to which it belongs occur. Instead, it is confined to comparatively narrow limits.

"Respecting the geographical distribution of the cretaceous group . . . . throughout the British Islands, a large part of France, many parts of Germany, in Poland, Sweden, and in various parts of Russia, there would appear to have been certain causes in operation, at a given period, which produced nearly, or very nearly the same effects. The variation in the lower portion of the deposit seems merely to consist in the absence or presence of a greater or less abundance of clays or sands, substances which we may consider as produced by the destruction of previously existing land, and as deposited from waters which held such detritus in mechanical solution. The unequal deposit of the two kinds of matter in different situations would be in accordance with such a supposition. But when we turn to the higher part of the group, into which the lower portion graduates, the theory of mere transport appears opposed to the phenomena observed, which seem rather to have been produced by deposit from chemical solution of carbonate of lime and silex."—*Sir H. T. De La Beche's Manual*, p. 259.

The limitation of this formation to a single period and to a narrow area, is thus wholly irreconcilable with the theory that geological causes act at all periods and with a uniform energy. If that postulate were true, chalk should exist, and on as great a scale in the different groups of the primary and earlier classes of the secondary formations, as it does in the series to which it gives its chief characteristic. It should occupy a proportional place also among the tertiary strata, and be in the process of formation at the present time. No indications appear, however, of such formations since the commencement of the tertiary period. Can a more decisive proof be demanded of the error of that postulate? Can a proposition be advanced in more direct and palpable repugnance to facts?

Rock salt, in like manner, instead of being interspersed like sandstone, limestone, and shale, through the whole succession of the strata, as the theory of the uniform activity and energy of geological causes requires, is mainly confined to a single era. There are examples, indeed, of the rise of salt springs, as in this State, from the New York or Silurian system. Even they, however, are generally associated with the new red sandstone, or the groups with which that is immediately connected; and rock salt itself occurs chiefly in that formation. Though found in every quarter of the globe, it is not, like sandstone and shale, a universal deposit, but exists only in patches, or districts widely separated from each other. It is in some localities several hundred feet in thickness. Geologists, however, instead of being able to point out any exemplification in the processes that are now going forward of the mode in which it was formed, have not hitherto succeeded in presenting any probable theory of its origin.

"It is not surprising that the origin of rock-salt has been a subject of much inquiry among geologists; yet nothing like a rational theory has yet been offered. It is far easier to show that the most simple and obvious hypothesis is wrong or imperfect than to propose a probable one. The origin of gypsum is not less mysterious, even with every conjecture we can make respecting the presence and acidification of sulphur ; yet this inquiry has never excited the same anxiety. No rational explanation has yet been suggested ; and I have none to offer. But we must seek for the greater ambition of geologists on the subject of salt, in their wish to derive these deposits from the waters of the ocean in a simple and direct manner ; seizing on one obvious analogy only, to the neglect of other possible modes of explanation. That it has been the produce of the ocean is possible, since the rocks among which it is found are indebted for their existence to the same source. Yet no obvious method *of accounting for its peculiar appearances or limitation* can be engrafted on that general admission ; while it were as well for geology, and in other matters than this, if they who deposit pure rock salt in the Mediterranean at this day, would learn at least as much of chemistry as the 'Chemist' of three blue bottles. The desiccation of saline lakes will not account for it, because subterranean salt is far more pure than that which must be the produce of the evaporation of the sea. The mode in which it is disposed will not admit of this explanation ; and still less can any system of evaporation account for the concretionary structure of the salt of Cheshire.

"To these difficulties it must be added that the depth of sea-water required to produce in this manner some of the larger masses known in Europe, is incomprehensible. It might also be asked why marine organic bodies have never been found in or near it, and wherefore it is accompanied by gypsum. As it is lastly true that the strata which lie above it have been deposited from the ocean, it is impossible to comprehend how, under these circumstances, evaporation could have taken place. The subject is beset with difficulties—fortunately for the cultivators of a science which would lose the greater part of its attractions were there nothing left for them to explain. As to the theory which derives it from volcanic actions, it seems useless to discuss such a question, when no volcanic rocks accompany these deposits in the sandstone, and when, with some very slender exceptions, deposits of salt are not found attending on this class of rocks. Were this the cause, it would remain also to be explained why it is limited to the red marl."—*Macculloch's Geology*, vol. ii., pp. 293, 294.

"We shall not call in question that gem-salt, either pure or mixed with muriatiferous clay, may have been deposited by an ancient sea; *but everything evinces that it was formed during an order of things bearing no resemblance to that in which the sea at present*, by a slower operation, *deposits a few particles of muriate of soda on the sands of our shores.*"—*Humboldt's Narrative*, vol. ii., p. 262.

It is thus the product almost exclusively of a few periods, and of causes or circumstances so obscure and peculiar that no satisfactory theory can be formed of their nature. It presents a resistless confutation, therefore, of the postulate, that the causes of geologi-

13

cal effects are always in activity, and giving birth to their several results on the same scale. Why, if that be true, are not masses of rock salt found at every stage in the series, from the primary formations to the close of the tertiary? Why are they not now in the process of deposition in the bays and gulfs of the sea?

Coal is likewise the product of peculiar causes and a limited period; and of causes or conditions, that, so far from being understood, are as much in debate among geologists, as the origin of rock salt. That it was formed beneath the ocean and mainly of vegetables that had their growth on the land, are the only points in respect to which they are in any considerable measure agreed. It is held by one class that those vegetables grew where the coal lies, and by another that they were transported from a distance by rivers and currents. Some maintain that it had its origin in peat; and others in arborescent ferns and forest trees. That the principal beds are of a single period, proves that the causes by which they were generated acted only at that epoch; and that they are confined to a few limited areas, shows that they acted only in those scenes, and confutes the doctrine accordingly that the geological agents by which the strata were formed, have acted at all periods, and given birth to their effects at a uniform rate.

Coal ought, on that theory, to be found in as great

abundance in the primary and tertiary series as in the secondary, and to be forming as visibly and rapidly at the present period as any other geological effect that is now taking place.

But besides these and other classes of effects that were peculiar to the eras when they were brought into existence, and sprung from causes that are no longer in activity, it is equally apparent that some of the geological agents that are still producing changes on the earth's surface, instead of operating at all times with the same energy, must have acted during the formation of the strata with far greater intensity and on a much wider area than at present. This is admitted by many geologists.

"Although it is maintained in one of the most popular geological systems that the powers of nature are as active and energetic at the present as in ancient periods, still, after a survey of the whole subject, and of the evidence on which those views rest, doubts of their correctness remain in the minds of most geologists. That a more quiescent state would now prevail, and that the former violence of the elements should be restrained, or rather become more feeble by a more equable balance of the forces which act and react on each other, is agreeable to reason and the benevolence of the Great Architect of the universe."—*Emmons's Geology of the Second District of New York*, p. 17.

Thus the ocean, either from chemical elements immixed in it, the motion of its waters in tides and currents, or other causes, must have had a power of diffusing the materials of the strata that were introduced into it, over wide areas, that is altogether unknown at the present period. There are many strata of sandstone, limestone, and shale, that originally extended, there is reason to believe, without interruption, many hundreds, and perhaps even thousands of miles, the elements of which, therefore, as they were deposited at the same epoch over the whole area, must have been interfused through the whole body of the waters. And where the beds, after solidification, are fifty, one hundred, or perhaps several hundred feet in thickness, as the materials cannot all have been supported by the waters at the same time, the agents by which they were transported to the place of deposition must have continued in activity for a considerable period. But no such power of holding matter in solution or suspension, and distributing it over vast areas, is now displayed by the ocean. The clay, sand, gravel, and ashes that are now introduced into it by streams or volcanic eruptions, are thrown down near the points where they enter its waters, and produce no change whatever on its bottom generally. The slight force with which it now acts, and the narrow spaces to which its effects are confined, scarcely present an analogy to the vast scale on which it operated at earlier periods and the massy results to which it gave birth. To take the power with which it now acts as the gauge of its energy at former epochs, is as unauthorized and unphilosophical, as it were to make the slight effects which it now produces the measure of those of all other ages.

Next: The action of the ocean on the continents and islands in the erosion of mountain ranges, denudation of hills, or level tracts of strata, and scooping of valleys, which took place on a stupendous scale at former epochs, has no parallel in its present agency. Instead of sweeping over the land in resistless deluges, cutting passages for itself through rocky barriers, and ploughing channels betwixt the hills and across plains, it is now confined to its decreed place, and its proud waves are stayed by the limits God has assigned it. No greater contrast can be conceived than that which the limited energy with which it now acts in its narrow sphere, presents to the resistless power with which in former ages it swept the continents and islands, tore asunder their rocky ranges, cut deep gorges through the strata, and transported to new positions vast masses of the loose earths that form the present surface.

The fires, in like manner, that burn in the depths of the earth, and have acted a more important part than any other agent in producing the changes that have taken place on the surface, exerted their power on an immeasurably greater scale in former ages than at present.

This is seen from the immense formations at early epochs of granite, of which none, so far as is known, is now in the process of production.

It is seen from the vast masses of porphyry, greenstone, basalt, and other rocks of that class that are of volcanic origin, which are wholly the product, it is generally held, of the secondary, or the first stages of the tertiary period.

It is seen also from the great number of volcanoes in every part of the globe, once active and disgorging immense masses of lava, that have now for many ages been wholly extinct. The number that now burn without intermission is very small. They once amounted, there is reason to believe, to many thousands.

It is demonstrated in a still more striking manner, in the universal changes they produced in the surface in the upheaval and dislocation of the strata, and the elevation of the hills and mountains. These great effects are now referred by geologists universally to subterranean fires, or the evolution of heat by processes causing an intense fusion and expansion of the materials on which it acted; and the energies by which they were wrought must have immeasurably surpassed the most powerful that are now exerted in earthquakes and volcanic eruptions. All the expansive forces that have shaken the earth for ages united, would have been wholly inadequate, there is reason to believe, to throw up the Andes, the Himalaya, or the Alps. This is admitted by many geologists, who nevertheless maintain that vast periods have been occupied in the formation of the strata.

"If now we withdraw ourselves from the turmoil of volcanoes and earthquakes, and cease to measure them by the effects which they have produced upon our imaginations, we shall find that the real changes they cause on the earth's surface are but small, and quite irreconcilable with those theories which propose to account for the elevation of vast mountain ranges, and for enormous and sudden dislocations of strata, by repeated earthquakes acting invariably in the same line, thus raising the mountains by successive starts of five or ten feet at a time, or by catastrophes of no greater importance than a modern earthquake. It is useless to appeal to *time;* time can effect no more than its powers are capable of performing ; if a mouse be harnessed to a large piece of ordnance, it will never move it, even if centuries on centuries could be allowed ; but attach the necessary force, and the resistance is overcome in a minute."—*H. T. De La Beche's Manual*, p. 131.

The vast changes indeed that have been produced on the earth's surface, so far transcend the forces that are now in activity, as to render the supposition that they have resulted from their operation, an extravagance unworthy of the support of men of judgment and science.

This great postulate of their theory is thus, like the

other, wholly irreconcilable with the facts of geology, and the laws of chemical and mechanical forces. So far from having resulted from the agents that are now producing changes on the crust of the globe, and acting with their present energy, all the great processes by which the principal rocks, from the earliest to the latest, have been formed, have sprung from causes and conditions that were peculiar to the epochs when they were produced, and are no longer in existence; while the energy exerted at former periods by some of the agents that are now in activity, and the spaces on which they acted, were immeasurably greater than at present. The overthrow of that postulate involves the confutation accordingly of the inference founded on it of the vast age of the world. As the strata cannot have been formed by the feeble agents and slow processes which that postulate represents, the inadequacy of those agents to a rapid production of such stupendous effects, is no proof that immeasurable periods—which would add nothing to the strength or efficiency of such causes—must have been occupied in their production. That an insect would be unable to drag a heavy mass of matter from its place, though the effort was prolonged for countless ages, presents no ground for the conclusion that a similar period would be required for its removal by an elephant or a steam locomotive. Yet it is on such a transparent fallacy that the whole deduction proceeds of the vast age of the world, from the tardy rate at which geological causes are now giving birth to their several effects.

These main foundations of their theory being thus overthrown, the only ground that remains for its support, is that which is supposed to be furnished by the vegetable and animal relics that are imbedded in the strata. But their inference from them of the great age of the world, is equally unauthorized and unphilosophical.

In the first place, it is, like their other arguments, founded, in a great measure, on their theory of the agents and processes by which the strata were formed; not on the nature, condition, or mass of those relics themselves; and is built, therefore, on an assumption of the point which it professes to demonstrate.

In the next place: Neither the masses of those fossilized relics, nor the conditions in which they are preserved, present any decisive, or probable evidence that the immense periods which geologists assume were occupied in their growth and deposition. In respect to the coal formations, for example, lignites, and other vegetable fossils, the supposition of vast periods is not requisite at all to account for the growth of sufficient masses of vegetables to constitute such deposits. The vegetables existing on the globe at a single epoch, were they gathered into spaces commensurate with those that are occupied by the mineralized vegetables, are enough, not improbably, to constitute deposits of equal bulk. The difficulty, accordingly, of accounting for their vast dimensions, does not lie at all in their quantity, but in their transportation to the places of their deposition. But that is not obviated in any degree, by the supposition that great periods were occupied in its accomplishment. That supposition, indeed, is forbidden by the condition of the coal strata. That the leaves, stems, and trunks, of which they are formed, neither grew in the places of their deposition, nor were transported there gradually through a series of ages, is clear from the fact that they had undergone no decay, but retained their structure and forms uninjured when the process of their fossilization commenced. Had a long period passed during the accumulation of a stratum, those that were first deposited would have been decomposed, and changed into vegetable mould. The lowest layers, however, of beds that are ten, twelve, or fourteen feet in thickness, exhibit no traces of such a decomposition. The forms of the stems and leaves are there as distinct and perfect as in the layers at the upper surface. Had they been transported, and slowly accumulated there by streams and currents charged by detritus from continents or islands, there would have been a large mixture in them of earthy particles, such as now takes place in the deposition of trees, plants, and leaves at the mouths of rivers. But no such foreign ingredients are intermingled with them. The main beds consist, throughout their whole mass, of pure vegetable matter. These facts demonstrate, therefore, both that they were transported from other sites, and that their accumulation, deposition, and the first steps of their fossilization, were accomplished with great rapidity.

Nor are vast periods any more necessary to account for the animal relics that are buried in the strata. So far from it, the slightness of these remains presents a resistless demonstration that no such incalculable series of ages, as geologists assume, can have elapsed during their deposition. It is infinitely incredible, had the ocean and extensive continents and islands, been peopled through such immeasurable periods as thickly as they now are, that their relics would not have been imbedded in vastly greater numbers and masses in the strata. This is too apparent to admit of dispute in respect to all vertebrate animals, both of the land and the sea. If all the relics of those classes that have hitherto been found in different localities, are taken as a measure of the quantity that lies buried throughout the globe in the strata to which they belong, the whole mass can scarcely exceed the number that subsists at the present epoch—certainly not the crowds that people the land and sea in the lapse of one or two centuries. Of this any one may convince himself, who considers how countless the multitudes were of the wild animals that lived on this continent three centuries ago, or how innumerable they and the flocks and herds of tame animals are at the present period: what infinite hosts of fish people the waters of the torrid zone; and what armies of cod, mackerel, herring, and other tribes swarm at certain seasons on the coasts of New England, New Brunswick, and Nova Scotia. Multitudes equivalent to these, a few times repeated, would equal, there is reason to believe, the whole of like classes that are entombed in the strata. The difficulty in accounting for their deposition, accordingly arises, not from the greatness, but rather from the slightness of their numbers, compared to the period during which they may have been accumulating. Two or three centuries seem as adequate to their production as fifteen or twenty.

Such is the fact also with the relics of testaceous and infusorial animals, which exist on a scale, and are multiplied with a rapidity as much greater proportionally, than the vertebrate classes, as their dimensions are less than theirs. The seas along the shores in every part of the globe, but especially in the equatorial and temperate climes, swarm with infinite hosts of testaceous animals. Thus Mr. Darwin relates:

"The kelp" of the sea in high southern latitudes, sometimes—"grows to the length of sixty fathoms and upwards.

. . . Captain Fitz Roy found it growing up from the depth of forty-five fathoms.

"The number of living creatures of all orders whose existence intimately depends on the kelp, is wonderful. A great volume might be written describing the inhabitants of one of these beds of sea-weed. Almost all the leaves, except those that float on the surface, are so thickly incrusted with corallines as to be of a white color. We find exquisitely delicate structures, some inhabited by simple hydra-like polypi, others by more organized kinds, and beautiful compound Ascidiæ. On the leaves also, various patelliform shells, trochi, uncovered molluscs, and some bivalves, are attached. Innumerable crustacea frequent every part of this plant. On shaking the great entangled roots, a pile of small fish, shells, cuttlefish, crabs of all orders, sea-eggs, star-fish, beautiful holuthurniæ, planariæ, and crawling nereidous animals of a multitude of forms, all fall out together. Often as I recurred to a branch of the kelp, I never failed to discover animals of new and curious structures."—*Darwin's Voyage of the Beagle*, p. 240.

But the infusorial tribes pervade the waters at every point, and in some localities on a scale in numbers as far transcending that of the larger animals as their bulk is less. They swarm in such incalculable multitudes in some localities, as to give their color to the whole mass of the water over large areas.

"During a run of fifty leagues, the sea was constantly of an olive green color, remarkably turbid, but it then changed to a transparent blue. The green appearance of the sea in these latitudes I formerly ascertained to be occasioned by an innumerable quantity of small molluscous animals of a yellowish color contained in it. A calculation of the number of these animals in a space of two miles square and 220 fathoms deep, gave an amount of 23,888,000,000,000."—*Scoresby's Journal of a Voyage to the Northern Whale Fishery,* 1822, p. 18. See also pp. 351, 353.

"We entered on a zone where the whole sea was covered with prodigious quantities of medusas. The vessel was almost becalmed, but the molluscæ were borne towards the southeast with a rapidity four times that of the current. Their passage lasted near three-quarters of an hour. We then perceived but a few scattered individuals following the crowd at a distance, as if tired with the journey."—*Humboldt's Narrative,* vol. i., p. 72.

These and other forms of infusorial animals existed not improbably in far greater multitudes at those epochs in the formation of the strata, when the waters of the seas were charged alternately with much greater quantities than at present of silex and lime. The vast scale on which they exist, and the rapidity with which they succeed each other, is such, therefore, that instead of a long series of ages being requisite to account for the masses in which they are accumulated in certain localities, it would be inexplicable had such incalculable periods passed, that their relics had not risen to an immeasurably greater bulk. The cause, if supposed to act through an innumerable series of ages, would as far transcend the magnitude of the effect, as the vertebrate and testaceous animals of such incalculable periods would exceed in number the relics of their classes that are imbedded in the strata.

The whole ground on which they have founded their induction of the great age of the globe, is thus swept from beneath them. They not only have not established their theory by legitimate and adequate proofs ; they have not advanced a solitary consideration that yields it support. Their whole argument proceeds on postulates that are gratuitously assumed, and that are in blank contradiction both to all the great facts of the science and the laws themselves of matter. That so mistaken a system should have gained the assent and advocacy of so large a body of studious and talented men, is truly a matter of astonishment. The fact, indeed, that they universally and unhesitatingly concur in assigning a vast period to the formation of the strata, is sometimes alleged as a proof of the validity and amplitude of the evidence on which their judgment is founded. The unanimity and ardor with which they maintain it, and the disquietude and not infrequently discourtesy with which they receive a doubt of its truth, are certainly remarkable. Their concurrence, however, is seen to be entitled to but little weight, when it is considered that it is almost absolutely confined to this branch of their speculations—that there is not another question in the whole range of their system, in regard to which they do not entertain a wide diversity of opinion. They are not agreed, for example, whether the world, at its creation, was in a gaseous or in a solid form. They are not agreed in respect to the processes by which granite, gneiss, schist, and the other primary rocks were produced. They are not agreed in respect to the point at which the secondary series commences, the order of the strata, the sources from which some of their elements were drawn, nor the agencies to which they owe their peculiar structure. They differ in respect to the point at which vegetable and animal life commenced, and the forms which it first assumed. They entertain the most diverse and absurd opinions respecting the origin of limestone, coal, gypsum, chalk, magnesia, iron, and salt. They hold conflicting views in regard to the state of the globe at the epoch of the different formations, the forces by which the strata were dislocated, the causes by which the mountains were upthrown, the period at which land animals were first called into existence, and the origin of the races that now inhabit the globe. They differ likewise, to the extent of countless ages, in regard to the period that has elapsed during the formation of the strata. In short, beyond the simple facts that the strata have been formed since the creation of the earth, that chemical and mechanical forces of some kind were the principal agents in their deposition, and that the fossilized forms that are imbedded in them once belonged to the vegetable and animal worlds—there is scarce a topic of any moment in the whole circle of the science, in respect to which they do not maintain very diverse opinions; there is scarce a solitary point so fully ascertained as to be placed beyond doubt. Their unanimity in assigning a vast round of ages to the world, while they thus disagree in repect to *the nature of the processes to which they suppose those incalculable ages were requisite,* instead therefore of giving strength to their induction, indicates that the grounds on which it rests are mistaken. What can be more absurd than to suppose that an inference erected on such a mere mass of gratuitous assumptions and disputable theories, can be entitled to the rank of a philosophic induction? What can be more preposterous than to dignify a branch of knowledge in which there is so little that is settled, and so much that is in debate, with the lofty title of an accurate science? It cannot, as a whole, rise any higher, in a demonstrative relation, than the parts of which it consists; the conclusion cannot acquire any greater validity, than the postulates possess from which it is drawn.

They have not then, as their theory represents, unfolded and established a series of facts that are at variance with the scriptural history of the creation, and that render it certain that the earth had, at the epoch at which that dates its existence, already subsisted through innumerable ages; nor is there anything in their discoveries that detracts in the least from that inspired narrative. So far from it, as their speculations are built throughout on hypotheses, not upon facts; as their inference is drawn from supposititious conditions and imagined processes, not from causes and conditions that are real and capable of being verified; the fancy that they have convicted the sacred record of error, and demonstrated the vast age which they assign to the world by unanswerable evidence, is as groundless and mistaken as it were to imagine that the scriptural account of the creation is confuted by Buffon's hypothesis, or that Newton's theory of the motions of the planets is overthrown by Descartes' fancied vortices. The history of the creation in Genesis remains untouched. If it is to be controverted, it must be by proofs, not by assumptions; by arguments founded on a real, not on a supposititious world. When, however, the question of its truth is tried by its proper criteria, it will be found—as we shall show,—that instead of being confuted, it is corroborated by all the facts of the strata, and all the laws that govern the action of geological forces.

QUESTIONS.

What is the second objection to the theory respecting the uniform action of the causes by which the strata and other rocks that constitute the surface of the earth were formed? If their theory were true, would rocks, and formations of all kinds that were produced in the early ages of the globe, continue to be produced on a similar scale now? Is it a fact, however, that none of the most important classes of rocks are now in the process of formation? What is the first and most important species to which no accessions are now making? Describe it. What is the second? Describe it and its extent. What is the third? How extensive is it? What other elements of the earth's crust are not now in the process of augmentation? Are sand, gravel, and pebbles important constituents of the earth's crust? How were they probably formed? Is there any reason to believe, that one of this infinite multitude of granules, or large masses, has been formed for ages? How is it with lime? Are there any additions made to the mass? How is it with chalk? Was the formation of that, confined to a limited period? Is that admitted and maintained by geologists? How is it with rock-salt? Is that distributed like sandstone and limestone through the whole series of the strata; or is it confined within narrow limits? Is coal confined mainly to one great division of the strata, called for that reason, the carboniferous, not distributed through the whole?

Is it apparent also, that some of the geological agents that are still producing effects on the earth's surface, are not now acting with more than a moderate share of the energy with which they exerted their powers during the formation of the strata? Is this admitted by geologists? Is this true of the ocean? What is the first class of effects in respect to which this is apparent? What is the second class of effects in respect to which it is manifest? Is it true in regard to volcanic fires? Point out proofs of it. Is this admitted by geologists? What is the testimony of Sir T. H. De La Beche, respecting it? Do these several considerations show that this postulate of their theory, instead of being legitimate, is inconsistent with the facts of geology, and the laws of matter? What else do they allege to sustain their theory of the great age of the world? What is the first objection to their argument from the vegetable and animal remains that are buried in the strata? What is the second objection? Are there positive proofs in the condition of the great mass of fossilized vegetables, that they cannot have been accumulated and buried by a slow process, but must have been enveloped in the earthy matter in which they are interred, in vast masses at once, before decay had commenced? Is there any reason to suppose vast periods were requisite for the generation of the animals that are entombed in the strata? Is the number of those relics greater than the sea and land might have supplied in a very few centuries? Is it not incredible that if millions of ages, as geologists maintain, had passed while the fossiliferous strata were forming, an incalculably greater number would not have existed, and their relics been incorporated in the strata? Is not this preëminently certain in respect to the testaceous and infusorial tribes? State some of the proofs that they swarm in infinite numbers, both in the cold and the warm latitudes?

Is the whole ground on which they found their inference of the great age of the world, thus swept from beneath them, and the whole fabric of their theory shown to be based upon unauthorized assumptions, instead of facts?

CHAPTER XIII.

The Materials of the Strata, derived from the Interior of the Earth.

THE great question in theoretical geology on which the conclusion in regard to the age of the world—founded on the structure of its rocky crust—depends, respects the sources from which the materials of the strata were derived. If they are held to have been such that immeasurable periods were required for their removal and deposition in their present form, then an existence of corresponding length is to be ascribed to the earth. If they are held and shown to have been such that but a brief period was necessary to their transference and arrangement in the positions in which they now lie, then there are no geological grounds for assigning it a longer existence than that which is ascribed to it by the Maker himself in the history he has given us in his word of its creation.

Whatever views, however, may be entertained on that subject, it will be admitted by all who regard the earth as the work of the All-wise and Almighty Creator, that they were specifically designed by him, and the causes and conditions from which they sprang arranged for the purpose of giving them existence They are not the offspring of chance. They are not the accidental work of causes that might not have acted, or that might have generated a wholly different product, without affecting the end for which they were created. The marks of intelligence and benevolence with which they are everywhere stamped, and the important office they fill in determining the condition of the race, forbid such a supposition. It is by them, in an eminent degree, that the world is fitted to be the residence of such an order of beings as men;—beings that are fallen, that are to be divided into different communities, and subsist under separate governments; that are capable of civilization, of arts, of commerce, and of great advances in knowledge; that are to gain the means of subsistence and comfort by toil and ingenuity; and that are to be placed in a great diversity of conditions, that they may in every possible form act out their natures, and show the moral dispositions with which they are animated towards God and one another. This constitution of the earth has, accordingly, exerted a most decisive influence on their physical, social, and moral condition. It is in a very large degree because its crust is what it is, in the proportion of the land and water; in the form and position of the continents and islands; in the direction and height of mountains; and in the nature and situation of rocks, soils, and minerals, that the life and career of the human family have been what they have; and that the condition of the several branches of which it consists is now what it is, in respect to knowledge, arts, government, and religion. A different arrangement of even a few of its features would have made it in important respects a different world, changed the relations to each other of large portions of its population, given a different direction to their pursuits, generated other empires, and issued in a different history. Had the Alps, for example, instead of separating Italy from France, divided France from Germany, it would have given a different caste to the whole history of ancient and modern Europe. Had the Himalaya, with their lofty table lands, in place of dividing Hindostan from Thibet, been interposed between Germany and Russia, the climate, the productions, and the population would have been essentially changed, and the agency of the different tribes on one another, both in Europe and Central Asia, been altogether unlike what they have been. Had Africa, instead of projecting from Europe to the south, stretched to the west, and joined this continent, it would have given a different turn, in a great degree, to the affairs of the whole world. America might then have been known, perhaps, to both Europe and Asia many ages ago; and been invaded by hostile armies from Africa, or Africa been conquered by the tribes of this western world. Europe and the Atlantic side of North America would then have been isolated from the southern part of the globe, and could have had no such commerce, and thence no such arts, and therefore no such eminence in wealth, cultivation, and power, as they now enjoy. Had South America extended to the Pole, and had the islands that lie southward from Malacca joined that peninsula, and rising into a continent stretched down to the region of perpetual ice, the three great southern oceans would have been isolated; there then could have been no circumnavigation of the globe, and consequently there could have been no general commerce.

The existence also of such strata as constitute the surface of continents and islands, and their upheaval and dislocation in their present form, have had an almost equal influence on the pursuits and character of the nations that occupy them. Had it not been for the metals that were imbedded in them, there could have been neither arts nor commerce. Had it not been, for example, for the tin, iron, lime, and coal that were deposited beneath the soil of Great Britain, she could neither have had such an agriculture, such manufactures, nor such navigation. Had not the strata in which they and other important minerals are lodged, been elevated from their original position, broken into fragments, and exposed at the surface, they would have remained unknown, or from their inaccessibleness been without use; and she would have had but a barren soil and a scanty and uncultured population. It is thus by the provision of these means from which all the implements and enginery, and most of the materials of the arts are drawn, that man is armed with his power over the earth and sea, and made capable of appropriating them to his use, and rendering them the instruments of subsistence, comfort, and progress in all the forms of cultivation.

It is apparent, therefore, from the momentous influence it was thus to exert, that the investiture of the earth with such a surface was expressly designed by the Creator, and held an important place in the great system of measures by which it was to be prepared to be the habitation of men. It was an indispensable condition to his placing them in such situations, and exercising over them such a providential administration as he has; and thence a necessary condition to their being subjected to such a discipline, made capable of such pursuits and acquisitions, and exerting such agencies as have constituted the great features of their physical, social, political, and in an important sense, also, their moral history. No part of the constitution of the world has drawn after it a more important train of consequences. No part of it bears more clear and emphatic proofs that it had its origin in the sovereignty, wisdom, and benevolence of its author, and held a conspicuous place in his great scheme, as the Ruler of the world. Whatever, then, the causes were of the formation of the strata, they are to be regarded as having been expressly assigned to that work, and armed with the requisite power for its accomplishment; and whatever the sources were from which the materials of the strata were drawn, they were arranged by him in their several places, with a direct reference to the agents by which they were to be transferred to their present positions, and the uses to which they are now appropriated. The means and conditions were fitted to the results that were to be attained, with the same intelligence and skill that mark the adaptation of other physical causes to the effects which God employs them to produce.

This great truth is to be borne in mind in our inquiries in respect to the agents and processes to which the strata owe their existence. Instead of having come into being aside from the great purposes of the Almighty, or sprung from causes whose proper office was to produce a different class of effects, they are the work of agents, and the result of conditions that were expressly appointed for their production, and that, on completing them, had accomplished their mission. They are themselves as absolute proofs of the existence and agency of such causes in such conditions, and for that end, as the world itself is of the existence and agency of its cause. The fact that the agents by which they were produced, ceased to give birth to such effects, is a proof also that those agents are either no longer in existence, or at least no longer in activity in the circumstances that are requisite to the generation of such products. And the limitation of the effect to the point at which it terminates, was accordingly as much a matter of arrangement, as the agency was of the causes by which that effect was carried to that extent.

With these views, then, of the place which the present constitution of the globe holds in the great scheme of the divine administration, and the certainty that it is the result of causes and conditions that were expressly ordained to its production, let us inquire whence it was that the materials were derived that constitute the present surface of the earth, that has been formed since the creation of the globe itself.

Two theories have been entertained by geologists on this subject. The first is that which was advanced by Werner, who maintained that the whole rocky and earthy mass of the strata was originally held in solution by the waters of the ocean, and was gradually deposited by the agency of chemical and mechanical causes. But that is now universally rejected; as the waters of the ocean are wholly inadequate to the solution of such a quantity of matter; as there are no chemical forces by which such a mass and combination of elements could be at once held in solution in any volume of water however great; and no known laws of chemical agents by which such mixed substances held in solution could be separated and assorted in such a manner as to form strata differing in their composition like those of the crust of the earth. Instead of furnishing any explanation of the problem which it professes to solve, it embarrasses and confounds it by false assumptions and palpable contradictions to the laws of matter.

The other theory is that now generally held, which represents the materials of the strata as having been drawn from pre-existing continents and islands of granite, that were gradually disintegrated, borne down by streams to the sea, and spread by tides and currents over its bottom. But this, as was shown in a former chapter, is equally groundless and unphilosophical; as there are no proofs that such continents and islands ever existed; while it is certain from the elevation which is ascribed to them, and from the laws that govern the disintegration and transportation of such masses, that they cannot have been the source of the materials from which the strata were formed.

But if the materials of the earth were neither originally held in solution in the waters of the ocean, nor derived by disintegration from pre-existing continents and islands, it is manifest that, at least in the main, they must have been drawn from the interior of the globe. We shall, accordingly, endeavor, to show that that was their origin; and that it supersedes the necessity of assigning to the earth any earlier date than that which is ascribed to it by the history in Genesis of the creation and deluge.

In order to accomplish this, it is not necessary that we should demonstrate directly *from the strata themselves*, that they were thrown up from the depths of the earth, and arranged in their present form *within the period* that is implied in the Mosaic history of the world from its creation to the remodification of its surface at the deluge. All that it is requisite for us to prove, is simply that it was compatible with the laws of nature, and therefore possible and probable; as that being shown, the consistency of the facts of geology with the Scriptures is established. And that we shall accomplish by proving first, that all the ingredients that enter into the composition of the different species of rocks and soils, originally existed in masses in the interior of the earth; next, that vast volumes of them have been thrown up from the depths where they were first placed, and become parts of the present surface of the earth; and thirdly, that there have been agents in the proper conditions, and of sufficient force, to have ejected the whole body of the sedimentary strata, and within the periods during which, according to the sacred narrative, they must have been formed. If these points are established, as the formation of the strata will be shown to have been practicable within the period that elapsed from the creation to the change of the earth's surface at the period of the deluge, no ground will exist in the strata themselves, for referring the creation of the world to an earlier date than that which is assigned it by the sacred history. This we shall, accordingly, now proceed to prove.

In the first place, then, there is the most ample certainty that all the various substances that enter into the composition of the present surface of the earth existed originally, and still exist within its depths. The chief of those substances are silica, alumine, lime, soda, potash, iron, magnesia. Of these, silica exists in far the greatest quantity; constituting, probably, at least one-half of the whole mass of the rocks and soils. Its proportion in granite is usually about seventy-five per cent., to thirteen or fourteen of alumine, eight or nine of potash, nearly two of iron, a trace of lime, and one or two other ingredients. This rock is now universally regarded as having been thrown up from beneath the primary stratified deposits, and must have come, therefore, in a large measure from a depth in the earth, and demonstrates accordingly the existence in its interior of the several elements that enter into its composition. Felspar, mica, and hornblende, instead of simple minerals, are formed by the union of those elements in different proportions. In felspar there are of

Silica, . : .	64·04	Potash, . . .	13·66
Alumina, . . .	18·94	Lime, . . .	0·76
	Oxide of iron, . . .	0·74	

In hornblende, the proportions are usually

Silica, . . .	45·69	Magnesia, . .	18·79
Alumina, . . .	12·18	Protoxide of iron, .	7·32
Lime, . . .	13·83	—— of magnesia, .	0·22
	Fluoric acid, . . .	1·50*	

Several of these elements, however, enter in much larger proportions into the composition of lavas. Thus of the felspathic minerals in volcanic rocks, there are in

	Silica.	Alumine.	Lime.	Magnesia.	Soda.	Iron.	
Anorthite,	43·79	35·49	18·93				and a trace of iron, magnesia, soda, and potash.
Labradorite,	53·48	26·46	9·49	1·74	4·10	1·60	and a trace of potash.
Andesin,	59·60	24·28	5·77	1·00	6·53	1·58	1·08 potash.
Albite,	69·36	19.26	0·46		10·50	0·43	—— "
Orthoclase,	65·72	18·57	0·35		1·25		14·02 "
Adularia,	65·59	17·97	1·34		1·01		13·99 " †

In the volcanic rocks or lavas themselves these ingredients exist in still different proportions. Thus in trachytes and other volcanic rocks, silica ranges from 49·21 to 73·46; alumina from 12·04 to 20·80; iron

* H. T. De La Beche's Geol. Observer, pp. 34, 35.

† H. T. De La Beche's Geological Observer, p. 352. Daubney's Description of Volcanoes, p. 13.

from 1·49 to 11.84; lime from 0·45 to 8·83; magnesia from 0·39 to 7·96; potash from 1·42 to 7·16; and soda from 4·29 to 7·98, with sometimes a trace of manganese.*

In the recent lava of Kilauea, Hawaii, silica ranges from 39·74 to 59·80; protoxide of iron from 16·91 to 33·62; and soda from 4·83 to 21·62.†

In basalt, silica ranges from 44·50 to 59·5; alumina from 11·5 to 17·56: iron from 4·64 to 20.‡

In all these volcanic rocks, which it is universally held are ejected from deep abysses in the earth, all the great elementary substances of which the strata consist are thus conspicuous ingredients. They present the most decisive proofs, therefore, that the various substances that enter into the composition of the strata were placed by the Creator originally in masses in the interior of the earth.

But besides the place which lime holds in these volcanic rocks, it has in some instances been thrown up in masses from the interior of the planet. Thus Mr. Emmons describes many veins, dykes, and larger bodies in the northern section of this State that are undoubtedly of igneous origin.

"The origin of primitive limestone, I apprehend, is precisely the same as that of all the granitic compounds. It is

* De La Beche's Geol. Observer, p. 353.

† Dana's Geology of the U. S. Ex. Exped., p. 200.

‡ De La Beche's Geol. Observer, p. 396.

not as some, perhaps, would be ready to suggest, produced by the overflowing of a molten mass of granite on a sedimentary limestone, thereby decomposing it ; and by which portions the most intensely acted on would be raised in a vaporous state, and made to penetrate the mass of cooling granite above. Geologists, in speaking of limestone, seem to be averse to the admission that it may form *a portion of the interior of the earth,* or even to admit that it may exist there at all ; but there seems not a particle of sound reason against the doctrine that it may be as common in the earth as silex, or any of the simple or compound rocks. There is, in fact, more reason to make this inference, for many of the phenomena of nature speak of its being, and proclaim its existence. From what I have seen of it, I am disposed to consider it as one of the igneous products, having its origin in a mode corresponding to all the unstratified rocks, and differing from them merely in the materials of which it is composed."—*Emmons's Geology of the 2d District of New York*, p. 26.

He accordingly cites a number of localities in which large masses, dykes, and veins of limestone project up from beneath into granite, in such a manner as to render it indisputable that they were forced from below in a state of fusion like the veins and dykes of granite, quartz, trap, and other species that have been driven up from beneath by heat into the primary and secondary formations.

Iron, also, has been ejected from the interior of the

earth in masses, as is seen from its existence in rocks that are of igneous origin. Thus of the magnetic oxide Mr. Emmons states:

"Masses of ore appeared to be coeval with the rock which incloses them; or such a view comports best with many facts and phenomena which are brought to light in mining. If this is sustained by future investigations, it will necessarily follow that the original formation must have been influenced by the same agents as those which were concerned in the production or modification of the materials composing the rock. The rock which incloses the ore is clearly unstratified; from which we are also to infer the igneous origin of the inclosed mass of ore. We are clearly driven off from every other mode of formation: the theory of electro-magnetic agency appears out of the question."—*Emmons's Geology of the 2d District of New York*, p. 90.

Other passages might be quoted from him and others, that present the same fact. We have thus the most indisputable proofs that all the great elements of the strata—silex, alumine, lime, potash, soda, magnesia, and iron—existed originally in the interior of the earth. The materials were lodged there on a vast scale, for the formation by their transferrence to the surface of precisely such composite rocks as those which now constitute the covering of the globe.

Immense masses of these substances that were

originally deposited in the depths of the interior, have actually been ejected to the surface, and now form a part of the earth's rocky vesture. Thus all the unstratified rocks—granite, porphyry, greenstone, serpentine, hypersthene, basalt, and all the varieties of trap, as well as the lavas and tuff of modern volcanoes, are universally admitted to be of igneous origin, and to have been elevated from the interior of the earth; and they together constitute a very considerable part of the crust that rises above the level of the sea. The Andes of South America, for example, extending from the Isthmus to Cape Horn, with a breadth of from 30 or 40 to 500 miles, cover, it is supposed, about one sixth of that continent, and rising from three or four thousand to fifteen or eighteen thousand feet, irrespective of the highest peaks, have undoubtedly—with the ranges that lie eastward of them in Venezuela, at the sources of the Oronoco, and in Brazil—several times the bulk of the other parts of the continent that lie above the line of the ocean; and they consist mainly of granite, porphyry, trachyte, andesite, basalt, and other igneous rocks, of which silex, alumine, lime, iron, potash, and soda, are the chief constituents. All these immense masses were thrown up to the surface, it should be considered, subsequently to the deposition of the principal stratified rocks; as is seen from the fact that they bear on their sides and summits vast bodies of the primary, secondary, and tertiary strata, that, anterior to their upheaval, were spread over the areas, at the bottom of the sea, they now occupy. Their elements existed in the depths of the earth, therefore, at the period of the formation of the strata, and constituted probably but a small portion of the immeasurable stores that were there treasured up. They prove, accordingly, that there was at that epoch an ample stock of them in the recesses of the earth for the formation of the strata. Nor have they been exhausted by the vast quantities that have been transferred to the surface. They continue to be thrown up by all the active volcanoes, and hold as large a place in the composition of their lavas, as in those that were ejected ages ago: and they continue still, there is every reason to suppose, to exist in exhaustless abundance in the interior of the globe. That a large share of the volcanoes from which they were once emitted, have sunk into inactivity, is owing to the exhaustion of the combustible or chemical agents in which their fires had their origin; not to the want of silica, alumine, lime, soda, and potash, that were, it is to be presumed, the subjects on which their fires acted, rather than the direct cause itself of their combustion.

We have the most ample evidence, therefore, that sufficient stores of them were originally treasured up in the depths of the earth to furnish the materials of the sedimentary strata. There is enough of them there now—for aught that can be shown or rendered probable—to furnish a similar rocky covering to a score of such worlds as ours.

QUESTIONS.

What is the great question on which the conclusion in respect to the age of the world depends? What condition of the sources from which the materials of the strata were derived, would prove that a long series of ages was required for their formation? What condition would show that they might have been formed in a brief period? Is the structure of the earth in its present form, to be considered as having been expressly ordained by the Creator and for most important ends? Has this peculiar constitution and structure of the earth, exerted a great influence on the condition and life of man? Show how. Would a different arrangement even in a few leading features have made the earth a different world, to its population? Exemplify it in respect to the Alps. Show what effects would have followed, had the Himalaya been placed between Germany and Russia. What effects might have resulted, had Africa, instead of projecting to the South, stretched Westward and joined this continent? What change in navigation would have been produced, had this continent extended to the Southern Pole? Has the fact that the strata consist of such elements as they do, and are thrown up into such positions, exerted a vast influence on the condition and pursuits of the human race? Exemplify it in respect to Great Britain. Are these great features of the globe then, to be regarded as not merely casual, and of little significance; but as among the most essential in the constitution of the world, in order to fit it to be the residence of such a race of intelligences? Are they the work of causes that were especially fitted for their production? And does the fact that those causes have long since ceased to act, show that they were commissioned to produce but a limited effect, and that that effect has been accomplished?

What is the theory which Werner advanced respecting the formation of the strata? Is that now rejected? What is the theory now generally held? Is that also mistaken? If the materials of the strata then, were neither originally held in solution by the waters of the globe, nor drawn from the surface of granite continents by disintegration, and transported to the ocean by streams: from what other quarter must they have been derived? What then is the view of their origin which we are to maintain? If we show that the materials *may* have been thrown up from the interior of the earth, and with such rapidity that the strata may have been formed, betwixt the creation recorded in Genesis, and the deluge, or the second and third century after the event; will that be sufficient to vindicate the sacred record from the charge of being contradicted by the facts of the strata?

What then is the first consideration that proves that they might have been formed in that period? What are the chief substances of which the strata consist? Which of these enters most largely into the composition of rocks and strata? Does it exist in inexhaustible quantities in the interior of the earth? In what proportion does it enter into the composition of granite? What other elements are united with silica in that rock? In what proportion do they exist in volcanic rocks? Has granite, as well as the volcanic rocks, been thrown up from the interior of the earth? Is lime sometimes thrown up in masses? State instances. Is iron also ejected from the depths of the earth? Cite examples. Have we then proof that all the main elements of which the strata consist, are lodged in vast masses in the recesses of the earth?

What is the second consideration which proves that the strata may have been derived from that source? Enumerate the great classes of rocks that have thus been ejected from the depths of the globe?

What great ranges of mountains on this continent, consist mainly of these rocks? When were they thrown up; before, or subsequently to the deposition of the principal series of the strata? Do they show that immense masses of the elements of which they consist, must have been created by the Almighty in the deep regions of the earth, out of which they have been thrown to the surface? Do these elements continue to be ejected by all the volcanoes that are still active? Do these facts sufficiently prove that there originally were ample stores of them there to furnish materials for the construction of the strata?

CHAPTER XIV.

The Materials of the Strata; derived from the Interior of the Earth.

There were chemical and mechanical agents also in existence and activity at that period, of sufficient power to transfer those materials from the depths of the earth to the surface, and unite them in the forms in which they now subsist in the strata. That such agents have existed and acted in the deep abysses of the earth where those substances were deposited, and with far greater energy and on a far larger scale than was requisite to that effect, is seen from the fact that it was by their action that all the mountains of the globe, and in a great degree the whole mass of the continents and islands, were raised from beneath the ocean to their present elevation. And the masses thus moved that lie beneath the line of the sea, are probably hundreds of times greater than those that rise above that line. The base of the mountains or bottoms of the columns that were upheaved, lie probably many times the distance below the surface that their summits stretch above it. The force that was exerted in upheaving them was, therefore, immeasurably greater than was requisite to the elevation to the surface of the contents of any one of the strata that can be supposed to have been thrown up at a single effort. The whole mass of a mountain, however great in weight, was to be lifted at once. Of the materials of a stratum forced up in a continuous current, like the waters of a spring or the lava of a volcano, only a small portion was to be supported at the same time. The weight at any moment, for example, of the column of lava borne upwards in the cavity of Etna or Hecla, at a period of the most violent eruption, is but that of a feather to the mountain itself, compared to the vast and inconceivable weight that was uplifted at the elevation of the Alps from the fathomless abysses of the earth in which their massy granites were elaborated. The lofty pinnacles and mounds of that range are themselves, indeed, but trifles, probably, in comparison of the vast bed extending down an immense depth in which they are rooted, that must have been elevated at the same moment along with them. Agents, then, have in fact been acting in the depths of the planet, and elevating the substances deposited there to the surface, that were of even greater energy than is ordinarily exerted in volcanoes, and than was necessary to the gradual ejection of the materials of the strata in the long series of ages that was occupied in their formation.

The forces, however, that are exerted in volcanic eruptions, and the volume of matter ejected by them on the surface in brief periods, is sometimes immense. Thus the current of lava thrown up in 1783 by Skáptar Jokul, one of the principal volcanoes of Iceland, was like that of a great river, and soon filled up deep valleys and spread over extensive plains.

"On the 11th of June, Skáptar Jokul threw out a torrent of lava which flowed down into the river Skapta and completely dried it up. The channel of the river was between high rocks, in many places from 400 to 600 feet in depth, and near 200 in breadth. Not only did the lava fill up this great defile to the brink, but it overflowed the adjacent fields to a considerable extent. The burning flood, on issuing from the rocky gorge, was then arrested for some time by a deep lake which formerly existed in the course of the river between Skaptardal and Aa, which it entirely filled. . . . On the 18th of June, another ejection of this liquid lava rushed from the volcano, which flowed down with amazing velocity over the surface of the first stream. By the damming up of the mouths of some of the tributaries of the Skapta, many villages were completely overflowed with water, and thus great destruction of property was caused. The lava, after flowing for several days, was precipitated down a tremendous cataract called Stapafoss, where it filled a profound abyss, which that great waterfall had been hollowing out for ages, and after this the fiery current again continued its course.

"On the 2d of August, fresh floods of lava still pouring from the volcano, a new branch was sent off in a new direction; for the channel of the Skapta was now so entirely choked up, and every opening to the west and north so obstructed, that the melted matter was forced to take a new course, so that it ran in a southeast direction, and discharged itself into the bed of the river Haverfisfliot, where a scene of destruction scarcely inferior to the former was occasioned. These Icelandic lavas—like the ancient streams that are met with in Auvergne and other provinces of central France—are stated to have accumulated to a prodigious depth in narrow rocky gorges; but where they came to wide alluvial plains, they spread themselves out into broad burning lakes, sometimes from twelve to fifteen miles wide, and one hundred feet deep. When the fiery lake which filled up the lower portion of the valley of the Skapta had been augmented by new supplies, the lava flowed up the course of the river to the foot of the hills from whence the Skapta takes its rise. . . . The eruption did not entirely cease till the end of two years.

"The extraordinary volume of the melted matter produced in this eruption, deserves the particular attention of the geologist. Of the two branches which flowed in nearly opposite directions, the greater was fifty, and the lesser forty miles in length. The extreme breadth which the Skapta branch attained in the low countries, was from twelve to fifteen miles; that of the other about seven. The ordinary height of both currents was 100 feet, but in narrow defiles it sometimes amounted to 600."—*Lyell's Principles*, vol. i., pp. 342–344.

The matter thrown out of this volcano principally in a few days of a single season, was thus enough probably to spread a stratum ten or twelve feet in thickness over six or seven thousand square miles.

The eruptions from Kilauea, Hawaii, are also on a vast scale:

"The discharge from the large lake during the night of the 17th, must have been equal to fifteen million cubic feet of melted rock. This undoubtedly found cavities to receive it on the line of the eruption. It is impossible to calculate the discharge from the smaller, or Judd's lake, but supposing it had continued as rapid as it was at the first filling, it would have thrown out, by the time I was there next day, upwards of two hundred million cubic feet of lava. It will readily be perceived, with such a flood, it would be possible within the lapse of a period comparatively short, geologically speaking, for a mound the size of Mauna Loa to be heaped up. However large the above numbers may seem to be, we have reason to suppose from appearances, that the 'boiling up' and overflow of the terminal crater of Mauna Loa must have been far greater; so much so, indeed, that the outpourings of Kilauea cannot bear a comparison with it. Its whole height of more than six thousand feet above the plain of lava, appears to be entirely owing to the accumulation of ejected matter."—*Wilkes's Narrative of the U. S. Exploring Expedition*, vol. iv., p. 178.

In an eruption which commenced on the 30th of May, 1840, and continued three weeks, a far greater mass was ejected.

"The first appearance of the lava at the surface occurred in a small crater about six miles from Kilauea. The next day another outbreak was distinguished farther towards the coast. Other openings followed, and by Monday, the 1st of June, the large flow had begun which formed a continuous stream to the sea, where it reached on the 3d of June, destroying the small village of Nanawale. This flood issued from several fissures along its whole course, instead of being an overflow of lavas from a single opening ; the lowest being at an elevation of 1,244 feet, as determined by Captain Wilkes, at a point twenty-seven miles distant from Kilauea, twenty-two miles from the first outbreak, and twelve from the shores. . .

"The lavas rolled on sometimes sluggishly and sometimes violently, receiving at times fresh force from new accessions to the fiery stream, and then almost ceasing its motion. It swept away forests in its course, at times parting and inclosing islets of earth and shrubbery, and at other times undermining and bearing away masses of rock and vegetation on its surface. Finally, it plunged into the sea with loud detonations. The burning lava on meeting the waters was shivered, like melted glass, into millions of particles, which were thrown up in clouds that darkened the sky, and fell like a storm of hail over the surrounding country. Vast columns of steam and vapors rolled off before the wind, whirling in ceaseless agitation, and the reflected glare of the lavas formed a fiery firmament overhead. For three weeks this terrific river disgorged itself into the sea with little abatement. Night was converted into day on all eastern

Hawaii. The light rose and spread like morning upon the mountains, and its glare was seen on the opposite side of the island. It was distinctly visible for more than one hundred miles at sea, and at the distance of forty miles fine print could be read at midnight. . . .

"From the period, thirty-six hours, which the lava required to reach the sea, an average velocity of four hundred feet an hour is readily deduced, as stated by Captain Wilkes. Yet as the lavas issued from various fissures along the course, the result cannot be correctly compared to an *overflow* of fluid ; it is rather the rate of progress of the eruption than of the motion of a flowing liquid.

"The thickness of the stream of lava was estimated by Dr. Pickering as averaging ten or twelve feet. In some places it was not over six feet. The whole area, judging from the surveys, covers about fifteen square statute miles ; and reduced to feet, and multiplying by the depth, 12 feet, gives, for the amount of ejected lava, 5,018,000,000 cubic feet ; to which, if we add for the previous ejections of the same eruption, three more square miles, it gives 6,023,000,000 of cubic feet for the whole amount of lavas which reached the surface.*

"We have a still more accurate means of estimating the amount of lavas which passed from Kilauea, in the actual

* This calculation, however, if we understand it, respects only the mass of the lava that remains on the surface between Kilauea and the shore. It takes no notice of the vast cataract that plunged into the ocean during the three weeks of the eruption. If that were taken into the account, the whole sum that was ejected would be seen to be immensely greater than this estimate.

cubic contents of the emptied pit. The area of the lower pit, as determined by the surveys of the Expedition, is equal to 38,500,000 square feet. Multiply this by 400 feet, the depth of the pit after the eruption, we have 15,400,000,000 cubic feet for the solid contents of the space occupied by lavas before the eruption, and, therefore, the actual amount of the material which flowed from Kilauea. This is two and a half times the amount obtained from the estimated extent of the eruptions. The difference may be accounted for partly on the ground that fissures were filled as well as surfaces overflowed, and also that there may have been eruptions beneath the sea not estimated.* This amount is equivalent to a triangular ridge eight hundred feet high,

* Here there is an omission also from the estimate, of that portion of the lava that was precipitated into the sea. It is assumed also that no lava was ejected except what was drawn from Kilauea; and that no accessions were made to the stock in that reservoir during the progress of the eruption by fresh emissions from the abysses beneath; the first of which was possible and the last certain, and on a great scale. The estimate must necessarily be in a large degree conjectural; but if conformed to the data furnished by Captain Wilkes, must greatly transcend Mr. Dana's calculation. Captain Wilkes represents the breadth of the stream at its entrance into the ocean as three-fourths of a mile, or 3,960 feet; and the rush of the current to the sea as at the rate of 400 feet an hour. Let us suppose the breadth of the column precipitated into the sea to have been 3,500 feet, its average depth 10 feet, and the length of the current that made the plunge in twenty-four hours, 9,000 feet; the mass, at that rate, precipitated into the ocean in twenty days, would be 6,300,000,000 cubic feet; to which, if the mass remaining on the surface, as estimated by Mr. Dana, 5,018.000,000, be added, they will form an aggregate of 11,318,000,000 cubic feet. If to these the proportion he supposes to have been absorbed by fissures be added, the whole sum will be near 20,000,000,000.

two miles long, and over a mile wide at base."—*Dana's Geology of the U. S. Ex. Expedition*, pp. 188–192.

The materials of the strata, however, were not thrown up from the interior in the form of lava—as they exhibit no marks of fusion—but of mud or a liquid tide, much like that, probably, which is ejected by the mud volcanoes of Italy, South America, and the Crimea. It seems probable that the first volcanic ejections were neither in the form of molten lava, nor attended with flames or excessive heat. If materials like those of the granitic masses which now constitute the general floor on which the stratified and volcanic rocks rest, originally formed the exterior of the globe, as their crystallization has taken place since their creation, they may be supposed to have existed at first in the form of particles, and were not improbably at the surface promiscuously mingled with each other, so as to form on the first continents and islands, a proper soil for the plants which were made to spring from them. As all the rocks, indeed, of which we have any knowledge, whether crystalline or stratified, have been formed since the creation of the elements of which they consist, we may justly assume that the surface of the earth to the depth which they now occupy, whatever that may be, was in its primitive state, in the form of dust, or without cementation in hard masses. If such was its state, the water of the ocean would naturally have descended into it, and as long as it met with no other substances than those that constitute granite, as it would have excited little more chemical action than sea water now does on pulverized granite, its chief effect would have been simply to moisten and soften the mass, and render it susceptible of a more easy displacement when subjected to the impulse of a powerful force from beneath. On the supposition, then, that the water descended to a depth equal to that of the present volcanic fires, which is, probably, at least fifteen or twenty miles below the surface, ere it came in contact with elements like iron, for example, and sulphur, which it could excite to powerful chemical action, and that it was then decomposed, a violent heat developed, and vast volumes of expansive gases generated; the effect would have been an upheaval of the softened mass at the points where that action became energetic, and at length the opening of a passage to the surface, by chasms extending, perhaps, long distances, through which the imprisoned forces beneath would have found vents; and the main discharges from which, at first, would obviously not have been molten lava, nor mud raised to a great heat, but the softened earth itself nearest the surface, and subsequently from greater depths. All the force of a powerful volcano may thus be supposed to have been employed for a long time in the seasons of its activity, in the propulsion to the surface of such unfused materials as form the great elements of the strata, ere burning lava began to be ejected; and this supposition is corroborated by the fact, that it was not till the primary and secondary strata had been formed that the igneous rocks began to appear on the surface.

Another important effect of such a process would have been, that that portion of the earth's surface which was expanded upwards beneath the ocean, would have been exposed by its elevation to the violent action of waves and tides, and currents, and swept off and spread, like that ejected from the depths below, over the surrounding surface. On the intermission of such an eruption, the chasm would speedily have been obliterated by the action of the waters on the softened mass, and soon, perhaps, no other indications of it remained, than the greater thickness near it of the stratum it had formed, than at a distance; as strata usually thin out regularly from the point or line where they attain their greatest depth.

Views very similar to these were several years since suggested by Mr. Bakewell, an eminent English geologist, for the purpose especially of accounting for the limestone and chalk formations. Thus, he says:

"In referring to the vast magnitude of ancient volcanoes,

I have stated that they had, doubtless, an important office to perform in nature; and can it be unreasonable to believe that *the earth itself is the great storehouse where the materials that form its surface were prepared, and from whence they were thrown out upon the surface in an igneous, aqueous, or gaseous state, either as melted lava, or in aqueous solution, or in mechanical admixture with water in the form of mud, or in the comminuted state of powder or sand?* Inflammable and more volatile substances may have been emitted in a gaseous state, and become concrete on the surface.

"These primæval eruptions, judging from the size of the ancient fissures and craters, may have been sufficient *to cover a large portion of the globe.* Nor can it be deemed improbable that still larger and more ancient craters have been entirely covered by succeeding eruptions. In proportion as the formation of the surface advanced, these eruptions might decline and be more and more limited in their operation.

"It is not necessary to suppose that these subterranean eruptions consisted only of lava in a state of fusion. The largest active volcanoes at present existing, throw out the different earths intermixed with water in the form of mud. Nor should we limit the eruptions of earthy matter in solution or suspension to volcanic craters; the vast fissures or rents which intersect the different rocks, may have served for the passage of silicious solutions to the surface. We know of no instance in nature of silicious earth being held in aqueous solution, except in the waters of hot or boiling springs; and hence it seems reasonable to infer that many silicious rocks and veins have been deposited from subterranean craters at a high temperature. Calcareous or cretaceous matter is also ejected during aqueous volcanic eruptions. According to Ferrara, streams of liquid chalk, or chalk in the state of mud, were ejected from the mud volcano of Macaluba, in Sicily, in 1777, which in a short space formed a bed several feet in thickness. Beds of limestone may have been formed by similar calcareous eruptions, in which the lime might be sometimes in solution, and sometimes mechanically suspended ; and the numerous remains of testaceous animals in limestone appear to indicate that the calcareous solutions were favorable to the growth of animals whose coverings contain so much calcareous matter. Nor is it necessary to suppose that these aqueous eruptions were always sudden, and attended with violent convulsions, for when a passage was once opened they may have risen slowly, and have been diffused in a tranquil state, and by gradual deposition or condensation, may have enveloped the most delicate animals or vegetables without injuring their external form.

"If the geologist can admit such a condition of the ancient world as above described—a condition which on a smaller scale might be proved to have existed since the period of authentic history ; if he will further admit, that before the formation of chalk, a great portion of what is now England and the northern continent of Europe, was covered by a deep ocean, interspersed with islands and surrounded by ancient continents—and this few modern geologists will deny—then if we allow submarine aqueous eruptions of calcareous matter either in solution or mechanical suspension, and eruptions of silicious solutions from thermal waters, to have been poured over the bottom of this deep and ancient ocean, we shall have all the circumstances required to form thick beds of chalk, interspersed with layers and nodules of flint. . . .

"My object in directing the attention of geologists to this subject, is to show that *strata may be formed more rapidly* than they are generally disposed to believe; and that the feeble operations of natural causes in our own times, however similar in kind, bear no proportion in their intensity to the mighty agents that have formed the ancient crust of the globe."—*Bakewell's Geology*, pp. 351–355.

A similar suggestion in respect to the origin of limestone was made by Mr. Featherstonhaugh, in his Report in 1835.

"The general deposits of calcareous matter on the globe have been by some persons attributed to the exuviæ of animals, without stopping to inquire whence those animals derived the solid parts they have left behind them. As we know not that animals have the power of forming lime from other mineral elements, we are compelled to suppose that the calcareous matter forming their osseous structure, their testaceous and crustaceous coverings, preceded them. In considering the primitive rocks, we have perceived that forces of great power, and unknown in modern times, have been in action in the earlier periods of the planet—forces which even now continue occasionally to act, though feebly and rarely. As to the manner in which the statuary limestones were produced, there is much ambiguity. We know, however, that mineral springs, both thermal and cold, deposit carbonate of lime in great quantities, as they come in contact with the atmosphere. The prodigious deposits of this character form a cold mineral water in the Sweet Springs valley in Virginia, which presents one of the most rare geological phenomena; the no less interesting travertine deposited by the Hot Springs of the Washita in Arkansas, both of which localities I visited this last year; and similar phenomena in various parts of the world, render it quite possible that some extraneous calcareous deposits, lying amidst the primitive rocks, *have come from the central parts of the earth in a state of aqueous solution*, and have subsequently received their high crystalline character from being in contact with ignigenous rocks in an incandescent state. With springs of such a character in action, the animals of those times could be at no loss for calcareous matter in favored localities.

"In the grauwacke we have beds of limestone, derived, for aught we know to the contrary, like the statuary limestone in the primitive series, from solutions ejected from below, alternating with schistose and sandy beds of probable mechanical origin."—*Featherstonhaugh's Report*, 1835, *on the country between the Missouri and Red Rivers*, pp. 20–25.

Such as we have already shown, is the theory in respect to the origin of limestone advanced by Dr. Emmons. We cite from him another passage.

"The opinions of geologists in relation to the origin of limestone have been hitherto unsettled. From the great amount of limestone in the strata which may be inspected, it has been supposed that animals possessed the power of forming it, or of combining its elements. This view or theory seems to be wholly unnecessary; for what reason have we to infer that it is a material less common *in the interior of the earth* than silex or alumine? And if it is common, it may find its way to the surface by the same means as the materials composing other rocks.

"Leaving here the opinions of other geologists, I will state that there are two points which it will be my object to establish: 1st, That it is a rock of igneous origin; and 2d, That it is unstratified, which follows from the establishment of the first point: or, if the last proposition is placed first—viz. that the rock is unstratified, its igneous origin seems to follow with equal certainty; so that the points to be proved are really reduced to one."—*Emmons's Geology of the Second District of New York*, p. 38.

He proceeds, accordingly, to establish these points by proofs drawn from the rock in a great number of localities.

Mr. Hall adopts the same theory to account for the formation of some of the sandstones of the western district of this State.

"If we might be permitted to hazard a conjecture as to the changes and their causes going on at the time of the deposition of these different divisions of the Medina sandstone—we should incline to the belief that the lower shaly deposit was the product of *a mud volcano*, rapidly ejected and spread over the surface, rendering the sea turbid and discolored to such a degree as to prevent the existence of any organic forms. Afterwards the cessation of the volcanic action allowed the deposition of the grey quartzose mass ; the materials having perhaps the same origin as the grey sandstone which was formed previous to the commencement of the Medina. Although at this period there was no matter ejected from the volcano, still it may have produced oscillations of the surface, causing alternate deep and shallow water, or deep water in some places and shallow in others. Subsequently, towards the close of the grey deposit, the volcano broke forth again with renewed energy, destroying all the organic forms which had come into existence during this comparatively quiescent period, and overwhelming the whole with another deposit of mud like that below. Again, after a time the subterranean action appears to have become more quiet, gradually subsiding, and allowing an increase of sandy matter from some other source. Lastly, towards the termination of the deposit of mud, and when the sand had increased considerably, we find an abundance of vegetable forms, . . . and the whole series terminating with the grey division, marked by that singular fossil, the Dictuolites."—*J. Hall's Geology of Western New York*, p. 40.

We have the most decisive evidences, therefore, that the great agents that have acted in the depths of the earth where the substances of which the strata consist were originally deposited, were abundantly adequate to transfer them to the surface in the state that was requisite to their conversion into the rocks into which they were formed.

QUESTIONS.

What is the third fact which shows that the strata may have been derived from the interior of the earth? What proofs are there of it? Was the force by which the mountains were upheaved far greater than was requisite to eject a current of lava or other liquid matter from the deep recesses of the earth? Is the force, however, exerted in volcanic eruptions sometimes very great? Give an example of it in Iceland. Give an example in Hawaii. Were the materials of the strata however lavas? What was their state, probably, when ejected into the ocean? Have the crystalline, as well as other rocks, been formed since the creation? What was the form, probably, of the earthy matter which originally constituted the exterior of the globe? Would the water of the ocean, resting on such a bottom, naturally descend in it to a great depth? If in descending ten, fifteen, or twenty miles—the supposed depth of the present volcanic fires—it came in contact with extensive depositories of iron and sulphur, would it not have excited them to a chemical action that would have decomposed it, developed intense heat, generated vast volumes of gas, and thereby caused an upheaval of the soft and pliant mass of earthy matter above; and at length, by forcing passages to the surface, driven it in torrents and rivers into the ocean? Would that part of the surface that was upheaved be acted on also by the waves and currents, and its matter swept off and spread over the bottom of the surrounding sea? Have views like these of the sources from which the matter of the strata was drawn, sometimes been presented by geologists? What is the intimation which Mr. Bakewell presents in respect to it? What are Mr. Featherstonhaugh's suggestions respecting the source from which the treasures of lime were drawn that form the immense beds of that mineral? What other writers have presented similar views? Are there ample proofs, then, that the great agents that have acted in the interior of the earth have been of adequate strength to force the substances to the surface of which the strata are constructed?

CHAPTER XV.

The Materials of the Strata—Derived from the Interior of the Earth.

THESE agents were adequate to the transferrence of the materials of the strata from the interior to the surface, in the period that is represented in the Mosaic record as having intervened betwixt the creation of the earth and the remodification of its surface at the flood. Sixteen hundred, eighteen hundred, or two thousand years were as ample for the work, as sixteen or eighteen thousand, or the immeasurable round of ages which geologists represent as having been occupied in the derivation of the materials of the strata from granitic mountains and continents that were to be disintegrated and transported to the ocean by the feeble agents that are now reducing the rocks to dust, and conveying their detritus to the sea. That the materials for such a process were deposited in the depths of the earth throughout its whole circuit, is seen from the fact, that the whole mass of the granite which is now elevated into the atmosphere, and which lies beneath the stratified formations, has, in the judgment generally of geologists, been raised to fusion by heat from beneath, and received its present crystalline form since the deposition of the primary strata. There is no reason to suppose that a particle of that rock was brought into existence in its present state by the creative fiat. It is the work of powerful chemical and mechanical forces that have since acted on the silex, alumine, potash, soda, lime, iron, magnesia, and other ingredients of which it is constructed. But if that took place in the manner we have supposed, by the evolution of heat in the depths of the earth, the first effect of which was the propulsion to the surface of vast masses of silex, alumine, lime, potash, soda, magnesia, iron, and other elements that enter into the composition of the strata, in the form of minute particles, moistened or rendered liquid by water, then, manifestly, the causes of the propulsion of these materials to the exterior existed beneath every point of the surface, and were as universal as the strata themselves are that have been formed from them. They were undoubtedly, therefore, at least as adequate to the production of the latter effect as they were of the former. Indeed, if the views we have presented of the process are correct, the fusion of the granitic elements, which originally lay at the surface, could not have been produced by the evolution of heat in the abysses beneath, without first producing chasms and vents at innumerable points, and forcing up into the superincumbent oceans immense volumes of the moistened materials that lay between the surface and the great subterranean laboratory from which the heat and the explosive forces generated by it proceeded.

Let us suppose the waters of Lake Superior to be drained, and its bed scooped down through the whole series of stratified and crystallized rocks that lie beneath it, till a region were reached at a depth perhaps of fifteen or twenty miles, where, let it be assumed, a vast magazine is treasured up of volcanic materials. Let us then suppose the chasm to be filled by successive layers, each hundreds or thousands of feet in thickness, of silex, alumine, lime, potash, soda, iron, magnesia, and a proportionate share of the other elements that entered into the composition of the strata, in minute primitive particles. Let us suppose the waters of the lake then to be readmitted to its bed, and gradually to descend through it till they reached the magazine of volcanic matter, and generated an expansive force by which the superincumbent mass should be pushed upwards; it is manifest that that portion of the upper layer, at the points where the impulse from below was the greatest, would be the first that would be raised above the general level and mixed with the waters of the lake; and that if it were silex, it would, on being subjected to the proper agencies, form quartz rock or sandstone; if alumine, with an intermixture of silex, it would form marl, or some species of schist; and if lime, limestone. The effect of the impelling force from beneath, however, especially if large volumes of gas were driven upwards, would soon be to open a passage to the surface by a vein or chasm, through which a current of the moistened or liquid matter would be driven up into the waters of the lake, and diffused over its bottom; and if that process were continued, a portion of each layer in the series would be raised to the surface and spread in a stratum over the bed of the lake —before a stream of melted lava would mount through the passage and pass into the waters, or shoot into the atmosphere. But such a stupendous enginery acting, with slight intervals, at innumerable points throughout the circuit of the globe, would have been amply adequate to throw the whole materials of the strata on the surface in the lapse of fifteen, sixteen, or eighteen hundred years. Such a period would, indeed, seem excessive rather than too short for such a work. Such powerful agents, acting at points not more numerous than those at which igneous rocks and lavas have been driven to the surface, would undoubtedly have been sufficient for that effect.

We have thus the most ample evidence of the existence at that period of the requisite materials and agents in the proper conditions for the accomplishment of that work. We shall now proceed to show that this view of the origin of the strata is corroborated and verified by a variety of considerations.

It is confirmed by the great number of the points

at which igneous rocks and lavas have been forced up to the surface. The number of volcanoes that burned during the formation of the secondary and tertiary strata was not only far greater than at present, but in the ratio probably of hundreds to one. Their traces are seen on a vast scale in many regions where no eruptions have taken place for centuries. Thus they are very numerous in Central and Southern France, sixty cones being distinguishable in the single province of Auvergne. They exist in great numbers in Germany, Hungary, Transylvania, and Styria. In Northern, Central, and Southern Italy they are very frequent; in Sicily, also, Sardinia, and the neighboring islands. Traces of them are seen in Spain and Portugal. Their relics exist on a great scale in the islands of the Grecian Archipelago, and throughout Asia Minor. They are seen also in Syria, Southern Arabia, Persia, Northern and Eastern Asia, and the islands of the Chinese seas. Most of the islands of the Atlantic, and—except those of coral—nearly the whole of the vast crowd that stud the Indian and Pacific oceans, have been the seat of volcanoes; and craters that no longer burn are found in great numbers along the whole line of the mountains that skirt the Pacific coast, from the Arctic ocean to Cape Horn. If the number still active in different parts of the globe is, as is supposed, from one hundred and seventy-five to two hundred, the whole series that have burned at successive periods must undoubtedly amount to many thousands.

But the number of points at which igneous rocks—granite, porphyry, basalt, and trap—have been forced up to the surface, is immensely greater. Some, or all of them, are found in almost every considerable district of the globe. Though there are no traces in the British islands of modern volcanoes, granite, porphyry, greenstone, hypersthene, basalt, and trap form the crust, or lie immediately beneath the soil in England, Scotland, Ireland and the Hebrides and Orkneys, in thousands of places, indicating that there has been at least an equal number of passages from the molten abyss beneath, through which first the materials that lay above it, and then a portion of its own contents, have been driven up to the surface. In this country no lavas occur throughout the wide space betwixt the Mississippi and New Brunswick, or the great lakes and the Atlantic; yet granite, porphyry, hypersthene, hornblende, greenstone, serpentine, basalt, and trap, rise to the surface, or tower into the atmosphere in myriads and perhaps hundreds of thousands of places, so distinct from each other as to show that the passages through which they generally made their way to the surface were separate from each other. They are equally numerous also on other portions of the globe. Half as many channels of ejection from below, and probably a much smaller number, would have been adequate for the transfer to the surface, in a very few centuries, of a sufficient mass of materials for the formation of the strata. That such a vast number of openings have been formed from the interior, through which immense volumes of matter have been thrown up and incorporated in the crust of the globe, demonstrates, at least, the possibility and probability that it was through them or others of a like nature that the silex, alumine, lime, soda, iron, potash, and other elements of which the strata are built, were forced up into the oceans and seas from which they were deposited.

It is corroborated by the deposition of the great elements—silex, alumine, and lime—of which the strata consist, in separate layers, instead of a promiscuous mixture;—silex constituting sandstone chiefly; lime forming limestone and chalk; and alumine, potash, and soda, which are conspicuous ingredients of felspar, entering, in a large measure, into the composition of shales, clays, and marls. That the ingredients of the strata are treasured up in masses separately from each other in the depths of the earth, is demonstrated, as we have already shown, by their being often separately ejected and embodied in the igneous rocks. Their distribution into separate strata is explicable, therefore, on the supposition that they were drawn from such depositories, and not on any other theory of their origin. Had they been formed, as geologists generally maintain, from the detritus of granitic mountains and continents that was transported by rivers to the sea, instead of being separated from each other and arranged in distinct layers, they would have been deposited in a confused mass together. But if ejected successively from different depositories in the recesses of the earth, they would naturally continue separate, in a great degree, on their transfusion into the waters of the sea, and be deposited in beds by themselves. They would receive that disposition, whether they were drawn from repositories placed in a series beneath each other, like that in which they are arranged in the strata, and thence had egress in succession at the same channel, or whether each one, descending in a column into the depths of the earth, was thrown up through a passage that was limited to itself. Either of these hypotheses furnishes a solution also of the partial intermixture of the strata sometimes seen at their juncture, or the passage of one into another, of which the common theory presents no explanation. The ejection of their elements through the same or different passages, in immediate succession, would naturally cause a mixture of those of their particles that were held in suspension in the waters of the ocean at the same time, or in close succession to each other. That this view of their origin thus naturally accounts for these conspicuous characteristics of the strata, that are inexplicable on any other theory, is a strong proof of its truth.

It is confirmed by the solution it furnishes of the diffusion of the strata over wide spaces. On the theory held by geologists, the spread of a stratum of gneiss, quartz, sandstone, arenaceous limestone, or any other similar deposit over a large area, is wholly inexplicable. It is inconsistent with the forces that govern the transportation and deposition of pebbles, gravel, and sand in water, that, being borne down to the sea by streams and rivers, they should be transfused through its mass and deposited equally over hundreds, and even thousands of square miles. As the currents by which they are supposed to be borne forward are checked by the resistance they meet on entering the ocean, gravel and sand of every description are immediately carried by their weight to the bottom, and are no more subject afterwards to be transferred to other places than any other parts of the shore or bed of the sea. That the waves, currents, and tides should remove them and spread them into strata over regions scores and hundreds of miles in length and breadth, is physically impossible. If, however, the materials of the strata were thrown up from the depths of the earth into the waters of the ocean in the form of the primitive minute particles in which Newton and other philosophers regard matter as originally created, their diffusion over wide spaces would naturally result from their lightness and mobility under the action of the tides, currents, and waves of the sea. Driven up into the mass of the waters by the impulse that forced them from below, they would be borne off by the current the stream in which they entered created, and continue for a period to float, like the impalpable particles that are held in solution or suspension by the Mississippi, Ganges, and other great rivers; and when thrown to the bottom, would form at first a liquid mud that would, by its own gravity, spread on every side and seek a level, as water at the surface, though partially thickened with light mud, flows in every direction till it finds a level. Silex or lime forced up in that form through numerous channels, widely distributed, into the ocean that spread from Vermont to the Rocky Mountains, would naturally have been diffused, by the forces to which it would have been subjected, over as large an area as is occupied by any of the sandstones or limestones of that region; and the layers in which it would at length have been deposited, would naturally have thinned out also from the centres from which they were spread, so as to vary at different points in thickness, as the sandstones, limestones, and shales of that region vary.

The union of their particles in granules and grains took place probably at their deposition. The causes that determined them to assume those forms are not known. That they were peculiar, however, to that era, is seen from the fact that grains of silex and felspar are no longer formed where those substances are deposited from water. The supposition that they assumed the shapes in which they now exist in the strata, at the time of their deposition, or cementation into solid rock, is as compatible, for aught that is known, with the laws of their formation, as the supposition that their concretion into grains took place at an earlier period.

These views are confirmed by the explanations they furnish of the elevations and subsidences of portions of the crust of the globe, which appear to have taken place during the formation of the strata, and that occasionally occur still.

Had the earth been, as is very generally maintained by geologists, in a state of "fusion from intense heat" when it began to be overspread with its solid crust; and if, as they hold, its interior (with the exception of a stratum of a few miles' thickness on its surface) has continued in that condition, no such elevation or depression of parts of its rocky covering could have taken place; nor could there have been an ejection of any of its liquid elements to the surface by volcanic forces. In order to an elevation of any portion of its solid crust, or propulsion of a part of its interior matter to the surface, a fresh evolution of heat and generation of gases, creating a pressure outward, would be necessary. But such a molten condition of the interior would preclude the possibility of either of those processes. A fresh evolution of heat and generation of expansive gases could only take place by a fresh and powerful action on each other of chemical substances and agents, by which portions of their elements would assume new forms, enter into new combinations, and release, in the process, vast volumes of heat that had before remained latent. But in such an ocean of molten lava no substances or agents of that nature would exist. Every particle of its matter being—by the supposition—already in intense fusion, it would have reached the maximum of the chemical agency in that form of which it was capable, and given out all the latent heat and discharged all the gases which it could yield. The chemical action accordingly of its several parts on each other having terminated, they would have sunk into repose and been incapable of any further change by virtue of their own powers, than a gradual loss of their caloric by conduction through their rocky envelope to the ocean and atmosphere without. All elevation of any part of the crust of the globe, or a propulsion of lava to the surface by the agency of such a molten ocean, would consequently be impossible. How could forces of such vast energy as would be requisite to lift a portion of the earth's crust, thirty, forty, or fifty miles in thickness, and extending through several degrees in length and breadth, be generated by a chemical agency, when there were no chemical substances or agents within the globe capable of acting on each other in such a manner as to develop an additional measure of heat, and expand the matter of which they consisted into larger dimensions? How could passages be forced outward to the surface, and immense volumes of gas and melted matter be driven with resistless violence to the surface, when the mass within was necessarily in a state of absolute repose, and no elements existed in it that were capable of yielding a fresh expansive force? A volcano ejecting a fiery flood from such a world would be as impossible as it would from a vacuum.

That theory, therefore, not only furnishes no solution of the elevations and depressions to which the crust of the earth has been subjected; but it exhibits those and all other processes of the kind as impossible. No volcanoes could have existed, no earthquakes could have taken place, no elevation of mountains, no dislocation of the strata could have been wrought by the action of forces from within had its constitution and conditions been what that hypothesis represents. That none of the great number of practical and speculative geologists and chemists who have advocated that view have caught a glimpse of consequences that would result with such certainty from the condition of the earth which they suppose, and the laws of chemical action, is truly surprising. They appear to have adopted the theory without looking at the implications which it involves.

On the view, however, of the earth's structure which we have advanced, all the phenomena of earthquakes and volcanoes, and the upheaval, depression, and dislocation of the surface, are naturally explainable. If vast masses of chemical substances were placed in separate repositories in the depths of the earth, that were susceptible, on being acted on by water, electricity, or other agents, of giving out immense measures of heat, generating vast volumes of gas, and exciting a combustion, by which the matter with which they were in contact would be raised to intense fusion, the expansion their action on a large scale would create, would, of necessity, either upheave the crust of the globe that rested on them, or force a passage through the crust, and relieve itself by an expulsion of the imprisoned matter till an equilibrium were restored. If the materials by which that heat and combustion were excited, were at length exhausted, and the temperature subsided to its original point, a space would then be left vacant in the interior commensurate with that which was originally occupied by the volume of matter that had been ejected to the surface; and if that space, instead of a great depth, were spread like a stratum over a wide level, the weight of the incumbent mass might, from the distance of the points on which it rested, force it to descend and fill up the vacuum. An elevation, a depression, and a dislocation of the surface, would thus naturally result from such an action of those causes; and there is no other view on which an upheaval or depression of a part of the earth's crust can be accounted for. As an upheaval and expulsion of matter to the surface could only result from a fresh evolution of heat producing an expansion of the substances on which it acted; so a subsidence could only result from a diminution or discontinuance of that expansion, by a diminution or cessation of the evolution of heat, in consequence of which, the upward pressure ceasing, a vacancy would be created, and the superincumbent crust, deprived in a measure of its support, would sink under the force of gravity till it met a firm basis. How could an area of the surface sink down a distance towards the centre, unless the space into which it descended had become vacant? If the support that had always upheld it remained unaltered, to what cause would it owe its depression? But how could a cavity of dimensions adequate for such a movement be produced in the depths of the earth, except by a transferrence of the materials, that originally occupied it, to the surface? And how could they be transferred to the exterior, except by an expansion of the matter that lay beneath or behind them, and occupation of the space from which they were expelled? How, on the other hand, could that expansion cease, and the matter that had last filled the recess it had created, subside into its original dimensions, except by a discontinuance of the chemical action of which that expansion was the effect? And what could occasion such a discontinuance, except the exhaustion of the chemical substances in which that action and the evolution of heat it had caused, had their origin? There are no other known causes and processes from which those results could spring? As then, wherever a subsidence has taken place, the vacancy into which the depressed crust descended must have been created by the expulsion to the surface of the substances that had originally occupied it, wherever those ejected substances were not, in some measure at least, in the form of lava, they must—so far as they were not purely gaseous—have been unfused, and consisted, therefore, either of dry or moistened particles, or been held in suspension or solution in water. But there are many localities in which elevations and subsidences appear to have taken place where no traces are seen of lava, or any species of igneous rock. The substances, therefore, which at those localities have been thrown up to the surface from the space into which the subsiding crust descended, *must have been unfused, and entered, in the manner we have supposed, into the composition of the strata.* In what other form can they have been ejected? or what other disposition can have been made of them? No unfused silex, alumine, lime, magnesia, soda, or potash, are found on the surface, except that which is incorporated in the sedimentary strata and the loose soils that rest on them.

This view of the causes of the elevation and depres sion of the earth's crust admits of their occurrence as often during the formation of the strata as appearances indicate that they have taken place, and suggests the reason that subsidences have been followed by upheavals, as well as upheavals by subsidences. If the chemical and combustible elements in which a volcano has its origin, are distributed in layers so varying in breadth and thickness that the quantity exposed to the action of the fire is at sometimes far greater than at others, or the layers or masses in which they are arranged are separated by barriers that for a time intercept the progress of combustion, variations will naturally occur, like those which actually take place in its activity, and transitions at times from violent ebullition to repose and apparent extinction, and from repose to sudden and violent eruption. It would give rise also to such alternate elevations and depressions as portions of the earth's crust appear to have undergone. An exhaustion of the materials to which the fire had access, would be followed by a season of inaction, a discontinuance of the upward pressure, and thence a descent of the mass above, from the loss of its support, into the vacant recess; but the fires reaching a new depository of combustibles, perhaps by a slight train, perhaps by the shock of an earthquake breaking down barriers, or opening fresh chasms, it would burst out afresh, rage with its primitive violence, and produce a new upheaval of the crust that lay between it and the atmosphere. But how could such alternations of activity and repose take place if the whole interior of the globe were maintained uniformly at the same point of intense fusion? How could a second upheaval occur, if, instead of an occasional augmentation, a perpetual diminution of heat took place—as must, were the common theory true—by conduction to the ocean or air through the surrounding strata?

That these and other kindred processes to which the earth has been subjected, which are wholly inexplicable on the theory generally held by geologists, thus admit of a satisfactory explanation on the view we have advanced of the earth's structure and the derivation of the strata, is a decisive proof that that view is correct.

This view of the origin of the materials of the strata, and the consequent subsidence of the crust of the earth into the vacuum their removal had created, suggests an explanation of the accumulation of the vast mass of tree-ferns and other vegetables in the localities where they have been converted into coal. That the materials from which the coal was formed did not in the main grow where the coal lies, is apparent from the immense bulk that was required for beds that are of any considerable thickness; and from the fact that that of which the bottom of the strata was formed, exhibits no more marks of having undergone decomposition or decay than that which lay at the top. The traces of stems, branches, and leaves, are as distinct and perfect in the lower divisions of the strata, as at the centre or surface. The whole, therefore, of which a layer was constituted, must have been deposited at once. How, then, were they conveyed thither? How, for example, was the immeasurable mass of which the principal stratum was formed extending from the Delaware to the Mississippi, and from the Appalachians nearly to the lakes, and of a depth in many places of ten, twelve, or fourteen feet, conveyed to that area? Not by rivers. All the vegetable matter that was ever borne on the streams of the continent, multiplied thousands and millions of times, would be inadequate to constitute such an immense bed. All the trees and plants that grow in the line of the rivers of a continent, in such positions as to expose them to be uprooted and borne off by floods, is but an inappreciable fraction compared to the whole that springs from the vales, plains, and mountains; and would never in the lapse of ages amount to enough, could they be concentrated at one point, to form a coal bed of any considerable thickness and extent. But that those of which the strata were formed were not transported to the places of their deposition by the agency of rivers, is apparent from the absence from the coal of all earthy sediment. Had rivers at periods of flood been the agents of their transportation, they would have been intermixed, like the trees that are carried by the Mississippi to its mouth, with a mass of mud, that would have precluded their conversion into a stratum of pure coal. The only force that could have swept them together in such an immeasurable mass unmixed with other matter, was that of the ocean rushing over a vast tract of fern-forests, and other vegetables, that was rapidly sinking beneath it. And that might have accomplished it. Let us suppose, for example, that immediately antecedent to the deposition of the principal stratum of the great bed of Pennsylvania, Virginia, Ohio, and Indiana, the continent eastward to the Atlantic, and westward to the Rocky Mountains, stood above the ocean and was covered with a rich vegetable growth. As none of the mountains that now stretch across it had then risen above the surface, had it suddenly sunk a half mile or mile beneath the line of the sea, the waters rushing over it with resistless force, would have uprooted or wrenched off all trees and vegetables of any considerable size; and bearing them forward in a confused mass, accumulated them chiefly on a line where the waters of the two oceans met. If the subsidence began so much earlier on the Pacific than the Atlantic side, that their waves met or finally sank to repose on the line of that coal bed, the relics with which they were charged would have centered there. As they would naturally have been much entangled, that part which lay lowest would, on being saturated with water by the pressure to which it was subjected, have become so heavy as to have sunk, and dragged down such as was bound with it; the next tier would soon have followed, and the whole at length have reached the bottom, where its own weight, increased by the water with which its cells would have become filled, and the vast pressure of the ocean, would speedily have reduced it to a solid mass. Such processes are certainly adequate to the production of such effects, and they are processes which all geologists admit have indisputably taken place. Why, then, should not the solution which they furnish of the accumulation of the materials of the coal strata, which is inexplicable on the prevailing theory, be accepted as legitimate?

The causes to which we thus refer the transportation of the materials of the principal strata—silex, alumine, lime, and vegetables—to their places of deposit, are certainly of sufficient energy to have accomplished their formation with great celerity.

And a variety of proofs indicate that they were, in fact, formed in a very rapid manner.

Thus, that the vegetables which were converted into coal, were deposited and buried by the strata that lie above them within a short space, is seen from the fact, already stated, that the outlines of the stocks, branches, and most delicate leaves, are preserved in every part of the bituminized mass unobliterated; which could not have occurred had they been exposed for long periods to the wear of the restless waters, and the action of decomposing forces.

That the strata, also, above them were deposited almost immediately, is shown by the trees, trunks, and branches that project out of the coal, and are imbedded in the sandstone, shale, and limestone that lie above. Many of them rise to such a height as to pass through six, eight, or ten strata, and show by the perfect preservation of their forms, that they were enveloped to their tops before they had begun to undergo decay. The wood is usually silicified, while the bark is converted into coal. In some localities large fields, or forests of trees and stems standing erect in the places in which they grew, are found enveloped in a series of sandstones, shales, and limestones; indicating that five, six, or seven of those strata were deposited in very quick succession; as otherwise those trees would exhibit marks of decay. How could they have been thus preserved, if, as the common theory represents, hundreds, and perhaps thousands of years were employed in their burial, and they were during that period exposed to the action of destructive agents, sufficiently powerful, as is held, to disintegrate solid rocks and convert them into the strata? Six, eight, or ten of the layers were sometimes formed, not improbably, in half the number of years. The rapidity with which they were deposited in those instances was, at least, such, that if it were the ordinary rate, sixteen or eighteen hundred years would be ample for the deposition of the whole series.

The condition of the fossilized animal relics indicates also that the strata in which they are entombed were deposited with rapidity. The perfect preservation, in many localities, of the forms of fish, shows that they were covered by the strata in which they are imbedded before decomposition had begun, or they had been exposed to mutilation by other fish.

"The perfect condition in which the impressions of fish are found in the rock of Monte Bolca, and their extraordinary abundance, seem to show that the catastrophe which destroyed them was a sudden one, such as might have been brought about by the evolution of some of the noxious gases exhaled from volcanoes. I have myself observed the speedy extinction of life which takes place when carbonic acid is introduced into a vessel in which fish of several different kinds are collected; the first operation of the gas causing them to leap out of the water with convulsive energy, but in a few seconds, all muscular energy being suspended, all the fish without any further effort sinking lifeless to the bottom of the tub."—*Daubney's Description of Active and Extinct Volcanoes,* p. 146.

The skeletons of those of considerable size are often unmutilated, and dispersed through strata that cover extensive areas. That would naturally happen, if the clay or lime that enveloped them was thrown down in a few hours, or even a few days; but could not, had scores, and, perhaps, hundreds of years, as the common theory represents, been occupied in their deposition. Do dead fish now float in the ocean, or welter at the bottom, months and years without decay, and without mutilation by the living? Do their skeletons long remain unbroken, if exposed to the dash of breakers, and the wear of powerful waves, currents, and tides? If not, why should it any more, in contravention of the most certain physical laws, be supposed that they did then?

The condition in which the solid parts of testaceous and other similar animals are found, indicates with equal clearness that they were rapidly inclosed in the mass in which they are imbedded. Shells and corals, in infinite numbers, are found wholly unbroken.

"The old fresh-water and sea-bottoms present us with the occurrence of animal remains so preserved, and amid such substances, that the sudden influx of waters charged with much fine matter in mechanical suspension may have destroyed multitudes of aqueous animals in some given area. At least their remains are so entangled amid this matter as to lead to this inference. That fixed creatures or others of slow movements could thus readily be overwhelmed, would be expected under such conditions at all geological periods. When, for example, in the vicinity of Bradford, the Apiocrinites of that locality is found rooted upon a subjacent calcareous bed, one of the oolitic series, and entangled in a seam of clay, its parts sometimes beautifully preserved, it may be inferred that it was destroyed by an influx of mud from which it could not escape. In like manner, also, the preservation of long uninjured stems of various encrinites found amid the Silurian and other older deposits, on the surfaces of limestone and other rocks, and having had a covering of fine sediment, would appear to be explained. Sometimes, as in the Lias of Golden Cope, near Lyme Regis, multitudes of belemnites, some with even the ink-bag of these molluscs preserved, so form a seam of organic remains, that the observer is led to infer a sudden destruction of thousands of them over a moderate area. Ammonites are also sometimes found in great numbers, distributed in a depth of only a few inches, over areas of a square mile or more, as if suddenly destroyed. . . . It sometimes happens that the shells of molluscs show that when their animals were entombed, the space occupied by their bodies prevented the entrance of the sediment which enveloped them. . . . Multitudes of examples are found in certain areas and deposits where the presence of the animals in their shells should seem required. When we consider the probable voracity of numerous creatures in fresh and sea waters, and the multitudes of scavenger animals consuming decayed animal matters at all geological times, the discovery of certain aqueous reptiles preserved entire amid rocks, even with the contents of their intestines preserved, leads us to infer that their entombment, if not also their death, was sudden. And this appears the more probable when we find, as often happens, that in the same deposits the same kinds of aqueous reptiles are dismembered, as if by predaceous animals feeding upon them. While, at times, in the lias of Western England, the skeletons of Ichthyosauri and Plesiosauri, are so well preserved, that all or nearly all the bones are in their proper places ; at others the bones of these reptiles are dispersed, though not always far removed from the place where the animals died. In fact the appearances presented are precisely those of decomposition having been so far advanced, that the scavenger animals could feed upon the carcases, and drag the bones short distances, so as somewhat to scatter them."—*De La Beche's Geological Observer*, pp. 515, 516.

The preservation of such multitudes of animals of all orders unmutilated, which admits of no solution, except on the supposition that they were suddenly destroyed and immediately buried, thus indicates decisively that the strata in which they are enveloped were deposited with rapidity. Is there any reason to believe that the unfossiliferous strata were not constructed with equal expedition? None whatever. All their features indicate that they had their origin in the same causes, and were formed under the same conditions.

QUESTIONS.

But were these agents of sufficient energy to transfer those substances to the surface in the period that is represented in Genesis, to have passed between the creation and the modification of the earth's surface at the flood? Was that period as adequate, as any greater one? Is it clear that the requisite materials existed within the globe at every point where they were needed, to be ejected for the construction of the strata? What is the proof of it? Is it clear that where those substances were deposited, expulsive forces must have been generated and thrown them out in vast masses on the surface? Give the proof of it. By what supposition in respect to Lake Superior, can this be illustrated?

These facts show that the materials of the strata *may* have thus been ejected from the interior of the earth: are there any considerations which indicate that they were in fact derived from that quarter? What is the first? Are volcanic rocks found in almost every part of the globe? Mention some of the principal countries. Have igneous rocks been driven up to the surface in still more numerous places? Do these facts show that such agents have been at work in the depths of the planet in every considerable region, as might have ejected the materials of the strata, and spread them by the waters of the ocean wherever they are found? What is the next fact by which this is corroborated? Can the distribution of the different substances of which the strata consist into separate layers and groups, be accounted for on any other supposition, than that they were separated from each other in the depositories from which they were drawn? If thrown up successively from separate repositories, would they naturally be deposited from the waters of the ocean in separate layers? If introduced into the ocean in that manner, would the slight intermixture of them naturally take place, that is now seen in the strata? What is the third fact which gives confirmation to this view? Show how, if injected into the waters of the sea in the manner we have supposed, they would be diffused over wide areas. What may be presumed to have been their form when ejected into the ocean? Did their union in granules and larger bodies take place then probably or at a later period?

What explanations of important phenomena are furnished by these views that corroborate their truth? Could such elevations and depressions of the rocky surface of the earth as exist, have taken place, had the globe been as many geologists hold it once was, in a state of fusion? State the reason. How is it that heat and expansive gases are generated? Is all the latent heat evolved in matter that is in a state of perfect fusion? Were the interior of the globe in a state of fusion, would it necessarily be in a state of repose, so far as the generation of gases is concerned? Would volcanoes, be impossible in such a globe? Is this consideration overlooked by the geologists, who hold that the earth is now a molten ocean, except a thin rocky crust which forms its surface? Are the phenomena of earthquakes, volcanoes, and the elevation and dislocation of the surface, explicable on the views we have advanced? Show how these great processes may have been produced. Does this view of the causes of these great movements allow of their repetition as often as the strata indicate that they have taken place? Show how.

Do these views suggest an explanation of the great accumulation of vegetable matter in the localities where coal exists? Is it apparent that the materials generally, of which coal beds are formed, did not grow in the places where the coal lies? What is the proof of that fact? Is it clear also that the whole materials of a bed, must have been deposited at once, not slowly accumulated? What is the proof of that fact? Can they have been borne to the places where they were buried, by rivers? Why not? What then is the only force that could have swept them together? State in what manner it might happen. How does it appear that the materials of the coal beds were deposited in a short space? How does it appear that the strata which lie next above the coal, were immediately formed over them? What indicates that the strata in which the relics of animals are buried, were deposited with rapidity? What is the testimony of Mr. Daubney respecting it? Would the larger animals have decayed if they had not been immediately involved in the earthy and mineral matter in which their remains are preserved? Does the condition also of shells indicate that they were buried suddenly in the beds of mud which were their birth-place and residence; not swept from them by violent currents and long exposed to erosion and fractures before being interred in the strata in which they are now found? What is the testimony of Sir T. H. De La Beche respecting it? Do all these facts confirm the view we have advanced, by showing that the strata were formed with rapidity?

CHAPTER XVI.

The Materials of the Strata derived from the Interior of the Earth.

THIS view of the mode in which the materials of the strata were introduced into the oceans and seas, suggests the probable reason that those animals that were invested with a covering of silex or lime, swarmed at periods in certain localities, in infinite numbers. The infusion into the waters of the ocean at those points, of the elements of which their shells are formed, perhaps at a temperature equal to or above that of the equatorial seas, and that rendered their propagation practicable through the whole year, may have been the cause of their extraordinary multiplication. The slight animalcula whose silicious sheaths are in a few places accumulated in vast masses, cast their coverings periodically, and, like other creatures of that order, multiplied with a rapidity in an inverse ratio to their minuteness. The bulk of their relics is not greater, perhaps, in proportion to their power of increase, than that of some larger animals. There is, at least, no satisfactory explanation of their infinite multitude on any other theory. The supposition of vast ages during which they existed, is altogether inadmissible ; for they are not common to all geological times, but confined to periods of comparatively slight length ; and there are no indications that the strata formed contemporaneously with them, occupied a long round of ages. Myriads as innumerable as those of the infusoria that sometimes now animate every drop of the ocean through hundreds of cubic miles, casting their sheaths at slight intervals, would in a few years accumulate masses as great as those imbedded in the strata.

It suggests a more probable solution than any other of the origin of rock salt, and the saliferous marls from which salt springs arise. Those marls were undoubtedly ejected, like all others, from the interior of the earth ; and why should not the salt with which they are saturated have been ejected along with them? We know that soda exists in the depths of the earth, as it is a conspicuous element in many of the volcanic rocks; and chloride also, as it is an element of muriatic acid, which is one of the most common and abundant of the gases emitted from volcanoes.

"Muriatic acid seems to be generated during almost all the phases of volcanic action ; for although some have attempted to establish a class of volcanoes to which the production of muriatic acid was peculiar, yet it would appear that there were none from which this gas is not in greater or less quantity disengaged."—*Daubney's Description of Volcanoes*, p. 607.

Their ejection in combination, and in such conditions as to form rock salt, however it may transcend our comprehension, is no more incredible than many other processes, of the occurrence of which we have ample evidence. There is no other theory of its origin that is not perplexed with insuperable objections.

This view of the rapidity with which the strata were formed, is confirmed by the softness and pliancy which they appear universally to have retained, till the time of their upheaval. That they were so soft when elevated as to be susceptible of flexion without breaking, is seen from the curvatures and contortions to which those of every species, especially from gneiss up to the last of the shales, sandstones, limestones, and coal beds of the carboniferous system, have been subjected.

"Contorted strata are common on the skirts or flanks of many mountain chains, appearing to show that before the latter attained their existing forms, there was a pressure from the central parts outward, causing the lateral contortions.

"To produce this effect—as in the Alps, between Rigi and the Hospice of St. Gothard—we seem compelled to suppose the whole mass of the calcareous Alps—a series of mixed strata of limestone, argillaceous slates, shales, and sandstone, the former predominating—to have been in a yielding or comparatively soft state. We can scarcely suppose with any approach to probability, that the soft, yielding condition of this mass should have continued sufficiently long to enable a succession of small shocks, of no greater intensity than those of a modern earthquake, to have acted upon it. The whole strongly impresses us with the idea of a powerful exertion, forcing the limestone and associated beds outwards."—*H. T. De La Beche's Theoret. Geology*, pp. 113, 114.

In some instances they form a simple curve; in others a series of curves, like so many waves; in others still they are folded over like a half dozen of the letter S joined in a continuous line. The folding, in some localities, is on so great a scale, that the strata must either have been drawn from a distance, or else greatly expanded in length and breadth. In some parts of the Alleghanies the coal series within a half dozen square miles, would, if spread out on a level, cover two or three times that space.

" The most probable condition of contortion appears to be pressure of solid matter on yielding stratified substances, which, while they bend, also *slide* to a certain extent on the planes of stratification."—*H. T. De La Beche's Theoretical Geology*, p. 121.

No such softness and pliancy are retained by the stratified or crystallized rocks that now lie beneath the surface, however far they may be below the line of the sea. Though permeated by moisture, and, when first raised to the atmosphere, far more easily sawn or wrought with the chisel than after the water with which they are charged has evaporated, they yet are not sufficiently flexible to be bent without fracture. As, then, they must have continued in a pliant state till their upheaval was completed and they were moulded into their present form, it is manifest that their elevation must have taken place rapidly. It cannot have proceeded, as many geologists maintain, by such slow stages, as to have been prolonged through a series of ages. If protracted after emerging from the ocean through even a few years, the heat beneath of the molten mass of granite by which they were forced upwards, and the action of the sun and atmosphere, would have desiccated and hardened them to such a degree as to have rendered them incapable of being bent into curves and folds without breaking into fragments. We have the most decisive evidence, therefore, that their upheaval was accomplished in a brief period; and that the vast round of years which geologists have regarded as requisite to that process, is wholly imaginary.

Their upheaval and subjection in that pliant state to the powerful breakers, waves, and currents of the ocean, explain the denudations which they have undergone. Had they possessed their present hardness when rising through the ocean into the atmosphere, no such immense wearing away and such vast excavations as have been wrought in them would have been possible.

"Of the formations comprising the rocks of this portion of the State, II. and III., are a limestone and slate stratum, which are at all times more destructible than sandstone; but especially so must they have been in their soft and pulpy state at the time of their elevation from the bed of the ocean in which they were deposited. Hence they have been more deeply excavated than the harder ponderous beds of sandstone, of which formation IV. consists. We accordingly find formations II. and III. always in the deep and nearly level valleys, and IV. in the high and steep mountain ridges. Of the other rocks, formation V. consists chiefly of soft slates and calcareous slates. Formation VI., of limestone, which, like II., was evidently of a very soft consistence when first uplifted, and formation VIII. of a mass of slate and argillaceous rocks. This would all be liable to very extensive destruction whenever subterraneous uplifting forces should bring them within the reach of those tremendous currents, which those same uplifting actions set in motion." —*H. D. Rodgers's Report on the Geology of Pennsylvania*, 1838, p. 41.

The sea does not now wear the solid rocks that lie embosomed in it, or rise from its surface, except in a few positions where exposed to the most powerful breakers and currents; and there what it rends and wears away is scarcely appreciable, compared to the masses that meet the shock of its powerful enginery century after century without yielding. Myriads of ages would have contributed little towards grinding down strata of such hardness, scores, hundreds, and even thousands of feet in thickness, over wide areas, scooping out valleys, and ploughing the broad passages betwixt the hills, in the bottom of which rivers cut their channels. But that immense rending and denudation was the natural result of the rapid upheaval of the strata from a level beneath the sea, in a condition so pliant as to yield to the violent currents and waves which that process itself must have created, and the resistless sweep and dash of ocean-tempests and storms. Under the impulse of those powerful agents, the parts most elevated would at many points be instantly swept away, and where a whole continent, like that of South America, rose at the same time, so as to cause the ocean to recede with a resistless rush hundreds and thousands of miles, its currents would necessarily tear up and bear off the strata over extensive regions. Instead of vast ages and incalculable periods, a very brief time, therefore, would be ample for the accomplishment of all the great modifications of that class to which the strata have been subjected. The cuttings, accordingly, through hills, the excavations of valleys, and the removal of strata from large districts, and deposit of the detritus in others, are precisely such as would naturally result from the vehement commotion and violent currents of the ocean acting on such susceptible materials. On the prevalent theory, however, they are wholly inexplicable. If the strata on the tops and sides of the mountains and hills, and on the plains and depressed surfaces, were as hard at their upheaval from the ocean as they now are, no solution could be given of the vast degradation that has taken place at many points in rocky ranges and plateaus, the abrasion of solid masses from wide plains, and the scooping out of deep channels and valleys between the hills, arranged in the same relations to each other, and exhibiting the same outlines as those that are now wrought in yielding soils by deluges and floods that sweep over them.

The soft condition of the strata at their upheaval into the atmosphere, indicates the reasons also of the excavations within a brief period by rivers of their deep channels for miles through rocky strata. Thus the Niagara must naturally have cut its passage back from Lake Ontario to near its present fall in the lapse of a few years; inasmuch as the strata over which it passed were at first so pliant as easily to yield to the powerful impulse of the current and cataract. That that was their state, is indisputable, not only from the fact that the strata generally were unhardened at their upheaval, but that the same formations on the Helderberg and the Appalachians were actually subjected to curvatures and contortions, that show that under the surge and dash of such a mass of waters as the Niagara, they would have given way in a moment, and dissolving into their primitive particles, been borne off by the resistless current. To suppose that a long round of ages, or even a considerable number of years, could have been exhausted in excavating such a chasm in strata in that condition, is a consummate solecism. The length and depth of the channel, instead of proving that a long period elapsed during its excavation, present a resistless demonstration that no more time can have been occupied by it than passed between the upheaval of the strata and their acquiring such a measure of hardness as to enable them to resist, as they now do, the impulse of the waters. It is truly surprising that geologists, though aware of the evidences that the strata, at their elevation, were tender and plastic, should yet wholly overlook it in their theories of erosion and denudation, and proceed in their inferences respecting the time that was required for those processes, on the assumption that the rocks that have been swept off, or cut by deep gorges, must from the first have had all their present hardness.

The plastic condition of the rocks at the elevation of the mountains furnishes an explanation of the formation of the rounded stones, pebbles, and much, probably, of the gravel that are found in the vicinity of the great ranges, as the Cordilleras of South America, the Rocky Mountains, the Appalachians, and the Alps. At their sudden upheaval, chasms were opened in them doubtless, and explosions of gas, and not improbably of lava, took place, by which portions of the rocks through which they forced their way upwards were torn into fragments, and projected with a rotary motion into the surging and rushing waters of the ocean, in the whirl of which they were borne off to a distance ere they reached the bottom, and stripped in the process of their angles and points, and reduced to a circular or elliptical form. Their rounding was then soon completed by the ceaseless change of position and wear to which they continued to be subjected by the advance and recession of powerful waves, while the areas on which they lie were upheaving towards the atmosphere, and the ocean retreating to its present bed. It is noticeable that these vast bodies of stones, pebbles, and gravel lie at the eastward of the mountain range from which they were derived. Thus in Patagonia:

" Here—in Patagonia—in the tertiary formations—along hundreds of miles of coast, we have one great deposit, including many tertiary shells all apparently extinct. These beds are covered by others of a peculiar soft white stone, including much gypsum, and resembling chalk, but really of a pumiceous nature. It is highly remarkable, from being composed, to at least one tenth part of its bulk, of infusoria. This bed extends 500 miles along the coast, and probably for a considerably greater distance. At Port Julian its thickness is more than 800 feet! These white beds are everywhere capped by a mass of gravel, forming, probably, one of the largest beds of shingle in the world; it certainly extends from near the Rio Colorado to between 600 and 700 nautical miles southwest; at Santa Cruz, a river a little north of St. Julian, it reaches to the foot of the Cordillera; half way up the river, its thickness is more than 200 feet; it probably everywhere extends to *this great chain, whence the well rounded pebbles of porphyry have been derived.* We may consider its average breadth as 200 miles, and its average thickness as about fifty feet. If this great bed of pebbles, without including the mud necessarily derived from their attrition, was piled into a mound, it would form a great mountain chain!"—*Darwin's Journal of Researches in Natural History and Geology in the Voyage of the Beagle,* pp. 170, 171.

"Near the mouth of the Santa Cruz the bed of gravel is from twenty to about thirty-four feet in thickness. The pebbles vary from minute ones to the size of a hen's egg, and even to that of half a man's head. They consist of paler varieties of porphyry than those found further northward, and there are fewer of the gallstone yellow kind; pebbles of compact black clay slate were here first observed. The gravel covers the step-formed plains at the mouth, head, and on the sides of the great valley of the Santa Cruz. At the distance of 110 miles from the coast, the plain has risen to the height of 1416 feet above the sea, and the gravel, with the associate great boulder formation, has attained a thickness of 212 feet. The plain, apparently with its usual gravel covering, slopes up to the foot of the

Cordillera to the height of between 3200 and 3300 feet. In ascending the valley, the gravel gradually becomes entirely altered in character ; high up we have pebbles of crystalline felspathic rocks, compact clay-slates, quartzose schists, and pale-colored porphyries ; these rocks, judging from the gigantic boulders on the surface, and from some small pebbles imbedded beneath 700 feet in thickness of tertiary strata, are the prevailing kinds in this part of the Cordillera : pebbles of basalt from the neighboring streams of basaltic lava are also numerous."

* * * * * *

"The transportal and origin of this vast bed of pebbles is an interesting problem. From the manner in which they cap the step-formed plains, worn by the sea within the period of existing shells, their deposition, at least on the plains up to a height of 400 feet, must have been *a recent geological event.* From the form of the continent, we may be sure they have come from the westward, probably in chief part from the Cordillera, but perhaps partly from unknown rocky ridges in the central districts of Patagonia. That the pebbles have not been transported by rivers from the interior towards the coast, we may conclude from the fewness and smallness of the streams of Patagonia. . . . . That the pebbles in central and northern Patagonia have not been transported by ice-agency, ... we may conclude from the absence of all angular fragments in the gravel, and from the complete contrast in many other respects between the shingle and the neighboring boulder formation.

"Looking to the gravel on any one of the step-formed plains, I cannot doubt, ... that it has been spread out and levelled by the long continued action of the sea, probably during the slow rise of the land."—*Darwin's Geological Observations on South America*, pp. 20–22.

Beds of pebbles and gravel, formed of quartz, gneiss, and primary slate, are strewn in much the same manner on the Atlantic side of the Appalachians in Virginia.

"The loose aggregation and coarse materials of those beds give them so great a resemblance to the common diluvium of sand and gravel, generally forming the surface strata in this part of the State, as to render careful observation necessary in order to distinguish between them ; and even the closest inspection in some cases will not suffice for this purpose. This obscurity, however, does not apply to localities in which the tertiary beds are seen resting upon them, as in such cases the subjacent position of the sandstone or conglomerate determines its true geological character, the diluvial sand or gravel having its place above the tertiary.

"When the tertiary, ... having been removed, . . . has been replaced by diluvial sand and gravel deposited on the broken surface of the secondary," still, "a marked difference may be noticed in their composition, especially in the comparatively large amount of white felspathic earth blended with the coarser matter of the upper secondary. Indeed, at most localities, however large may be the pebbles imbedded in some of the layers, the intervening matter will be found to possess the character of a soft felspathic sandstone, and some portions of the mass will display this character throughout.

"The pebbles thus imbedded in the finer material of these beds, sometimes in layers of many feet in thickness, but oftener in narrow *courses*, are frequently of great size, measuring even as much as eight or ten inches in diameter. They are of very various origin; some being from the primary region, and consisting of quartz, gneiss, and primary slates, while others are from the formations further west, and especially that lying on the valley (west) side of the Blue Ridge, and which I have designated as the first of the series of rocks of our great Appalachian system. These fragments of formation i., remarkable for their bright white color and their great magnitude, serve to distinguish the mass in which they occcur from the overlying diluvium, in which nothing analogous has as yet been discovered. Forming thus a part of what may be considered as ancient diluvium belonging to the secondary era, they point to the extensive agency of the currents by which the heterogeneous materials of these upper secondary strata were swept together."—*Rodgers's Report on the Geology of Virginia*, 1839, pp. 36, 37.

See also p. 60 for a description of similar conglomerates and sandstones in the northern district east of the Blue Ridge.

That these immense masses were thus swept

towards the east, indicates that a resistless rush of the ocean took place in that direction at the upheaval of the mountains from which they were hurled by volcanic explosions, or torn by the surge and sweep of the waters. This and the transportation of the pebbles to such a distance, may have arisen in a measure from the elevation of the western side of the continent first. If, instead of being raised throughout at the same time, it was elevated first at the western side, so as to form a slope beneath the sea, descending one, two, or three miles towards the east, the sudden upheaval of the Cordilleras to within a few hundred feet of the atmosphere, would have thrown the vast mass of waters that before rested on the plains of Patagonia, Buenos Ayres, and Brazil, towards the Atlantic, so as to have drawn after them a current from the Pacific of hundreds of times the force with which it surges in an ordinary tempest, and swept the fragments ejected from the interior, and wrenched from the summit and sides of the mountain, to the distance of many miles; and its ceaseless waves would then, at every roll along the inclining bottom, have borne them still further into the depths. These stupendous processes, which were wholly impossible on the prevailing theory, might thus have been dispatched in a very brief period, instead of occupying the interminable ages which geologists assign them.

These views of the period at which the strata were formed, and of the causes of the submersion of the land beneath the sea, and the retreat of the sea from the land, indicate the reason that no human remains are found fossilized in the strata. Geologists generally allege the fact that no relics of the human race are buried in the rocks in which so many animals of the sea and land are entombed, as a decisive proof that man was not created till after these rocks were formed. That conclusion, however, is without any just ground. There is no reason to suppose that anterior to the flood, any of the human family lived in this hemisphere, in Europe, or in those parts of Asia or Africa, in which the strata have been examined. How, then, could their remains be entombed in the rocks of those regions? The strata, moreover, that now form the crust of the continents and islands, in the main, lay undoubtedly, previous to the deluge, beneath the sea, and were formed, at least chiefly, during the interval from the creation to that catastrophe. The primitive earth, occupied by the first pair and their descendants down to the flood, was then submerged—and doubtless by its own subsidence—and still continues to lie at the bottom of the ocean. For how could it have sunk beneath the waters to so great a depth, unless on the one hand by its being depressed below the line it had before occupied, and on the other, by a corresponding elevation of the bed of the former sea? But such a subsidence of that ancient earth would have caused the ocean to rush on to it from every side, and carried its population and all other movable things from its exterior towards its centre, where they would naturally have sunk along with the wreck of their dwellings, fields, and forests, and been buried beneath the mud and sand with which the rushing waters would have become charged. To suppose that their bodies could have disentangled themselves from such a complicated mass, and floated off against the current to the other hemisphere, is to contradict the physical laws to which they and the movements of the ocean must have been subject. The total absence from the strata of this country, of Europe, of Africa, and Asia, of the relics of those then destroyed, is precisely therefore what was to be expected from the time and mode of their destruction. How could their remains be entombed in those strata which had been deposited *before* the epoch of the deluge, that swept them to their watery sepulchre? How could they obtain a burial in the seas where these strata were formed, when their distance was so great as to preclude their being borne to them? How extensive the continent, or continents and islands, of that world were, we have no means of judging. It is highly probable that they were of but moderate dimensions at their elevation on the third day of the creation; and they may have been enlarged at subsequent periods, as the race multiplied, and still have been at the time of their submergence, at the deluge, greatly inferior in extent to the present dry land. On that supposition, portions of the present continents might have been elevated into the atmosphere sufficient to have borne the vegetable growths out of which the coal beds were formed, without rendering the aggregate of the dry land greater than it is now.

It is highly probable, also, that at the reappearance of dry land at the close of the deluge, the extent of the Asiatic continent, raised above the ocean, was comparatively small; and that the great processes by which the strata generally were completed, and the continents and islands elevated to their present positions, were continued through a considerable period after that event. And it may have been in reference to such a gradual reconstruction of the crust of the earth, that animals were preserved in the ark, notwithstanding—as there is reason to believe—there were to be new creations to stock the remote regions of Asia, and other continents and islands which were to be prepared to be peopled with animals more rapidly than those from the ark could multiply; or from their distance, the impassable barriers with which they were surrounded, and their different climates, were to require a creation on their own soil of peculiar genera and species. While, therefore, the animals preserved in the ark may have been sufficient in kinds and numbers to supply the wants of Noah and his family, and stock that part of the earth that was first raised above the sea; as other countries became fitted to support the same or other tribes, those with which they were peopled may have been called into existence by a new fiat. And on this supposition the existence in Europe, Northern Asia, Africa, and this continent, of the land animals whose relics are fossilized in the strata, is rendered consistent with the sacred history of the creation and deluge. These animals existed undoubtedly after the deluge, not anterior to it. Some of the species of Europe and Africa that were the most active, and best adapted to live in different climes, māy have migrated from the East; but most were probably created in the regions where they perished. If during the two or three hundred years that followed the flood, Northern Asia, Europe, Africa, and America, emerged from the ocean, portions of them being gradually drained of their waters, and portions again submerged, or overflowed by deluges occasioned by the sudden elevation of other tracts; there was ample space for the life and destruction of the land animals whose remains are buried in the upper tertiary strata, gravel, and soil of these regions that were formed after the elevation, at least in a considerable measure, of their great mountain ranges.

The fact that certain classes of animals appear to have passed out of existence during the formation of the strata, and other forms of marine life and land animals that had not before inhabited the same regions were called into existence, and in their turn swept away also, is indeed alleged by some as a decisive proof that vast periods must have been occupied by these changes. No conclusion, however, could be more unnatural. Vast periods surely were not required for the creation of animals. They are instantly called into being by the word of the Almighty; and not in single pairs, like the progenitors of the human race, but in crowds, as at the first creation of the tenants of the air and the water, when the waters were commanded to "bring forth *abundantly* the moving creature that hath life, and fowl that may fly above the earth in the open firmament of heaven;" and the earth was commanded to "bring forth the living creature after his kind, cattle and creeping thing, and beast of the earth after his kind;" which also, like the fish and fowl, were produced, doubtless, not solely in one locality, but wherever the earth was prepared to sustain them. Their creation shows, therefore, that instead of innumerable ages, only brief periods were required for their being called into existence. Nor is the extinction of certain classes any more a proof of a lapse of long periods; as all appearances indicate that their destruction took place by causes that were sudden and acted over great areas; such as the effusion of deadly gases into the ocean; the eruption of vast masses of silex, alumine, lime, and other substances from the depths of the earth, that thickened the waters of the sea, and generated chemical processes that were fatal to animal life. Nor is there any reason to suppose that there were long intervals between the extinction of one series and the creation of its successors. The seas and lands were again repeopled, doubtless, as soon as they became fitted to be the residence of the tribes with which they were next stocked. The change of their population, therefore, by these rapid processes, instead of demanding a long round of ages, may have been accomplished in a short time.

This supposition accounts also for the preservation of such of the relics of those animals as, instead of being entombed in the solid strata, were buried in the gravel or sands deposited above them, where they have been exposed to moisture and other chemical agents that were adapted to induce their decay. That bones of any species should be preserved in such conditions, through the vast series of ages which geologists assign to them—30,000 years, Sir C. Lyell assumes, have passed since the burial of the Mastodon found in the gravel near Niagara—is physically impossible. If the same chemical forces that acted on that skeleton disintegrated during that period immense masses of the most solid rocks, and bore their detritus to the sea—as that writer holds—how is it that those bones, which were far more easily decomposed, should have withstood their destructive agency and survived almost unimpaired? The two assumptions are incompatible with each other. Many of the skeletons that are found buried in low grounds, bogs, and swamps, are probably of a comparatively recent date. Others were doubtless of a much earlier age; but four thousand years are probably as long a period as any of them could have been preserved without undergoing a greater measure of decay.

Such are the facts and considerations that confirm the view we have presented of the formation of the strata. We might add many others; but these are sufficient on the one hand to demonstrate the total error of the theory generally entertained by geologists; and on the other, to show that the strata, so far from offering any contradiction to the Mosaic record of the creation and deluge, are in entire harmony with it, and indicate in all their great features that they were formed with a rapidity as great as that history implies.

It will, perhaps, be said that although the views we have advanced seem to be consistent with the laws of the physical world, and with the appearances of the strata; and to show that all the great processes by which the crust of the earth received its present form, may have been consummated within the period we have supposed—the 1,800 or 2,000 years that followed the creation—yet we have produced no absolute demonstration that such was the fact; and that, therefore, there is room to doubt that they were finished in that period, and to suppose that they occupied a far greater series of ages.

To this we reply, that it is not necessary to our object that we should demonstrate directly and absolutely *from the strata themselves*, that they were completed in that period. Our aim is to confute the representation, that the strata themselves present resistless evidence that they were formed at a far earlier epoch than that to which the Scriptures refer the creation of the world; and thereby to protect the sacred word from the charge and suspicion of giving a false history of that event; and that we accomplish by showing, in the first place, that the geological theory which ascribes an immeasurable age to the world, is altogether groundless and mistaken; and in the next, that the materials of the strata were placed originally in such conditions, and acted on by such agents as rendered their transfusion into the ocean, and deposition and upheaval in their present form in a period of eighteen hundred or two thousand years, consistent with the great laws of those substances and agents, and possible therefore; and thirdly, that their completion with such a rapidity is indicated and confirmed by their structure and condition. In accomplishing that, we do all that is necessary to vindicate the Scriptures from the charge to which the geological theory of an immeasurable age of the world has given rise, that they are convicted by the facts of science of error; and of an error so extraordinary and stupendous as to show that neither the history of the creation, nor any of the other professed communications from God, which they contain, can have been written by inspiration. And these propositions we have demonstrated. We have shown that the theory which ascribes a vast age to the world cannot be true, because it is not supported by any proofs; because if granted it could not account for the formation of the strata; because it is against the laws themselves of matter; and because it would preclude the occurrence of any of the great processes by which the crust of the earth has been formed and modified; such as earthquakes, the elevation of mountains, the eruption of volcanoes, the introduction of the materials of the strata into the ocean and dispersion over the areas where they lie, and the upheaval and dislocation of the strata after they were formed. A theory that presents such insuperable barriers to the accomplishment of these great processes cannot have any foundation in truth, nor present any solution of the facts which it is devised to explain. If the advocates of that theory are to demonstrate or render it probable that the earth has had a longer existence than is assigned to it by the Scriptural history of its creation, it must be by means wholly different from those which they have hitherto employed for the purpose.

The proofs are decisive also on the other hand, that the strata may have been formed within the period of eighteen hundred or two thousand years from the creation; and all the features of the strata indicate that they were built with as great a rapidity, and completed within as recent a date, as that supposes; and the establishment from the laws of the chemical and mechanical forces by which the structure and modification of the earth's crust have been produced, and from the nature and condition of the strata themselves, of the possibility of such a rapid formation, is all that is requisite to exempt the Scriptures from the imputation of error in their narrative of the creation and deluge. For if such a construction of the crust of the globe is consistent with the laws of those forces, and is probable, then neither the extent and thickness of the strata, the substances of which they consist, the relics they imbed, their upheaval and dislocation, nor any other peculiarities which they exhibit, present any contradiction to the sacred history of their origin and date; nor furnish any ground for an inference against the divine authority of that history, and the other parts of the sacred volume that are founded on it, and assume and ratify its truth.

It is not to invalidate this conclusion, to say that we have not absolutely demonstrated *from the crust of the earth itself*, that it was wrought into its present shape within that period. To set that conclusion aside, they who dissent from it must prove directly and absolutely that the strata cannot have been formed, the igneous rocks thrown on to the surface, and the mountains upheaved in the manner, nor consummated within the period we have represented. But that they cannot do, unless they can set aside the grounds on which we found that conclusion. But in order to that, they must show, first, that there are no proofs that any such stores of the various substances of which the present surface of the globe is constructed, were originally treasured up in its interior, as that—on the supposition that there were proper agents for their transferrence to the surface—the strata might have been formed from them. But that they cannot show. It is against the most palpable facts. It is against their own admissions. It were to overturn their own theories of the nature and origin of all the igneous rocks, which they themselves regard as of immeasurably greater bulk than the sedimentary strata. No certainty is more indisputable or holds a more important place in their speculations, than that the igneous rocks which were thrown up from the abysses of the planet are formed of identically the same substances as the sedimentary strata. They cannot deny, therefore, that all those elements were originally stored in repositories in the interior of the earth, and on a scale sufficiently vast to have supplied all the materials that were requisite for the construction of the sedimentary strata, as well as the crystallized and volcanic rocks.

As then that is indisputable, if they would set that conclusion aside, they must show that there were no agents that had access to those substances of sufficient power and activity to raise them into the ocean, that they might be deposited on its bottom and wrought into the strata in which they now exist. That, however, they cannot any more prove; as it is indisputable that such agents in fact existed, and actually raised to the surface the vast masses of those substances of which the igneous rocks are formed. This is acknowledged and maintained also by geologists, and is a conspicuous and important element of their theory. It is plain, moreover, that the fires of volcanoes, in forcing a passage from the deep recesses in which they were kindled to the atmosphere, must have driven up in an unfused state immense volumes of the substances that lay between them and the surface; and that those substances must have entered into the construction of the strata; as otherwise they would have formed a separate body; but no such masses exist on the surface. The igneous rocks and the sedimentary strata constitute the whole crust of the globe.

As then the requisite materials for the strata indisputably existed, originally, in the depths of the earth, and the requisite agents have existed and acted to transfer them to the waters of the ocean; it cannot be proved that they were not in fact drawn from those sources, unless it can be shown that if they had been introduced into the ocean in that manner, they could not have been so diffused through the waters and deposited as to have formed the existing strata. But that cannot be proved. So far from it, their diffusion and deposition in separate layers, like those of the strata, is precisely what would naturally and necessarily take place, from the unfused and uncemented condition of those substances on their infusion into the ocean, and from the action on them of gravity, and the motions and pressure of the water. To this, indeed, geologists cannot hesitate to assent; as they represent the materials of the strata as having been transported by the tides and currents from the circumference of the ocean, where they suppose them to have been introduced by rivers, or beat off from rocky shores, into its interior, and thrown down on the areas where they were formed into the strata.

As, then, neither of these great points of the view we have advanced can be disproved, no method remains of setting it aside, unless it can be shown that such a construction of the crust of the earth is inconsistent with or leaves unexplained some of the other great processes to which it has been subjected;

such as the upheaval and dislocation of the strata and the elevation of continents and mountains, or the incorporation in it of elements, such as the relics of vegetables and animals, that were not derived from the interior of the globe. But neither of these can any more be proved. Instead, all these extraordinary effects are precisely what would naturally result from such causes acting in such conditions, and could not have been produced by any other forces, nor in any other circumstances. They solve, accordingly, all the great processes that have taken place, and account for all the great results; while, on the prevalent theory of a molten globe invested by a granite crust —in which no new developments of an expansive force could take place, and thence no upheavals, no subsidences, no volcanoes, and no earthquakes—they are inexplicable and impossible.

As then those several positions are thus indisputable, it is clear that there are no means of proving that the strata were not in fact formed by those agents and processes. Instead, their construction in that manner is not only altogether possible and probable, but they are the only agents and processes that were adequate to their production. All the facts of geology are accordingly in harmony with the history given in Genesis of the creation and deluge. No means, therefore, exist of proving or rendering it probable that the world has existed through a longer period than that which is assigned to it by that inspired history; and the Scriptures consequently are vindicated from the charge to which the speculations of geologists have subjected them, of a contradiction to the discoveries and deductions of that science.

The result at which we have aimed is thus established on indisputable and ample grounds. The facts of geology, in place of contradicting, corroborate the narrative in Genesis; and the fancy that the Scriptures have been convicted of an error, demonstrating that they cannot have proceeded from the God of nature, turns out to be wholly groundless and unjust.

This great fact, free as it is from all rational doubt, of infinite moment to the credit of the Scriptures, and flashing an effulgent light over the whole domain of theology, demands the earnest consideration, especially of the ministers of religion. The inspiration and authority of the sacred volume are boldly assailed, on the ground of the theory held by geologists of the immeasurable age of the world. That theory is undoubtingly and exultingly claimed to be deduced from the facts of the science "according to the strictest rules of the Baconian philosophy;" and taken to be so, the conclusion is seen and felt by thousands and tens of thousands to be inevitable that neither the Pentateuch nor any other part of the Bible can have been written by the inspiration of the Almighty. That theory has been taught in lyceums, lecture-rooms, pulpits, and books, almost without obstruction for half a century, until it has gained the assent very generally of the press, and acceptance in all ranks of society. It has become, accordingly, a prolific source and powerful auxiliary of scepticism; and, unfortunately, has been aided in its mischievous influence, not only by the inconsiderate concessions of many religious men, but in a still worse manner by the unjustifiable and absurd methods by which it has been attempted to bend the history of the creation in Genesis into harmony with their speculations, which contradict it, and impeach it of fatal error. No duty, therefore, is more urgent on those in the sacred office, than the rejection of those lawless perversions of the word of God, and confutation of the theory which assails its inspiration and veracity. They should no longer acquiesce in the seduction of their people—and especially the young, who are eminently exposed to the danger—into doubt and unbelief, by the pretences of a superficial and but half matured science; but boldly and resolutely point out its palpable fallacies, its flagrant contradictions to the laws of nature, and its inconsistency with the principles and facts of geology; and show, on the other hand, the proofs that the works of God are in harmony with his word. No task is more incumbent on their profession; none can be easier or of more interest and benefit to their people.

And in this they will have the concurrence, we

trust, of good men among geologists themselves. The science manifestly needs a reconstruction. The completeness to which it has been advanced has been greatly over-estimated. There needs a clearer discrimination of that which is practical in it from that which is speculative—of the phenomena from the theories that are constructed to account for them. There needs a specific statement, which geologists have never yet given, of the axioms on which it is founded, and the principles by which reasonings and speculations respecting it are to be governed. There needs, especially, a rejection of unphilosophical assumptions and groundless hypotheses; and among them, the theory of a world created in a state of gas or of fusion, invested with a granite covering, and continuing molten in the interior, which is the basis of the inference of a vast age of the planet, must be abandoned, as against the constitution of nature, at war with the facts it is employed to explain, and involving the science in endless self-contradiction and error. The results that are to be accounted for must be contemplated independently of hypotheses, in the light of the great truths which they themselves reveal respecting their origin, and of the agents that were concerned in their production, and such views alone adopted as are in harmony alike with causes, conditions, and effects. An effort, in short, needs to be made by its cultivators to free the science from the artificial and unnatural adjuncts with which it is now disfigured and embarrassed, to define its true principles more clearly, to ascertain more adequately its facts, to limit its deductions to such as have a legitimate basis, and to unfold and verify its consistency—the certainty of which will advance proportionally with the progress that is made in real knowledge—with the revelation which God has given respecting the creation of the world, and the remodification through which it passed at the period of the flood.

And in this reconstruction we sincerely hope those who are devoted to the cultivation of the science in this country will take an active part. No finer field either for distinction or usefulness can present itself to the young men especially who are engaged in the profession. No superior theatre exists for the observation of the strata. There is none where they are found through their whole series on a larger scale; or yield more ample indications of the great processes by which they were formed. Let those, then, who have chosen the science as a profession, dismiss the unfortunate theories by which it has hitherto been embarrassed, and aim at a reconstruction of it under the guidance of the great principles we have suggested; and its facts will soon be unfolded in their proper relations, their true import be determined, and their consistency made apparent with the teachings of revelation. And this, instead of diminishing the interest and value of the science, will add to its attractiveness, its dignity, and its usefulness; and, in place of an enemy, show it to be what it legitimately is, a natural and efficient auxiliary of religion.

QUESTIONS.

Does this view of the mode, in which the matter of the strata was introduced into the ocean, suggest the reason that the waters were so prolific of minute animals that were invested with coverings of silex and lime? What is it? Does this view suggest a solution of the origin of rock-salt? What is it? Is its origin explicable on the common theory? What bearing on this view of the rapidity with which the strata were formed, has the softness which the strata appear to have retained at the time of their upheaval? What proof is there that they were then soft and pliable? What are the various forms in which the strata are bent? How is their being forced into this shape accounted for by De La Beche? Do their flexures and contortions show that their upheaval must have been completed before they lost their pliancy, and therefore, that it must have taken place rapidly? Does their upheaval while in a soft state furnish an explanation of the denudations they have undergone? What is the testimony of Professor Rogers, respecting it? Would the rapid elevation of hills and mountain ranges have created violent currents and agitations of the ocean, which would necessarily have torn the strata up, if soft, and washed them off, from large areas? Could however, such erosions and denudations as they have undergone, ever have taken place, if, at the time of their upheaval, they had possessed their present hardness? Does their softness at their upheaval suggest the reason that rivers in a brief period cut their deep channels through rocky strata? Might the Niagara have thus excavated its present bed back from Lake Ontario to the falls in a very brief period? Is there any reason to believe it would ever have worn the rocks away in such a form, had they not been in a plastic condition? Does the elevation of the mountains while in a plastic state, suggest an explanation of the formation of the large masses of rounded stones and pebbles that are found in their vicinity? Explain the manner in which they may have been formed? Do they abound on the slopes and at the feet of the Andes? Is it the judgment of geologists that they were derived from those mountains? State Mr. Darwin's views. Are they found in great masses at the feet of the Appalachians? Does the distance from the high ranges of the mountains at which they are lodged, show that the currents by which they were borne there, must have rushed with great violence?

Do these views indicate the reason that no human remains are found in the strata? Do geologists allege that as a proof that man did not exist till after the strata were formed? Is it a just ground for that conclusion? Is there any reason to suppose that Europe or this country was inhabited by man before the flood? As all our present mountains, as was shown in a former chapter, were raised from the ocean since the deluge, and as the strata with which they and the continents at large are covered, were formed beneath the ocean, is it not clear that the present continents and islands, all of which are covered with the strata, must have continued to be buried in the ocean, at least most of the time till the deluge; and if so, is not that a sufficient reason that no human relics are found in the strata? Is it not probable that the lands that were inhabited anterior to the flood, and were submerged at that catastrophe, were situated at a vast distance from Europe and this continent, and are now beneath the sea? If so, does not that explain the non-existence of human remains in the strata of Europe and America? Is it not clear then, that the fact that no human remains are found in the strata of Europe or America, is no ground for the inference that man did not become an inhabitant of the world, till after these strata were formed?

Is it not supposable that the area of the Asiatic continent at first raised above the ocean after the deluge, was of moderate extent, and that the great processes by which the strata were completed, and the continents and islands elevated to their present positions, were continued for a period afterwards? May it not have been because the earth was of but a narrow extent at its first emergence, and requiring but few animals to stock it, that so small a number was preserved in the ark? May it not be presumed that as other regions were fitted for the residence of living creatures, they may have been called into existence by new creations? Does this supposition render the existence of the land animals whose relics are fossilized consistent with the sacred history of the creation and the deluge? Did those animals undoubtedly live after the deluge? Would two, three, or four hundred years after the lands became generally inhabitable, have been sufficient for the growth of all the large animals, whose period is proved to have followed the deluge by the fact that their relics are buried in the upper strata and soil that were formed after the elevation of the great mountain ranges, which took place as was shown in Chapter VII, after the flood? Does the fact that certain classes of animals that once occupied the waters and the land, have disappeared, and others have taken their place, prove that long periods were occupied in those changes? May not the destruction of those classes that have perished, have taken place rapidly? Must not the creation of their successors have taken place instantaneously? Does the freedom of many of the relics of the bulky animals from decay, indicate also, that their period cannot have been more remote than three or four thousand years? Is it credible that bones of the Mastodon buried in the soil near Niagara, could continue there as Sir C. Lyell supposes, through thirty thousand years, without undergoing more than a slight decomposition? Does not the perishable nature of those relics confute the supposition that they can have dated at an earlier period than the ages that immediately followed the flood? Are these various facts then sufficient on the one hand, to confute the theory of the great age of the world; and on the other, to show that the facts of the strata are consistent with the history in Genesis, of the creation and deluge, and vindicate that record from the charge of error? Should it be said that though we have shown that the great processes of geology may have taken place in the manner we have indicated, we yet have not demonstrated that they took place in that manner; what is the reply that should be made? Is it enough for our object to show that the strata themselves do not prove the great age of the world? What are the points by proving which we have established that? State how those points have been proved? Is it enough for geologists to set aside our conclusion, that the facts of the strata are consistent with the history in Genesis, to say that we have not demonstrated from the strata themselves that they were formed since the epoch of the six days creation? What must they prove to set that conclusion aside? Must they not show that the strata cannot have been formed in the period and in the manner we have indicated? But can they show that the requisite materials did not exist in the depths of the earth? Can they show that there were no agents sufficiently powerful and active to raise those materials to the surface? Can they show that if they had been ejected into the ocean, they could not have been so diffused and deposited, as to have formed the existing strata? Or can they show that such a construction of the crust of the earth, is inconsistent with any of the other processes to which it has been subjected? If then, they cannot disprove any of those great facts, is it not manifest that they cannot prove that the strata were not formed in the manner we have represented? And if they cannot prove that, is it not clear that they have no ground for their assumption, that the facts of the strata are irreconcilable with the Mosaic history of the creation and deluge?

THE END.

doctrines of theology;—such in metaphysics as the idealistic atheism of Kant and Coleridge; the pantheism of Swedenborg, Schleiermacher, Schelling, and Hegel; the schemes of their disciples, Parker, Newman, Bushnell, Park, and Nevin; and the development theory of Neander and Schaff.

The Journal treats largely also of the principles of Biblical Interpretation, especially of the laws of figures and of symbols. A variety of other topics are likewise discussed in it, as may be seen from the titles of the articles in the several volumes.

CONTENTS OF VOL. I.

NO. I.

NO. II.

NO. III.

CONTENTS OF VOL. II.

CONTENTS OF VOL. III.

CONTENTS OF VOL. IV.

NO. I.

NO. II.

NO. III.

NO. IV.

CONTENTS OF VOL. V.

NO. I.

NO. II.

NO. III.

NO. IV.

CONTENTS OF VOL. VI.

CONTENTS OF VOL. VII.

NO. I.

NO. II.

NO. III.

NO. IV.

www.ingramcontent.com/pod-product-compliance
Lightning Source LLC
LaVergne TN
LVHW011150110826
845150LV00006B/1212

* 9 7 8 1 4 2 5 5 4 5 5 4 3 *